MW00933891

Legal Notice

ISBN-13: 978-1490435305
ISBN-10: 1490435301

This book is dedicated to all my students over the past 12 years, I have learned just as much from all of you as you have learned from me.

I'd also like to acknowledge Larry Ronaldson and Robert Folatico, thank you for introducing me to the rewarding field of SAT tutoring.

BOOKS BY DR. STEVE WARNER FOR COLLEGE BOUND STUDENTS

28 SAT Math Lessons to Improve Your Score in One Month
- Beginner Course
- Intermediate Course
- Advanced Course

320 SAT Math Problems Arranged by Topic and Difficulty Level

SAT Prep Book of Advanced Math Problems

The 32 Most Effective SAT Math Strategies

SAT Prep Official Study Guide Math Companion

ACT Prep Red Book – 320 ACT Math Problems with Solutions

CONNECT WITH DR. STEVE WARNER

www.facebook.com/SATPrepGet800

www.youtube.com/TheSATMathPrep

www.twitter.com/SATPrepGet800

www.linkedin.com/in/DrSteveWarner

www.pinterest.com/SATPrepGet800

plus.google.com/+SteveWarnerPhD

SAT Prep Official Study Guide Math Companion

SAT Math Problem Explanations For All Tests in the College Board's 2nd Edition Official Study Guide

---

Steve Warner, Ph.D.

Table of Contents

Actions to Complete Before You Read This Book

1. Purchase a TI-84 or equivalent calculator

It is recommended that you use a TI-84 or comparable calculator for the SAT. Answer explanations in this book will always assume you are using such a calculator.

2. Take a practice SAT from the Official Guide to get your preliminary SAT math score

Use this score to help you determine the problems you should be focusing on.

3. Claim your FREE book

Simply visit the following webpage and enter your email address to receive an electronic copy of *The 32 Most Effective SAT Math Strategies* for FREE:

www.thesatmathprep.com/DVDSAT.html

4. 'Like' my Facebook page

This page is updated regularly with SAT prep advice, tips, tricks, strategies, and practice problems. Visit the following webpage and click the 'like' button.

www.facebook.com/SATPrepGet800

INTRODUCTION

There are many ways that a student can prepare for the SAT. Teachers and tutors may have their own personal philosophies, but there is one thing that we all agree on - every student should be attempting the questions from the practice SATs given in "The Official SAT Study Guide."

Despite this, my colleagues and I have always wanted more from the infamous blue book. The problems in the Official Guide are fantastic – they are exactly the types of questions you will encounter on the SAT. The explanations to the problems, however, are not so fantastic. In the blue book there are no explanations at all, and if you do have access to the College Board's solutions then you have only a single solution which, in my opinion, may not always be the best way to solve that problem. This is why I have created this guide.

The book you are now reading contains solutions to the questions from all 10 SATs in the Official Guide. Note that in many cases several different solutions are provided for the same question. The reason for this is simple. If you really want to show a drastic improvement in your score it is highly recommended that you try to solve SAT questions in more than one way. After all, you will never see a given specific question on an SAT again. The important thing is to learn as many strategies as possible for attacking different types of problems. In fact, I always recommend trying to solve each problem that you attempt in up to four different ways

- Using an SAT specific math strategy.
- The quickest way you can think of.
- The way you would do it in school.
- The easiest way for you.

In this book, when an SAT specific strategy is used it will be mentioned right after that particular solution and the strategy number will be given that corresponds to the strategy in my other book "The 32 Most Effective SAT Math Strategies." Also in this book (as well as in all my other test prep products) the quickest solution is always marked with an asterisk (*).

Although I always suggest solving problems the way you would do it in school when practicing, I highly recommend that you avoid these methods on the actual SAT as much as possible. In this book I will generally include these more rigorous solutions last. It's good to solve problems rigorously to get a deeper understanding of the underlying mathematics and to increase your level of mathematical maturity, but when it comes exam time, more clever solutions will save time and keep you from making "careless" errors.

You can use "The Official SAT Study Guide" together with this solution manual as your only study source with excellent results as long as you use it correctly.

You should practice solving SAT math problems for about 10 to 20 minutes per day every day over a period of 3 to 4 months. Your main focus should be on problems that are just slightly above your current ability level in each topic. For example, if you are getting all Level 3 number theory questions correct, you should begin practicing Level 4 number theory questions.

Make sure to attempt each question BEFORE looking at the solutions in this book. I cannot legally reprint the full questions and answer choices, so you should turn to the question in the blue book to see the question itself as you review my explanations. I recommend reading my explanations for every question you attempt, not just the ones you got wrong. By reading my solutions you will be learning the same time-saving techniques I have been teaching all of my students for the last decade.

As you go over my solutions, mark off any questions that you get wrong. You should reattempt each question you get wrong every few days until you can get that question correct on your own.

In addition to daily practice you should take about one full practice test per month under timed conditions. I recommend saving the first 3 tests in the blue book, and the DVD test for this purpose (these four tests are all previously administered SATs).

Try to take these practice tests just as you would take the real test. You should be applying the techniques you have learned from this book, taking guesses when appropriate, pacing yourself properly (see the table below), using your TI-84 (or equivalent) calculator effectively, and leaving some time to redo as many questions as possible, preferably using a different method.

I recommend taking a guess on a multiple choice question whenever you can eliminate at least one answer choice. Always take guesses on grid in questions since you are not penalized for getting these wrong.

There are three math sections on the SAT. They can appear in any order. There is a 20 question multiple choice section, a 16 question multiple choice section, and an 18 question section that has 8 multiple choice questions and 10 grid-ins.

Let us call these sections A, B, and C, respectively. You should first make sure that you know what you got on your last SAT practice test, actual SAT, or actual PSAT (whichever you took last). What follows is a general goal you should go for when taking the exam.

Score	Section A	Section B	Section C (Multiple choice)	Section C (Grid-in)
< 330	7/20	6/16	2/8	2/10
330 – 370	10/20	8/16	3/8	3/10
380 – 430	12/20	10/16	4/8	4/10
440 – 490	14/20	11/16	5/8	6/10
500 – 550	16/20	12/16	6/8	8/10
560 – 620	18/20	15/16	7/8	9/10
630 – 800	20/20	16/16	8/8	10/10

For example, a student with a current score of 450 should attempt the first 14 questions from section A, the first 11 questions from section B, the first 5 multiple choice questions from section C, and the first 6 grid-ins from section C.

This is *just* a general guideline. Of course it can be fine-tuned. As a simple example, if you are particularly strong at number theory problems, but very weak at geometry problems, then you may want to try every number theory problem no matter where it appears, and you may want to reduce the number of geometry problems you attempt.

Blue Book Test 1
Fully Explained Solutions

Section 3

1. Algebra

Solution by plugging in the number: We substitute 4 in for x in all five answer choices.

(A) (5)(6) = 30
(B) (5)(3) = 15
(C) (2)(6) = 12
(D) (2)(5) = 10
(E) (0)(8) = 0

We see that 30 is the largest answer so that the answer is choice (A).

Remark: You can minimize the amount of time it takes to do these computations by doing everything in your head and just writing down the final answer. For example, for choice (A) you should add 4 + 1 to get 5, and 4 + 2 to get 6, and then multiply (5)(6) to get 30. Then just write down 30 next to answer choice (A). Repeat this for the rest of the answer choices.

* **Quick solution:** A quick scan of the first four answer choices will show that choice (A) has factors both of which are at least as large as both factors in each of the next three answer choices. Therefore we can eliminate choices (B), (C), and (D). Choice (E) is easily seen to be 0. So the answer is choice (A).

2. Algebra

* **Quick solution:** $B = 7$. So $A = 3(7) = 21$. So $C = 2(21) = 42$, choice (E).

Note: In the above solution A is an abbreviation for train A's speed in miles per hour, and similarly for B and C.

Algebraic solution: We are given that $A = 3B$, $C = 2A$, and $B = 7$. Therefore $A = 3(7) = 21$, and $C = 2(21) = 42$, choice (E).

3. Statistics

Solution by starting with choice (C): We begin by looking at choice (C), and we take a guess that $x = 3$. Then $5x = 15$ and $6x = 18$. So, the average is $\frac{3+15+18}{3} = 12$. This is too big. So we can eliminate (C), (D), and (E).

Let's try choice (B) next and guess that $x = 2$. Then $5x = 10$ and $6x = 12$. So, the average is $\frac{2+10+12}{3} = 8$. This is correct, so that the answer is choice (B).

For more information on this technique, see **Strategy 1** in ***"The 32 Most Effective SAT Math Strategies."***

* **Solution by changing averages to sums:** We change the average to a sum using the formula

$$\text{Sum} = \text{Average} \cdot \text{Number}$$

So $x + 5x + 6x = (8)(3)$, or equivalently $12x = 24$. Dividing each side of this equation by 12 yields $x = 2$, choice (B).

Note: The above formula comes from eliminating the denominator in the definition of average: Average $= \frac{\text{Sum}}{\text{Number}}$

For more information on this technique, see **Strategy 20** in ***"The 32 Most Effective SAT Math Strategies."***

4. Functions

* The given statement is equivalent to saying that the graph "passes the vertical line test." So any vertical line should hit the graph at most once. Only choice (D) satisfies this requirement.

5. PERCENTS

* 9 students studied butterflies, and there are 30 students total. Now we have $\frac{9}{30}$ = .3 (use your calculator for this). We change .3 to a percent by multiplying by 100. That is .3(100) = 30%, choice (C).

Some notes on converting between fraction, decimal and percent:

(1) To change a fraction to a decimal, simply perform the division in your calculator, as was done in the solution above.

(2) To change a decimal to a fraction using your TI-84 (or equivalent) calculator simply press the sequence of buttons MATH ENTER ENTER.

(3) To change a fraction to a percent, set up a ratio where the second fraction has denominator 100. Then cross multiply and divide. In this question we could have done this as follows:

$$\frac{9}{30} = \frac{x}{100}$$

$$30x = 900$$

$$x = \frac{900}{30} = 30.$$

(4) To change a decimal to a percent, multiply by 100 as was done above, or equivalently move the decimal point two places to the right (adding zeros if necessary).

(5) To change a percent to a decimal, divide by 100, or equivalently move the decimal point two places to the left (adding zeros if necessary).

(6) To change a percent to a fraction using your TI-84 (or equivalent) calculator simply divide by 100 and press the sequence of buttons MATH ENTER ENTER.

6. GEOMETRY

* The length of $\overline{CD}$ is 10. Since *AB* = *CD*, the length of $\overline{AB}$ is also 10. We therefore need to move down 7 to get to *t*, so that *t* = -7, choice (C).

Some details: Since $\overline{CD}$ is a horizontal segment, we compute the length of *CD* by subtracting the *x*-coordinate of *C* from the *x*-coordinate of *D*:

$$CD = 6 - (-4) = 6 + 4 = 10.$$

Similarly, since $\overline{AB}$ is a vertical segment, we compute the length of $\overline{AB}$ by subtracting the y-coordinate of B from the y-coordinate of A:

$$AB = 3 - t.$$

Since $AB = CD$, we have $3 - t = 10$. So, $-t = 7$, and $t = -7$.

7. ALGEBRA

* Let's solve each equation separately.

$$3x^2 = 12. \text{ So } x^2 = 4.$$
$$4y = 12. \text{ So } y = 3.$$

Therefore $x^2y = 4(3) = 12$, choice (D).

Note: We solved for x^2 here. There was no need to solve for x since only x^2 was needed.

8. GEOMETRY

* The diameters of circles A, B, and C are 4, 8, and 8, respectively. The diameter of the largest circle is then $4 + 8 + 8 = 20$. Therefore the radius of the largest circle is $\frac{20}{2} = 10$, choice (D).

Remark: The diameter of a circle is twice the radius, or equivalently, the radius of a circle is half the diameter.

$$d = 2r \quad \text{or} \quad r = \frac{d}{2}.$$

* **Quick solution:** The radius of the largest circle is the sum of the radius of circle A and the diameter of circle C. Note that the diameter of circle C is $2(4) = 8$. So we have $2 + 8 = 10$, choice (D).

Definitions: The **radius** of a circle is a line segment that joins the center of the circle with any point on its circumference.

The **diameter** of a circle is a line segment connecting the center of the circle with two points on the circumference of the circle.

9. Number Theory

The total length from 2 to 42 is 42 – 2 = 40. Since there are 5 subintervals between 2 and 40, the length of each of these subintervals is $\frac{40}{5} = 8$. There are 2 subintervals between 2 and x, so that

$$x = 2 + 8 + 8 = 18, \text{ choice (D).}$$

*** Quick computation:** $\frac{42-2}{5} = 8$. So $x = 2 + 8 + 8 = 18$, choice (D).

Note about intervals and subintervals: If $a < b$, the length of the interval from a to b is $b - a$. If there are n subintervals between a and b, the length of each subinterval is $\frac{b-a}{n}$.

10. Geometry

* Since there are 360 degrees in a circle, we have

$$90 + 30 + 110 + x = 360$$
$$230 + x = 360$$
$$x = 130, \text{ choice (C).}$$

Remarks: (1) 90 comes from the right angle in the picture.

(2) The 70 is not needed in this computation. It is just there to cause confusion.

11. Number Theory

Let's choose a positive integer whose remainder is 6 when it is divided by 7. A simple way to find such a k is to add 7 and 6. So let $k = 13$. It follows that $k + 2 = 13 + 2 = 15$. 7 goes into 15 two times with a remainder of 1, choice (B).

Important: To find a remainder you must perform division **by hand**. Dividing in your calculator does **not** give you a remainder!

Note: A slightly simpler choice for k is $k = 6$. Indeed, when 6 is divided by 7 we get 0 with 6 left over. Since this choice for k sometimes confuses students I decided to use 7 + 6 = 13 which is the next simplest choice.

Note that in general we can get a value for k by starting with any multiple of 7 and adding 6. So $k = 7n + 6$ for some integer n.

*** Quickest solution:** Let $k = 6$. It follows that $k + 2 = 6 + 2 = 8$. 7 goes into 8 once with a remainder of 1, choice (B).

Remark: The answer to this problem is independent of our choice for k (assuming that k satisfies the given condition, of course). The method just described does **not** show this. It is not necessary to do so.

For more information on this technique, see **Strategy 4** in ***"The 32 Most Effective SAT Math Strategies."***

For the advanced student: Here is a complete algebraic solution that actually demonstrates the independence of choice for k. The given condition means that we can write k as $k = 7n + 6$ for some integer n. Then $k + 2 = (7n + 6) + 2 = 7n + 8 = 7n + 7 + 1 = 7(n + 1) + 1 = 7z + 1$ where z is the integer $n + 1$. This shows that when $k + 2$ is divided by 7 the remainder is 1, choice (B).

Calculator Algorithm for computing a remainder: Although performing division in your calculator never produces a remainder, there is a simple algorithm you can perform which mimics long division. Let's find the remainder when 13 is divided by 6 using this algorithm.

Step 1: Perform the division in your calculator: $\frac{13}{6} \sim 2.166667$
Step 2: Multiply the integer part of this answer by the divisor: 2*6 = 12
Step 3: Subtract this result from the dividend to get the remainder:

$$13 - 12 = \mathbf{1}.$$

Definitions: The **integers** are the counting numbers together with their negatives.

$$\{\ldots,-4, -3, -2, -1, 0, 1, 2, 3, 4,\ldots\}$$

The **positive integers** consist of the positive numbers from that set:

$$\{1, 2, 3, 4,\ldots\}$$

12. Geometry

Solution by drawing a picture: Let's plot the first two points.

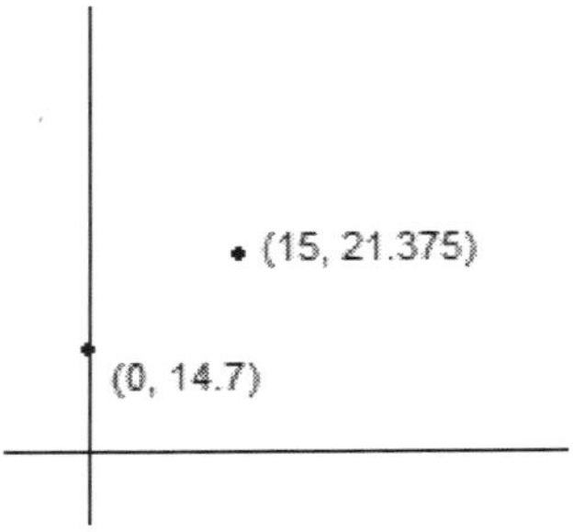

It should now be clear that the answer is choice (D).

For more information on this technique, see **Strategy 9** in ***"The 32 Most Effective SAT Math Strategies."***

* **Quick solution:** A quick glance at the table shows that as depth increases, pressure also increases. This means that the graph has a positive slope. Also, the first row of the table (Depth=0, Pressure=14.7) shows that the *y*-intercept is positive. The only graph that satisfies these two conditions is the graph given by choice (D).

Remark: The second sentence tells us that the pressure increases at a **constant rate** for every foot of descent. This, together with the fact that the entries under "Depth" in the table are equally spaced implies that the graph is a straight line.

* **Complete algebraic solution** (not recommended during the actual SAT)**:** From the first two rows of the table we see that the points (0, 14.7) and (15, 21.375) are on the line. Therefore the slope of the line is $m = \frac{21.375 - 14.7}{15 - 0} = \frac{6.675}{15} = .445$. Also, in the equation $y = mx + b$, we have that $b = 14.7$ (because (0,14.7) is the *y*-intercept of the line). So, the equation of the line is $y = .445x + 14.7$. The only answer choice that possibly matches this equation is choice (D).

For more information on this technique, see **Strategy 28** in ***"The 32 Most Effective SAT Math Strategies."***

Notes:

$$\text{Slope} = m = \frac{\text{rise}}{\text{run}} = \frac{y_2 - y_1}{x_2 - x_1}$$

Lines with positive slope have graphs that go upwards from left to right. Lines with negative slope have graphs that go downwards from left to right. If the slope of a line is zero, it is horizontal. Vertical lines have **no** slope (this is different from zero slope).

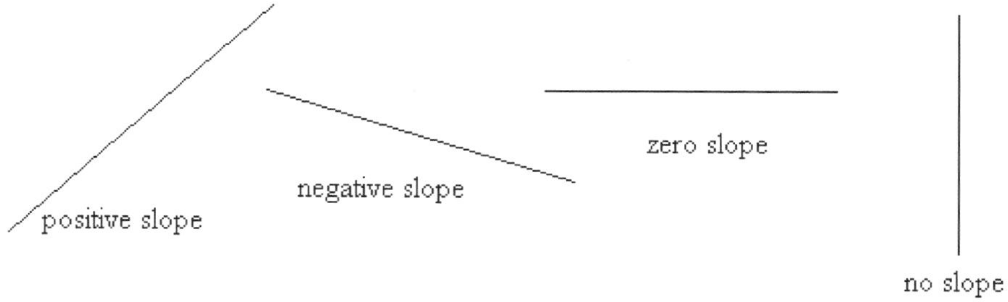

Slope-intercept form of an equation of a line:

$$y = mx + b$$

m is the slope of the line and b is the y-coordinate of the y-intercept, ie. the point $(0, b)$ is on the line. Note that this point lies on the y-axis.

13. Number Theory

Let's just compute the first 6 terms of the sequence. The first term is 1. The second term is (-2)(1) = -2. The third term is (-2)(-2) = 4. The fourth term is (-2)(4) = -8. The fifth term is (-2)(-8) = 16. The sixth term is (-2)(16) = -32, choice (E).

* **Quick list:** If you can keep multiplying by -2 in your head you can form a list very quickly:

1, -2, 4, -8, 16, -32

So the answer is choice (E).

Remark: The word **product** indicates that a multiplication is to be performed.

14. Algebra

* $2x - 5$ and $2x + 5$ are **conjugates**. This means that we can multiply them by just multiplying the first terms and last terms and adding these two together. So

$$(2x-5)(2x+5)=4x^2-25$$

So, $4x^2-25=5$, and therefore $4x^2=30$, choice (E).

Remarks:

(1) If a and b are real numbers, then $a+b$ and $a-b$ are called **conjugates** of each other. We have $(a+b)(a-b)=a^2-b^2$.

(2) In general, if a, b, c, and d are real numbers, we have

$$(a+b)(c+d)=ac+ad+bc+bd.$$

The process of expanding the product on the left to get the expression on the right is often called FOILing (here FOIL stands for First, Outer, Inner, Last).

15. Geometry

* First note that the slope of the line is negative so that we can eliminate choices (C), (D), and (E). Now observe that the figure does NOT say "figure not drawn to scale," so we can assume it is. To get from O to B it is consistent that you need to go right twice as much as you go down. So the slope can be $-\frac{1}{2}$, choice (B).

Note for the advanced student: The condition $|p|>|r|$ is quite confusing and can essentially be ignored in this problem (in the solution above the picture alone was used). For the advanced students $|p|=-p$ (since we move LEFT from the origin to get to point A), and $|r|=r$ (since we move UP from the origin to get to point A). Therefore the slope of the line is $-\frac{|r|}{|p|}$, and since the denominator is larger than the numerator we should move right more than we move down as we draw the line. Don't worry too much if this confuses you. These are just technical details that aren't necessary to solve the problem.

For more information on this technique, see **Strategy 6** in ***"The 32 Most Effective SAT Math Strategies."***

See the notes at the end of problem 12 from this section for more information on slope.

16. ALGEBRA

Solution by picking a number: Let's choose a value for b, say $b = 2$. Then we have

$$3a + 4(2) = 2$$
$$3a + 8 = 2$$
$$3a = -6$$
$$a = -2$$

So $6a + 6b = 6(-2) + 6(2) = \mathbf{0}$. **Put a nice big, dark circle around 0 so that you can find it easily later.** Substituting 2 in for b in each answer choice gives the following:

(A) 0
(B) 12
(C) 2(2) = 4
(D) 12(2) = 24
(E) 6(2) – 8 = 12 – 8 = 4

Since (B), (C), (D), and (E) each came out incorrect, the answer is choice (A).

Important note: (A) is **not** the correct answer simply because it is equal to 0. It is correct because all 4 of the other choices are **not** 0. **You absolutely must check all five choices!**

For more information on this technique, see **Strategy 4** in ***"The 32 Most Effective SAT Math Strategies.***

*** Algebraic solution:** Subtract b from each side of the equation to get

$$3a + 3b = 0.$$

Multiplying each side of the equation by 2 yields

$$2(3a + 3b) = 2(0)$$
$$2(3a) + 2(3b) = 0$$
$$6a + 6b = 0.$$

So the answer is choice (A).

17. Geometry

*** Solution using the fact that the figure is drawn to scale:** Note that the big triangle is an isosceles right triangle, that is it's a 45, 45, 90 triangle. So $AC = 10\sqrt{2}\sqrt{2} = 10(2) = 20$ (see Remark 2 below). We can assume that the figure is drawn to scale (since it does not say that it isn't drawn to scale). Therefore the length of the shaded rectangle is 10 and the width is 5. So the area of the shaded rectangle is 10(5) = 50, choice (C).

Remarks:

(1) An isosceles right triangle is the same as a 45, 45, 90 right triangle.

(2) We got AC by using the formula for a 45, 45, 90 triangle given at the beginning of any math section of the SAT.

(3) The formula for the area of a rectangle is also given at the beginning of any math section of the SAT.

For more information on this technique, see **Strategy 6** in ***"The 32 Most Effective SAT Math Strategies."***

Some nitpicky details: For completeness we give the details without assuming that the measurements in the picture are accurate.

We have $AE = CF = 5\sqrt{2}$ by the definition of midpoint. So each small triangle has legs of length 5. It follows that the width of the shaded rectangle is 5, and the length of the shaded rectangle is $20 - 5 - 5 = 10$.

Definition: The **midpoint** of a line segment is the point on the segment that divides the segment into two equal parts.

18. Functions

*** Solution by plugging in points:** Let's start with the point $(0,\frac{1}{2})$. Equivalently, $\frac{1}{2} = f(0) = ka^0 = k$.

So the function is now $f(x) = (\frac{1}{2})a^x$. Let's use the point (1,2) to find a. Equivalently, $2 = f(1) = (\frac{1}{2})a^1$ so that $a = 4$, choice (D).

For more information on this technique, see **Strategy 5** in ***"The 32 Most Effective SAT Math Strategies."***

19. Geometry

Solution by picking numbers: Let's let $e = m = 2$. We get the following two pictures.

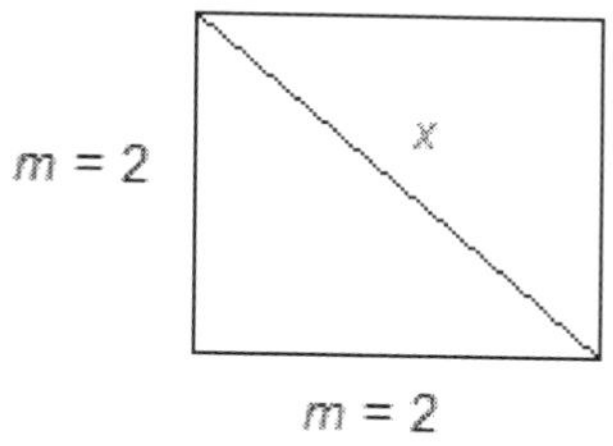

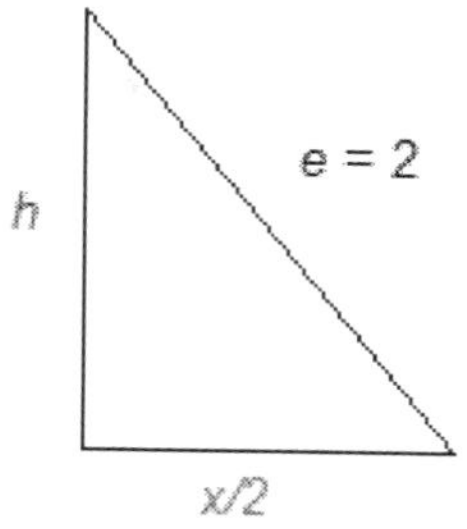

The picture on the left is the square base of the pyramid. Note that $x = 2\sqrt{2}$. We can see this by observing that the triangle formed from two sides of a square and its diagonal is an isosceles right triangle (or equivalently, a 45, 45, 90 triangle). So we can use the formula for the special triangle or the Pythagorean Theorem. Both of these formulas are given at the beginning of this math section.

The picture on the right consists of the triangle with vertices V (the top of the pyramid), the center of the square, and the front right vertex of the square. Note that the side labeled $\frac{x}{2}$ is half the diagonal of the square. It now follows that $\frac{x}{2} = \sqrt{2}$, and we can use the Pythagorean Theorem to find h.

$$2^2 = h^2 + (\sqrt{2})^2$$
$$4 = h^2 + 2$$
$$h^2 = 2$$
$$h = \sqrt{\mathbf{2}}$$

Put a nice big, dark circle around $\sqrt{2}$ so that you can find it easily later. Substituting 2 in for m in each answer choice gives the following:

(A) $\frac{2}{\sqrt{2}}$

(B) $\sqrt{3}$

(C) 2

(D) $\frac{4}{\sqrt{3}}$

(E) $2\sqrt{2}$

Uh oh! It appears as if none of the answers are correct. But actually, choice (A) is correct because $\frac{2}{\sqrt{2}} = \sqrt{2}$. You can see this by putting each of these numbers in your calculator and observing that you get the same decimal approximation. Alternatively, you can rationalize the denominator of $\frac{2}{\sqrt{2}}$ by multiplying each of the numerator and denominator by $\sqrt{2}$ as follows.

$$(\frac{2}{\sqrt{2}})(\frac{\sqrt{2}}{\sqrt{2}}) = \frac{2\sqrt{2}}{2} = \sqrt{2}.$$

Since (B), (C), (D), and (E) each came out incorrect, the answer is choice (A).

Important note: (A) is **not** the correct answer simply because it is equal to $\sqrt{2}$. It is correct because all 4 of the other choices are **not** $\sqrt{2}$. **You absolutely must check all five choices!**

For more information on this technique, see **Strategy 4** in ***"The 32 Most Effective SAT Math Strategies."***

* **Algebraic solution:** Let's draw two pictures as in the last solution.

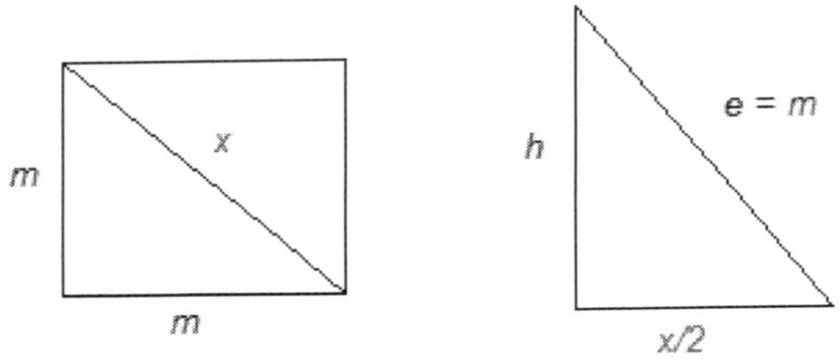

A diagonal of the square base has length $x = m\sqrt{2}$. So the length from the center to the lower right corner of the square is $\frac{x}{2} = \frac{m\sqrt{2}}{2}$.
Now notice that we have a right triangle whose legs are labeled by h and $\frac{x}{2} = \frac{m\sqrt{2}}{2}$, and whose hypotenuse is labeled by $e = m$. By the Pythagorean Theorem, $m^2 = h^2 + (\frac{m\sqrt{2}}{2})^2$. Now, let's square the rightmost term to get $m^2 = h^2 + \frac{m^2 \cdot 2}{4}$, or equivalently

$$m^2 = h^2 + \frac{m^2}{2}$$

Now multiply each term by 2 (to eliminate the denominator).

$2m^2 = 2h^2 + m^2$. So $m^2 = 2h^2$, and $h^2 = \frac{m^2}{2}$. Therefore $h = \frac{m}{\sqrt{2}}$, choice (A).

20. Number Theory

Solution by picking numbers: Let's pick a number for k, say $k = 10$, so that the salesperson's commission is 10% of the selling price of the car. The total sale price for the two cars is 2(14,000) = \$28,000, so that the commission is (28,000)(.1) = **2800**. Put a nice big, dark circle around this number.

Now let's substitute 10 in for k in each answer choice.

(A) 2800
(B) 70,000
(C) 280,000
(D) 14,000/120 ~ 116.67
(E) 28,010/100 = 280.10

Since (B), (C), (D), and (E) are all incorrect, the answer is choice (A).

Important note: (A) is **not** the correct answer simply because it is equal to 2800. It is correct because all four of the other choices are **not** 2800.

Remark: This is a percent problem, so an even nicer choice for k would be $k = 100$. Try solving the problem again with this choice for k.

For more information on this technique, see **Strategy 4** in ***"The 32 Most Effective SAT Math Strategies."***

* **Algebraic solution:** The total sale price for the two cars is 2(14,000) = \$28,000, so that the commission is $(28,000)(\frac{k}{100}) = 280k$, choice (A).

SECTION 7

1. DATA ANALYSIS

* We add up the first three rows of little houses to get 14. Since each little house represents 2000 homes, we get 14(2000) = 28,000 new homes, choice (E).

2. GEOMETRY

* Since vertical angles are congruent, we see that the triangle has angles that measure 35, 45, and w degrees. So $w = 180 - 35 - 45 = 100$, choice (B).

Definition: A pair of **vertical angles** is a pair of two angles formed by two intersecting lines and lying on opposite sides of the point of intersection.

3. NUMBER THEORY

Solution by starting with choice (C): We start with choice (C) and assume that 6 tables seat 5 people. This takes care of 6(5) = 30 people. So there are 84 – 30 = 54 people left. Since 54 is not divisible by 4 we can eliminate choice (C).

Let's try choice (D) next. Then 7 tables seat 5 people. This takes care of 7(5) = 35 people. So there are 84 – 35 = 49 people left. Since 49 is not divisible by 4 we can eliminate choice (C).

Let's try choice (E) next. Then 8 tables seat 5 people. This takes care of 8(5) = 40 people. So there are 84 – 40 = 44 people left. $\frac{44}{4} = 11$. So, 11 tables seat 4 people. Now we check: 8 + 11 = 19 is the total number of tables. This is correct so that the answer is choice (E).

For more information on this technique, see **Strategy 1** in ***"The 32 Most Effective SAT Math Strategies."***

* **Quick solution:** If we place 4 people at each table, this takes care of 4(19) = 76 people. There are 84 – 76 = 8 people left. So the number of tables that seat 8 people is 8, choice (E).

* **Algebraic solution:** Let x be the number of tables that seat 4 people, and let y be the number of tables that seat 5 people. Then we have that $x + y = 19$ and $4x + 5y = 84$. We multiply the first equation by -4 and then add the two equations:

$$\begin{array}{r} -4x + (-4y) = -76 \\ \underline{4x + 5y = 84} \\ y = 8 \end{array}$$

So the answer is choice (E).

4. Algebra

* **Algebraic solution:** We substitute 4 in for a, and then factor.

$$am^2 + am + a = 4m^2 + 4m + 4 = 4(m^2 + m + 1).$$

So, the answer is choice (D).

Solution by picking numbers: Let's choose a value for m, say $m = 2$. Then the expression becomes $4(2)^2 + 4(2) + 4 = 4(4) + 8 + 4 = 16 + 8 + 4 =$ **28**. Put a nice big, dark circle around this number. Now substitute 2 for m into each answer choice.

(A) $4(2^3 + 1) = 4(8 + 1) = 4(9) = 36$
(B) $4(2 + 1)^2 = 4(3)^2 = 4(9) = 36$
(C) $4(2^2 + 2) = 4(4 + 2) = 4(6) = 24$
(D) $4(2^2 + 2 + 1) = 4(4 + 2 + 1) = 4(7) = 28$
(E) $4(4(2)^2 + 2 + 1) = 4(4(4) + 2 + 1) = 4(16 + 2 + 1) = 4(19) = 76$

Since (A), (B), (C), and (E) all came out incorrect we can eliminate them. Therefore the answer is choice (D).

Important note: (D) is **not** the correct answer simply because it is equal to 28. It is correct because all four of the other choices are **not** 28. **You absolutely must check all five choices!**

For more information on this technique, see **Strategy 4** in ***"The 32 Most Effective SAT Math Strategies."***

5. Geometry

* The diameter of the circle has the same length as a side of the square. So the diameter is 2. The radius of a circle is half of the diameter. So the radius of the circle is 1. The area of the circle is $A = \pi r^2 = \pi(1)^2 = \pi$. The shaded portion is $\frac{1}{4}$ of the circle, so that the area of the shaded portion is $\frac{\pi}{4}$, choice (A).

6. GEOMETRY

* The slope of line ℓ is $\frac{\text{rise}}{\text{run}} = -\frac{4}{12} = -\frac{1}{3}$ (we can see this by looking at the graph – to get from the leftmost point to the rightmost point we move down 4 and right 12). So the slope of a line perpendicular to line ℓ is 3. Answer choice (C) is the only equation whose graph has a slope of 3. Therefore the answer is choice (C).

Remarks: (1) Perpendicular lines have slopes that are negative reciprocals of each other. The reciprocal of $\frac{1}{3}$ is $\frac{3}{1} = 3$. The negative reciprocal of $\frac{1}{3}$ is -3.

(2) The equation of a line in **slope-intercept** form is $\boldsymbol{y = mx + b}$ where m is the slope of the line and (0, *b*) is the *y*-intercept of the line.

(3) We can also find the slope of the given line by getting *y* by itself.

$$3y = -x + 12$$
$$y = -\frac{1}{3}x + 4$$

The line is now in slope-intercept form with $m = -\frac{1}{3}$.

For more information on this technique, see **Strategy 28** in ***"The 32 Most Effective SAT Math Strategies."***

7. GEOMETRY

* We use the **triangle rule** which says that the length of the third side of a triangle is strictly between the difference and sum of the lengths of the other two sides.

In this question, the difference is 5 – 5 = 0, and the sum is 5 + 5 = 10. Therefore the length of the third side is strictly between 0 and 10. So the length of the third side CANNOT be 10, choice (E).

For more information on this technique, see **Strategy 25** in ***"The 32 Most Effective SAT Math Strategies."***

8. Algebra

* **Algebraic solution:** If Candidate II received x votes, then Candidate I received $x + 28{,}000$ votes. So

$$x + (x + 28{,}000) = 2{,}800{,}000$$
$$2x + 28{,}000 = 2{,}800{,}000$$
$$2x = 2{,}772{,}000$$
$$x = 1{,}386{,}000$$

So Candidate I received 1,386,000 + 28,000 = 1,414,000 votes.

Now, $\frac{1{,}414{,}000}{2{,}800{,}000} = .505$. Finally, we move the decimal point to the right two places to change this decimal to a percent. So, the answer is 50.5%, choice (C).

Remarks: (1) Remember that x is the number of votes that Candidate II received. The number of votes that Candidate I received is $x + 28{,}000$.

(2) To get the **percentage** of votes that Candidate I received we divide the **number** of votes Candidate I received by the **total** number of votes cast, and then multiply this number by 100 (or equivalently, move the decimal point to the right two places).

9. Algebra

* **Quick solution:** Since 2(9) = 18, we see that the two sides of the equation will look identical if we let p = **9**.

Full algebraic solution: We square each side of the equation to get $2p = 18$. We then divide each side of the equation by 2 to get p = **9**.

10. Number Theory

* 1.783 is 2 to the nearest whole number, and 1.8 to the nearest tenth. Now just subtract in your calculator: 2 – 1.8 = **.2** or $\frac{1}{5}$.

11. Probability

Solution by guessing: Let's guess that there are 10 towels in the closet. Then $(\frac{2}{5})\cdot 10 = 4$ of the towels are brown. This is a bit too small. So let's guess that there are 15 towels in the closet. Then $(\frac{2}{5})\cdot 15 = 6$ of the towels are brown. This is correct. Therefore the answer is **15**.

Remark: Saying that the probability of picking a brown towel is $\frac{2}{5}$ is the same as saying that $\frac{2}{5}$ of the total number of towels are brown.

For more information on this technique, see **Strategy 3** in ***"The 32 Most Effective SAT Math Strategies."***

* **Algebraic solution:** Let x be the total number of towels in the closet. Then $(\frac{2}{5})x = 6$. We multiply each side of this equation by $\frac{5}{2}$ to get that $x = 6(\frac{5}{2}) = $ **15**.

12. Geometry

* Let's draw a picture.

In the picture above each tick mark represents one unit. I plotted A first, followed by D which is 4.5 units from A. Next I plotted C, so that C is 2 units to the left of D. Now, we have a little flexibility with where we plot B and E. I took a "guess" that it was okay to plot B at the nearest tick mark to the left of C. I am now forced to plot E 3.5 units to the right of C. Since E is to the right of D this configuration works. In this picture, we have that BC = **1/2** or **.5**.

Note: By adjusting where we place B, we see that there are infinitely many solutions to this problem. For example, we can simultaneously move B and E to the right so that B is as close as we like to C (without touching it), so that BC can be as close to 0 as we like. At the other extreme, we can simultaneously move B and E to the left so that E is as close to D as we like (without touching it), so that BC can be as close to 1.5 as we like. Putting these two results together we see that we must have $0 < BE < 1.5$, and we can grid in **any** number between 0 and 1.5 (but 0 and 1.5 themselves would each be marked wrong).

For more information on this technique, see **Strategy 9** in ***"The 32 Most Effective SAT Math Strategies."***

13. Number Theory

* It rained on $(\frac{3}{5})(30) = 18$ of the days in April. Therefore it didn't rain on $30 - 18 = 12$ of the days of April. Finally, $18 - 12 =$ **6**.

Formal Algebra: $3x + 2x = 30$, so that $5x = 30$ or $x = 6$. Then $3x = 3(6) = 18$ and $2x = 2(6) = 12$. Finally $3x - 2x = x =$ **6**.

14. Number Theory

Solution by guessing: Let's take a guess that the common difference is 10. Then, beginning with the third term, the terms of the sequence would be 17, 27, 37, 47,... So the sixth term is 47, too small.

So the common difference must be bigger. Let's guess 20 next. Then again beginning with the third term, the terms of the sequence are 17, 37, 57, 77,... This is correct. So let's keep going: 97, 117. There it is! The eighth term is **117**.

Note: The full sequence is -27, -7, 17, 37, 57, 77, 97, 117,...

For more information on this technique, see **Strategy 3** in ***"The 32 Most Effective SAT Math Strategies."***

* **Solution using slope**: A sequence with a common difference is called an **arithmetic** sequence. You can compute the common difference quickly using the same formula for the slope of a line between two points. Here the *x*-coordinates are the term numbers, and the *y*-coordinates are the term values. So in this example the two points are (3,17) and (6,77). The common difference is then

$$d = \frac{77-17}{6-3} = \frac{60}{3} = 20.$$

Finally, as before, the seventh term is $77 + d = 77 + 20 = 97$, and the eighth term is $97 + d = 97 + 20 = \mathbf{117}$.

Solution using the formula for an arithmetic sequence: We use the arithmetic sequence formula $a_n = a_1 + (n - 1)d$, where a_1 is the first term of the sequence, d is the common difference, and a_n is the nth term of the sequence. Note that we are given that $a_3 = 17$ and $a_6 = 77$.

$$77 = a_1 + (6-1)d = a_1 + 5d$$
$$17 = a_1 + (3-1)d = a_1 + 2d$$

Subtracting the second equation from the first gives us $60 = 3d$, so that we have $d = \frac{60}{3} = 20$. Now as in the other solutions, $a_7 = 97$, and $a_8 = \mathbf{117}$.

15. Algebra

* **Algebraic solution:** The given equation is equivalent to the two equations $x - 3 = .5$, and $x - 3 = -.5$. The solutions of these equations are 3.5 and 2.5, respectively. So the least value of x satisfying the given equation is $x =$ **2.5** or **5/2**.

Remark: An equation with an absolute value will most likely have two solutions. Don't be tricked into finding just one.

16. Number Theory

* Let's take a guess for W, say $W = 7$ (note that W must be at least 5 in order for Z to be a digit). Now working from bottom to top, we have $Z = W - 5 = 7 - 5 = 2$, $Y = W - 1 = 7 - 1 = 6$, and

$$X = W + Y + Z = 7 + 6 + 2 = 15.$$

This is too big because 15 is not a digit.

Let's try $W = 5$, Then $Z = W - 5 = 0$, $Y = W - 1 = 5 - 1 = 4$, and

$$X = W + Y + Z = 5 + 4 + 0 = 9.$$

This works, so that $WXYZ =$ **5940**.

For more information on this technique, see **Strategy 3** in ***"The 32 Most Effective SAT Math Strategies."***

17. Geometry

* Let's redraw the figure to scale.

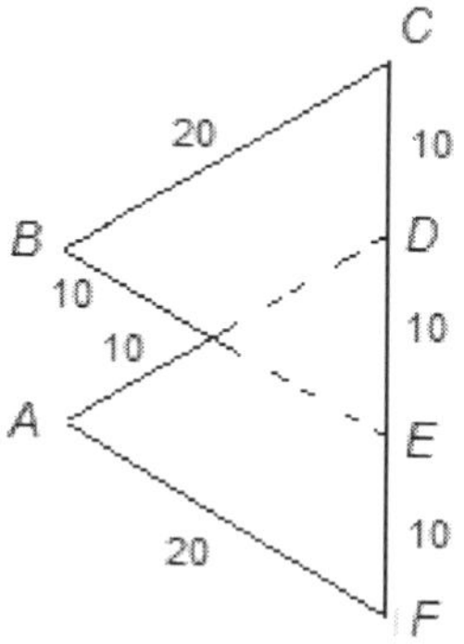

In the picture above, each side that contributes to the perimeter is labeled with its length. Note that it is given that $CD = DE = EF = 10$, and each of these sides has half the length of a side of the two big equilateral triangles. Thus $AF = BC = 20$, and the other two segments are 10 each. Therefore the perimeter is **90**.

For more information on this technique, see **Strategy 7** in ***"The 32 Most Effective SAT Math Strategies."***

18. Functions

* Note that from the graph (or the function) $g(-3) = 0$ and $g(3) = 0$. So $a - 1.2 = -3$ or $a - 1.2 = 3$. Therefore we have that $a = -3 + 1.2 = -1.8$ or $a = 3 + 1.2 = 4.2$. Since it is given that $a > 0$, the answer is **4.2**.

Remark: Graphically we see that the given graph touches the x-axis at $x = -3$ and $x = 3$. Therefore, the x-intercepts of the graph of g are the points $(-3,0)$ and $(3,0)$. Equivalently, $g(-3) = 0$ and $g(3) = 0$.

SECTION 8

1. DATA ANALYSIS

* According to the chart there are 4 honorable mention ribbons in painting, 2 in pottery, 5 in photography, 1 in metalworking, and 1 in silkscreen. Therefore the total number of honorable mention ribbons is $4 + 2 + 5 + 1 + 1 = 13$, choice (D).

2. GEOMETRY

* We can assume that the figure is drawn to scale. It looks like $\overline{BC}$ and $\overline{ED}$ have the same length. So $ED = 4$ and the answer is choice (E).

Remark: It also looks like $AB = AC = AD = AE$, but there is no answer choice saying that any of these are equal to 6.

Geometric solution: Since $\overline{AB}$, $\overline{AC}$, $\overline{AD}$, and $\overline{AE}$ are all radii of the circle, they are equal in length. Thus, $AB = AC = AD = AE = 6$. The angles BAC and EAD are **vertical angles** and are thus congruent. Minor arcs BC and ED have the same measure as angles BAC and EAD, respectively since these two angles are central angles (**central angles have the same degree measure as their intercepted arcs**). Thus, minor arcs BC and ED have the same measure. **If two minor arcs are equal in measure, their corresponding chords are equal in measure**. Therefore $ED = BC = 4$.

3. ALGEBRA AND FUNCTIONS

* The expression

5
2
6

is equal to $5^2 - 5 \cdot 6 + 6 = 25 - 30 + 6 = 1$, choice (A).

Order of Operations: A quick review of order of operations.

PEMDAS	
P	Parentheses
E	Exponentiation
M	Multiplication
D	Division
A	Addition
S	Subtraction

Note that multiplication and division have the same priority, and addition and subtraction have the same priority.

4. Geometry

* Let's plot the points and draw the square.

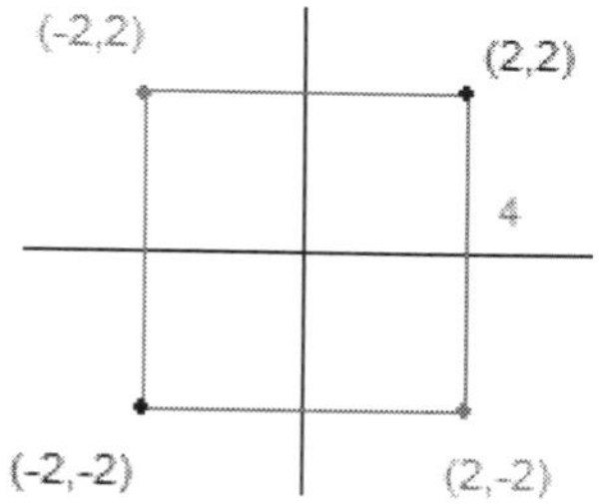

Note that the given points are plotted in black, and after drawing the square we see that the length of a side of the square is 4. Therefore the area of the square is $A = s^2 = 16$, choice (C).

For more information on this technique, see **Strategy 9** in ***"The 32 Most Effective SAT Math Strategies."***

5. Logic

* Let's use process of elimination. It is given in the second sentence that Chad is not the oldest. So we can eliminate Chad. The fourth sentence says that Steph is the youngest. So we can eliminate Steph. The fifth sentence implies that Owen is not the oldest. So we can eliminate Owen. By process of elimination Daria is the oldest, choice (B).

6. Geometry

* We can assume that the figure is drawn to scale so that the figure is a parallelogram. In a parallelogram two adjacent angles add up to 180 degrees. So $x + y = 180$, and $2(x + y) = 2(180) = 360$, choice (E).

For more information on this technique, see **Strategy 6** in ***"The 32 Most Effective SAT Math Strategies."***

Remark: In actuality there is no reason to believe that the given figure is a parallelogram. So the above solution is technically wrong. But on the SAT we can assume that a figure is drawn to scale unless stated otherwise. See below for a solution that uses only the given information.

Mathematically correct solution: $\overline{QR}$ and $\overline{PS}$ are two parallel line segments cut by the transversal $\overline{PQ}$. It follows that angles PQR and QPS are supplementary. Therefore $x + y = 180$, and $2(x + y) = 2(180) = 360$, choice (E).

Solution by picking numbers: We can let x and y be any two numbers that add up to 180. For example, let $x = 50$, $y = 130$. Then we have that $2(x + y) = 2\ (50 + 130) = 2(180) = 360$, choice (E).

For more information on this technique, see **Strategy 4** in ***"The 32 Most Effective SAT Math Strategies."***

7. Statistics

* For the first equation, we change the average to a sum using the formula

$$\text{Sum} = \text{Average} \cdot \text{Number}$$

In this question the Average is 12 and the Number is 3. Therefore the Sum is

$$x + y + z = (12)(3) = 36.$$

For the second equation note that the greatest number is z, and the sum of the other two is $x + y$. So when the greatest of these numbers is subtracted from the sum of the other two we get

$$(x + y) - z = 4.$$

The two equations together and simplified are

$$x + y + z = 36$$
$$x + y - z = 4$$

So the answer is choice (A).

For more information on this technique, see **Strategy 20** in ***"The 32 Most Effective SAT Math Strategies."***

8. ALGEBRA

Solution by guessing: Let's take guesses for x and y, say $x = 1$, $y = 2$. Then $3^{2x} \cdot 3^{2y} = 3^2 \cdot 3^4 = (9)(81) = 729$. This is too big, so let's decrease the value of y.

Let's try $x = 1$, $y = 1$ next. Then $3^{2x} \cdot 3^{2y} = 3^2 \cdot 3^2 = (9)(9) = 81$. So this works. Therefore $x + y = 1 + 1 = 2$, choice (B).

For more information on this technique, see **Strategy 3** in ***"The 32 Most Effective SAT Math Strategies."***

* **Algebraic solution:** $3^{2x} \cdot 3^{2y} = 3^{2x+2y} = 3^{2(x+y)}$ and $81 = 3^4$. So we have $2(x + y) = 4$ and so $x + y = 2$, choice (B).

Laws of Exponents: For those students that have forgotten, here is a brief review of the basic laws of exponents.

Law	Example
$x^0 = 1$	$3^0 = 1$
$x^1 = x$	$9^1 = 9$
$x^a x^b = x^{a+b}$	$x^3 x^5 = x^8$
$x^a / x^b = x^{a-b}$	$x^{11} / x^4 = x^7$
$(x^a)^b = x^{ab}$	$(x^5)^3 = x^{15}$
$(xy)^a = x^a y^a$	$(xy)^4 = x^4 y^4$
$(x/y)^a = x^a / y^a$	$(x/y)^6 = x^6 / y^6$

9. FUNCTIONS

* The maximum is where the graph is highest. The x-coordinate of this point is $x = 4$, choice (B).

Remark: If the question had asked for the maximum value the answer would be $y = 5$.

10. ALGEBRA

Solution by picking numbers: : Let's choose a value for k, say $k = 2$. Then we have $2 = \frac{x}{3}$ so that $x = 6$. Therefore $3x = 3(6) =$ **18**. Put a nice big, dark circle around this number. Now substitute 2 for k into each answer choice.

(A) 2

(B) 18

(C) $\frac{9}{2} = 4.5$

(D) $\frac{2}{9}$

(E) $\frac{2}{3}$

Since (A), (C), (D), and (E) are incorrect we can eliminate them. Therefore the answer is choice (B).

Important note: (B) is **not** the correct answer simply because it is equal to 18. It is correct because all four of the other choices are **not** 18. **You absolutely must check all five choices!**

For more information on this technique, see **Strategy 4** in ***"The 32 Most Effective SAT Math Strategies."***

Algebraic solution: Multiply each side of the given equation by 3 to get $3k = x$. Multiply each side by 3 again to get $9k = 3x$. So the answer is choice (B).

***Quickest algebraic solution:** Multiply each side of the equation by 9 to get $9k = 3x$, choice (B).

11. GEOMETRY

* A cube has 6 faces. Since 2 are painted black, 4 are painted white. Since the total area of the white faces is 64, the area of one white face is $\frac{64}{4} = 16$. So the length of a side of the cube is $s = 4$, and the volume of the cube is $V = s^3 = 4^3 = 64$, choice (A).

Formulas: If s is the length of the side of a square, then the area of the square is $A = s^2$. If s is the length of the side of a cube, then the volume of the cube is $V = s^3$.

12. Geometry

* The length of each small interval is $\frac{1-0}{4} = \frac{1}{4} = .25$. Thus, $x = .25$, $y = .75$, $w = -.5$, and $v = -.75$. Now we simply do each of the five computations.

(A) $v + y = -.75 + .75 = 0$
(B) $v + x = -.75 + .25 = -.5$
(C) $w + x = -.5 + .25 = -.25$
(D) $v - w = -.75 - (-.5) = -.75 + .5 = -.25$
(E) $y - x = .75 - .25 = .5$

We see that -.5 is the least answer, choice (B).

Note: See problem 9 in section 3 (p. 14) for an explanation of the computation of the length an interval.

13. Statistics

* If we let $n = 2$, the median will be 6. If we let $n = 13$, the median will be 7. The only way to make the median 6.5 would be to let $n = 6.5$. But 6.5 is not an integer, and so the median **cannot** be 6.5. Therefore, the answer is I and III only, choice (D).

Detailed look at the lists: For completeness, let's write out the lists described above with the median in each list in boldface. If $n = 2$, we get

2, 3, 4, **6**, 7, 10, 12

If $n = 13$, we get

3, 4, 6, **7**, 10, 12, 13

Finally, in order to make the median 6.5 our list would look as follows.

3, 4, 6, **6.5**, 7, 10, 12

Definition: The **median** of a set of numbers is the middle number when the numbers are arranged in increasing order. If the total number of values in the set is even, then the median is the average of the two middle values.

14. Counting

Solution by listing: Let's suppose the 5 available colors are red, blue green, yellow, and purple. Let's list all the possible combinations of colors. In what follows we list color 1 first, followed by color 2, and we abbreviate the colors by using their first letter.

rb	rg	ry	rp
br	bg	by	bp
gr	gb	gy	gp
yr	yb	yg	yp
pr	pb	pg	py

We can now easily see that there are 20 possible designs, choice (B).

For more information on this technique, see **Strategy 21** in ***"The 32 Most Effective SAT Math Strategies."***

Solution using the counting principle: There are 5 possible choices for Color 1. After Color 1 has been chosen, there are then 4 possible choices for Color 2. By the counting principle we get (5)(4) = 20 possible designs, choice (B).

Remark: The **counting principle** says that if one event is followed by a second independent event, the number of possibilities is multiplied.

* **Solution using permutations:** There are 5 colors, and we are arranging 2 of them. So there are ${}_5P_2 = (5)(4) = 20$ possible designs, choice (B).

Permutations: ${}_5P_2$ means the number of **permutations** of 5 things taken 2 at a time. In a permutation order matters (as opposed to the **combination** ${}_5C_2$ where the order does not matter).

$${}_5P_2 = \frac{5!}{3!} = \frac{1\cdot2\cdot3\cdot4\cdot5}{1\cdot2\cdot3} = 20.$$

In general, if n is an integer, then $n! = 1\cdot2\cdot3\cdots n$

If n and k are integers, then ${}_nP_r = \frac{n!}{(n-r)!}$

$0! = 1$ by definition.

On the SAT you do **not** need to know these formulas. You can do these computations very quickly on your graphing calculator. For example, to compute ${}_5P_2$, type 5 into your calculator, then in the **Math** menu scroll over to **Prb** and select **nPr** (or press **2**). Then type 2 and hit **Enter**. You will get an answer of 20.

15. Geometry

*** Solution by picking numbers:** Let's start with a rectangle with length and width both 10 (yes, it's a square), so that the area is $10^2 = 100$. Now if we increase the length by 30%, then the new length is 13. If we decrease the width by 30%, the new width is 7. So the area of the new rectangle is $(13)(7) = 91$. The area has decreased by 9%, choice (E).

Remark: We can visualize the above solution with the following picture.

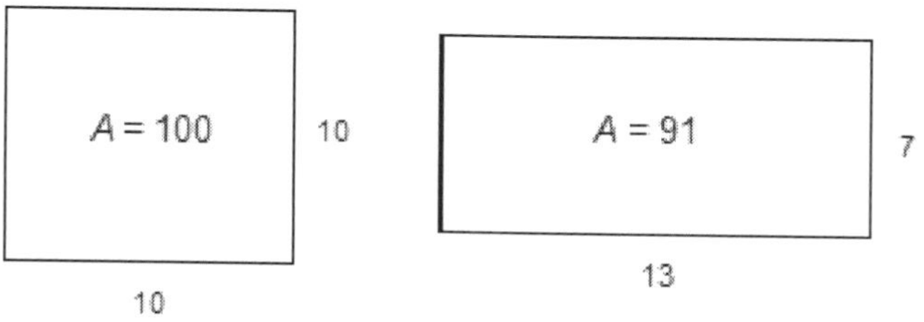

Note: We chose the length and width of the original rectangle so that the area was 100. This makes the computations very simple – remember that the word percent means "out of 100."

Algebraic solution: Let x and y be the length and width of the original rectangle, respectively. Then the original area is xy. The new length is $1.3x$ and the new width is $.7y$, so that the new area is $(1.3x)(.7y) = .91xy$. This is a decrease by 9%, choice (E).

16. Functions

On day $t = 10$, the number of bees was

$$n(10) = \frac{10^2}{2} - 20(10) + k = 50 - 200 + k = k - 150.$$

We can now proceed in two different ways:

Solution by starting with choice (C): Recall that $n(10) = k - 150$ (we did this computation above). Starting with choice (C) we compute

$$n(40) = \frac{40^2}{2} - 20(40) + k = \frac{1600}{2} - 800 + k = 800 - 800 + k = k.$$

This is not correct. Let's try choice (B) next.

$$n(30) = \frac{30^2}{2} - 20(30) + k = \frac{900}{2} - 600 + k = 450 - 600 + k = k - 150.$$

This is correct, so that the answer is choice (B).

For more information on this technique, see **Strategy 1** in ***"The 32 Most Effective SAT Math Strategies."***

*** Algebraic solution:** We set $n(k)$ equal to $k - 150$. So,

$$\frac{t^2}{2} - 20t + k = k - 150.$$

Strike off the k from each side of the equation, and then add 150 to each side to get $\frac{t^2}{2} - 20t + 150 = 0$. Multiplying through by 2 gives us

$$t^2 - 40t + 300 = 0.$$

This factors as $(t - 10)(t - 30) = 0$, giving the two solutions $t = 10$ and $t = 30$. So the answer is 30, choice (B).

Remarks: (1) At any time we can stop doing algebra and start plugging in the answer choices (beginning with choice (C)) in order to find the answer.

(2) When factoring the expression $t^2 - 40t + 300$, it is a safe guess that one of the factors will be $t - 10$. Since $\frac{300}{10} = 30$, the other factor must be $t - 30$.

(3) The equation $t^2 - 40t + 300 = 0$ can also be solved by completing the square or using the quadratic formula. Since it is absolutely not necessary to know these methods for the SAT, I have decided not to provide these solutions here. Students familiar with these methods may want to practice them, but I wouldn't recommend solving problems in either of these ways on the day of the SAT.

Blue Book Test 2 Fully Explained Solutions

Section 2

1. Number Theory

* **Quick solution:** $t = 2(10) + 2 = 20 + 2 = 22$, choice (D).

Note: To find t we only needed to look at the term immediately preceding t, namely 10. Here 10 is the "previous term." So twice the previous term is $2(10) = 20$, and 2 more than twice the previous term is $20 + 2 = 22$.

Observe: $2(1) + 2 = 2 + 2 = 4$, $2(4) + 2 = 8 + 2 = 10$, $2(10) + 2 = 20 + 2 = 22$, $2(22) + 2 = 44 + 2 = 46$,...

Remark: The word "twice" indicates that you should multiply by 2. The expression "2 more than" indicates that you should add 2. For example, "2 more than twice 10" is "2 more than 20" which is $20 + 2 = 22$.

2. Number Theory

* **Quick solution:** $\frac{24}{12} = 2$, choice (A).

Explanation: An hour is made up of 12 five minute blocks, so we divide by 12. More explicitly, there are 60 minutes in an hour, and $\frac{60}{5} = 12$.

A more formal solution: We begin by identifying 2 key words. In this case, such a pair of key words is "cartons" and "minutes."

cartons	24	x
minutes	60	5

Note that we converted 1 hour into 60 minutes. Notice that we wrote in the number of cartons next to the word carton, and the number of minutes next to the word minutes. Also notice that the number of cartons that can be filled in 60 minutes is written above the number 60, and the (unknown) number of cartons that can be filled in 5 minutes is written above the number 5. Now draw in the division symbols and equal sign, cross multiply and divide the corresponding ratio to find the unknown quantity *x*.

$$\frac{24}{60} = \frac{x}{5}$$

$$60x = 120$$

$$x = \frac{120}{60} = 2.$$

This is choice (A).

For more information on this technique, see **Strategy 14** in ***"The 32 Most Effective SAT Math Strategies."***

3. Data Analysis

* Cathy sold 20 cars in January, 18 cars in February, and 48 cars in May. She therefore sold 48 – (20 + 18) = 48 – 38 = 10 more cars in May than in the months of January and February combined. This is choice (A).

4. Data Analysis

Solution by setting up a ratio: 30 cars were sold in April, and the total number of cars sold during these six months was

$$20 + 18 + 22 + 30 + 48 + 42 = 180.$$

We can now set up a simple ratio as in the formal solution from question 2 in this section.

cars	30	180
degrees	*x*	360

Now draw in the division symbols and equal sign, cross multiply and divide the corresponding ratio to find the unknown quantity *x*.

$$\frac{30}{x} = \frac{180}{360}$$

$$180x = 10{,}800$$

$$x = \frac{10{,}800}{180} = 60.$$

This is choice (C).

For more information on this technique, see **Strategy 14** in ***"The 32 Most Effective SAT Math Strategies."***

* **Quick solution:** $\frac{30}{180} = \frac{1}{6}$, and $\frac{1}{6}$ of 360 is $\frac{360}{6} = 60$, choice (C).

5. GEOMETRY

* Simply rotate your test paper counterclockwise 90 degrees (one quarter turn). Sketch the figure in this position if necessary. Then observe that the answer is choice (D).

Helpful tip: You may want to observe what happens to just one corner of the figure as you rotate it, and use process of elimination.

For example, notice that the upper right corner of the figure has two boxes side by side. Upon rotation you get two boxes in the upper left corner, one above the other. Only choices (C) and (D) have this configuration. Thus, we can eliminate choices (A), (B), and (E).

Now look at the upper left corner which has a "4 box square." Upon rotation you get a "4 box square" in the lower left corner. Choice (C) does not have this configuration. Therefore the answer is choice (D).

6. ALGEBRA

Solution by guessing: Let's take a guess that the number is 3. Then twice the number is 6, and 3 more than twice the number is 9. This is a bit too small. So let's guess that the number is 3.5. Then twice the number is 7, and 3 more than twice the number is 10. That's right! But remember that the question is asking for 4 times the number. So we multiply 4(3.5) = 14, choice (D).

For more information on this technique, see **Strategy 3** in ***"The 32 Most Effective SAT Math Strategies."***

Algebraic solution: Let x be the number. Then $2x + 3 = 10$. So $2x = 7$, and $x = \frac{7}{2} = 3.5$. So $4x = 4(3.5) = 14$, choice (D).

Remark: There is actually no need to solve for x. We can simply multiply $2x$ by 2 to save a bit of time. See the next solution for details.

*** Quickest algebraic solution:** Let x be the number. Then

$$2x + 3 = 10$$

$$2x = 7$$

$$4x = 14.$$

This is choice (D).

Note that the remark at the end of question 1 from this section is relevant to this problem as well.

7. ALGEBRA

*** Solution by picking a number:** Let's choose a value for a which is less than 0, say $a = -2$. Then we have that $2a = 2(-2) = -4$, $4a = 4(-2) = -8$, and $8a = 8(-2) = -16$. In list form we have

$$-2, -4, -8, -16$$

We see that a = -2 is the greatest. So the answer is either choice (A) or (E).

Let's check one more number of a different "type," say $a = -.25$. Then we have that $2a = 2(-.25) = -.5$, $4a = 4(-.25) = -1$, and $8a = 8(-.25) = -2$. In list form we have

$$-.25, -.5, -1, -2$$

Again, we see that $a = -.25$ is the greatest. I'm convinced! The answer is choice (A).

For more information on this technique, see **Strategy 4** in ***"The 32 Most Effective SAT Math Strategies."***

*** A more definitive solution:** If a is negative, then multiplying a by a number greater than one makes the number **more** negative. That is, it makes the number **smaller**. So a is the largest of the four numbers. Therefore the answer is choice (A).

A picture for visual students: For those of you that prefer to "see" what's going on here, the following number line should be useful. 0 and the four numbers in the problem are labeled at the bottom of the number line. A few additional numbers have been included above the number line. These are not relevant to this particular problem.

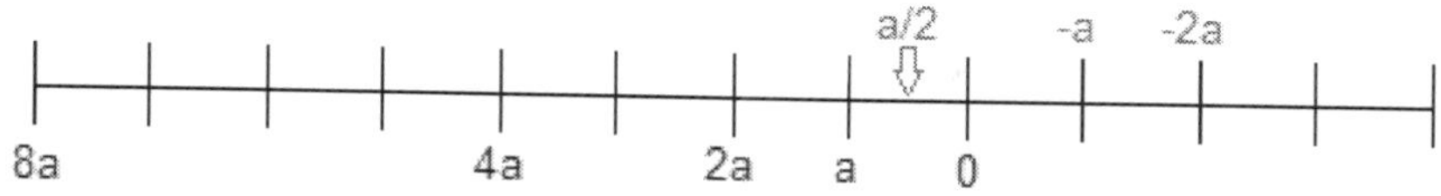

8. Geometry

* Let's split the figure into two rectangles.

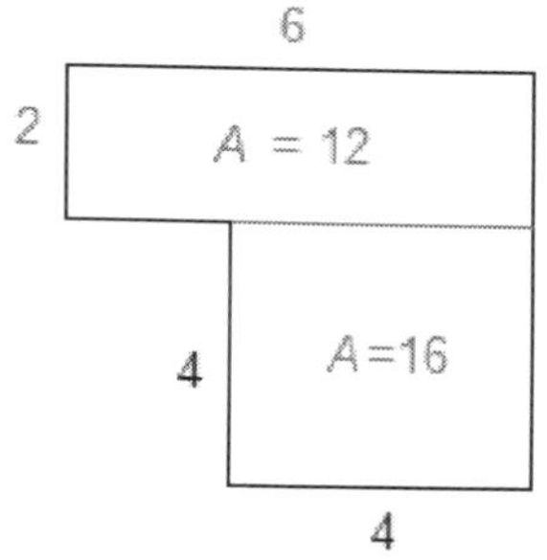

We see that the length of the top segment of the figure is 4 + 2 = 6, and the length of the upper left segment of the figure is 6 – 4 = 2. Thus, the area of the top rectangle is $A = (6)(2) = 12$, and the area of the bottom square is $A = 4^2 = (4)(4) = 16$. It follows that the area of the figure is $A = 12 + 16 = 28$, choice (B).

Two alternative solutions: The following two pictures show two other ways to solve this problem.

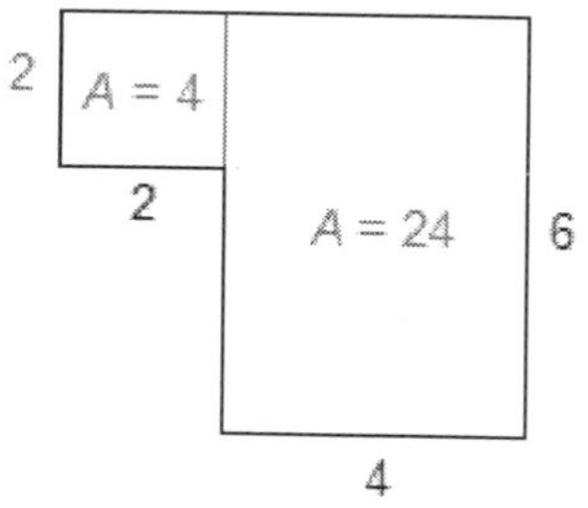

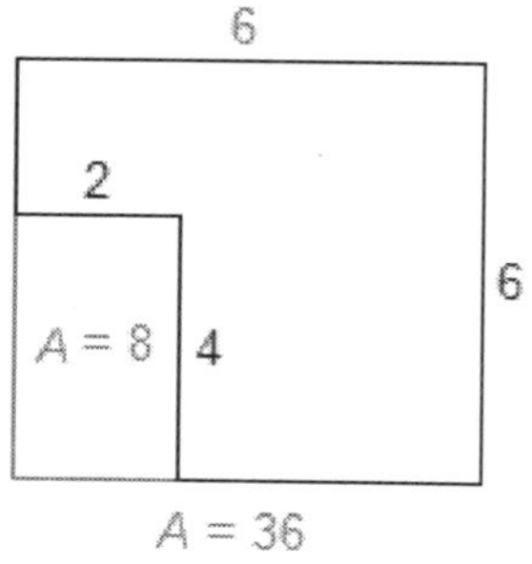

In the figure on the left, we see that the area is 4 + 24 = 28, choice (B).

In the figure on the right, the area of the large square is $A = (6)(6) = 36$, and the area of the smaller rectangle inside is $A = (2)(4) = 8$. So the area of the figure is $A = 36 - 8 = 28$, choice (B).

For more information on this technique, see **Strategy 23** in ***"The 32 Most Effective SAT Math Strategies."***

9. ALGEBRA

Solution by starting with choice (C): Let's guess that choice (C) is the answer and let $x = -5$. Then $(x - 2)^2 = (-5 - 2)^2 = (-7)^2 = 49$. This is too big.

Let's take a guess that choice (D) is the answer next. So we guess that $x = -3$. Then $(x - 2)^2 = (-3 - 2)^2 = (-5)^2 = 25$. This is correct. So the answer is choice (D).

Remark: The square of a number is **always** nonnegative. As an example $(-5)^2 = 25$ and **not** -25. Compare this to -5^2 which is equal to $(-1)(5^2) = (-1)(25) = -25$. For a review of **Order of Operations** see the end of the solution to Problem 3 in Section 8 of Test 1 (pp. 32-33).

For more information on this technique, see **Strategy 1** in ***"The 32 Most Effective SAT Math Strategies."***

* **Algebraic solution:** We use the **square root property**, and then solve for x.

$$(x - 2)^2 = 25$$
$$x - 2 = \pm 5$$
$$x = 2 \pm 5$$
$$x = 2 - 5 \text{ or } x = 2 + 5$$
$$x = -3 \text{ or } x = 7$$

Since it is given that $x < 0$, the answer is $x = -3$, choice (D).

Remark: The **square root property** says that if $b^2 = a$, then $b = \pm a$.

Common Error: When solving an equation with a "square" in it students will often apply the square root property incorrectly by only taking the positive square root. In this problem, the erroneous computation might look like this.

$$(x - 2)^2 = 25$$
$$x - 2 = 5$$
$$x = 7$$

This is not one of the answer choices, but nonetheless many students will choose choice (B) because it looks similar. DO NOT fall into this trap!

10. Geometry

*** Solution by using the fact that the figure is drawn to scale:** Clearly $\overline{PT}$ is more than half the size of $\overline{PS}$, so that $\frac{PT}{PS} > \frac{1}{2}$. Thus, the answer is $\frac{4}{5}$, choice (E).

Remember: On the SAT when the answer choices are all numbers, these numbers are usually given in either increasing or decreasing order.

For more information on this technique, see **Strategy 6** in **"The 32 Most Effective SAT Math Strategies."**

Solution using geometry: Triangles *PQT* and *PRS* are **similar**, and corresponding sides of similar triangles are in proportion. Therefore $\frac{PT}{PS} = \frac{QT}{RS} = \frac{8}{10} = \frac{4}{5}$. Thus, the answer is choice (E).

Definition of similar: Two triangles are **similar** if their angles are congruent.

Note that similar triangles **do not** have to be the same size.

Also note that to show that two triangles are similar we need only show that two pairs of angles are congruent. We get the third pair for free because all triangles have 180 degrees.

In this problem we have that angles *PTQ* and *PSR* are congruent and the two triangles share angle *P*.

11. Data Analysis

*** Solution by plugging in a point:** Let's pick a point and plug it into the answer choices. For example, note that when $W = 3$, we have $L = 30$. Substituting $W = 3$ into each answer choice gives the following.

(A) $L = 3$
(B) $L = 10$
(C) $L = 13$
(D) $L = 30$
(E) $L = 40$

Since choices (A), (B), (C), and (E) came out incorrect we can eliminate them. Therefore the answer is choice (D).

Important note: (D) is **not** the correct answer simply because it is equal to 30. It is correct because all four of the other choices are **not** 30. **You absolutely must check all five choices!**

Another note: Note that if we were to choose $W = 1$, then $L = 10$, and both choices (B) and (D) come out correct. We would then have to choose another point to figure out if (B) or (D) were the correct answer.

For more information on this technique, see **Strategy 5** in ***"The 32 Most Effective SAT Math Strategies."***

Solution using the slope formula: Let's compute the slope of the line. We first need two points. We can take any two, say (1, 10) and (3, 30). Therefore the slope of the line is $m = \frac{30-10}{3-1} = \frac{20}{2} = 10$. Only choices (D) and (E) are equations of lines with a slope of 10. Clearly the line does **not** cross the y-axis at $y = 10$. This eliminates choice (E) and the answer is choice (D).

For more information on this technique, see **Strategy 28** in ***"The 32 Most Effective SAT Math Strategies."***

For a review of **slope** see the end of the solution to Problem 12 in Section 3 of Test 1 (pp. 15-17).

Complete solution: Note that I do not recommend using this method on the SAT. I include it for completeness. As in the previous solution we see that the slope of the line is $m = 10$, and the line passes through the point (1, 10). We can now write an equation of the line in **point-slope form**.

$$L - 10 = 10(W - 1)$$

We can now put the line into slope-intercept form by distributing on the right hand side and solving for L.

$$L - 10 = 10W - 10$$
$$L = 10W$$

Therefore, the answer is choice (D).

Point slope form: The point-slope form for an equation of a line is

$$\boldsymbol{y - y_0 = m(x - x_0)}$$

where m is the slope of the line and (x_0, y_0) is a point on the line.

In the given problem $m = 10$, $W_0 = 1$ and $L_0 = 10$.

Remark: We're using the variables W and L in place of x and y here. So technically in this problem the point slope form would be

$$L - L_0 = m(W - W_0)$$

12. Statistics

* **Quick solution:** If n were to equal 6, then 5 and 6 would both be modes. But we are given that 5 is the only mode. So n CANNOT be 6, choice (A).

Note: If we list the numbers in increasing order we get the following.

$$5, 5, 5, 5, 6, 6, 6, 7$$

Now, if $n \leq 5$, then the list becomes

$$n, 5, 5, 5, 5, 6, 6, 6, 7$$

and we see that the median is 5. If $5 < n < 6$, then the list becomes

$$5, 5, 5, 5, n, 6, 6, 6, 7$$

and we see that the median is n. If $6 \leq n \leq 7$, then the list becomes

$$5, 5, 5, 5, 6, 6, 6, n, 7$$

and we see that the median is 6. Finally, if $n > 7$, then the list becomes

$$5, 5, 5, 5, 6, 6, 6, 7, n$$

and we see that the median is 6.

In particular, for every answer choice given the median is 6. So the information given about the median in the problem is not needed to solve the problem.

Definitions: The **median** of a list of numbers is the middle number when the numbers are arranged in increasing order. If the total number of values in the list is even, then the median is the average (arithmetic mean) of the two middle values.

The **mode** of a list of numbers is the number that appears most frequently in the list. More than one number can be a mode if there is a tie.

13. Number Theory

* There are 3 + 7 = 10 elements in the intersection of sets *Y* and *Z*, choice (C).

Let's find the number of elements in some other regions for extra practice.

	Region	**Number of Elements**
1	*X*	5 + 2 + 4 + 3 = 14
2	*Y*	3 + 2 + 7 + 3 = 15
3	*Z*	5 + 4 + 7 + 3 = 19
4	Only *X*	5
5	Only *Y*	3
6	Only *Z*	5
7	The intersection of *X* and *Y*	2 + 3 = 5
8	The intersection of *X* and *Z*	4 + 3 = 7
9	The intersection of *X*, *Y* and *Z*	3
10	*X* and *Y* but not *Z*	2
11	*X* and *Z* but not *Y*	4
12	*Y* and *Z* but not *X*	7

Note: The intersection of sets *Y* and *Z* consists of 2 regions. They are labeled by numbers 9 and 12 in the table.

Definition: The **intersection** of sets *X* and *Y* is the set $X \cap Y$ consisting of the elements common to both sets.

14. Algebra

Solution by picking a number: Let's choose a value for *t*, say $t = 2$. Then we have $m = t^3 = 2^3 = 8$, and $w = m^2 + m = 8^2 + 8 = 64 + 8 = 72$. **Put a nice big, dark circle around 72 so that you can find it easily later.** Substituting 2 in for *t* in each answer choice gives the following:

(A) $2^2 + 2 = 4 + 2 = 6$
(B) $2^3 = 8$
(C) $2^3 + 2 = 8 + 2 = 10$
(D) $2^5 + 2^3 = 32 + 8 = 40$
(E) $2^6 + 2^3 = 64 + 8 = 72$

Since (A), (B), (C), and (D) each came out incorrect, the answer is choice (E).

Important note: (E) is **not** the correct answer simply because it is equal to 72. It is correct because all 4 of the other choices are **not** 72. **You absolutely must check all five choices!**

For more information on this technique, see **Strategy 4** in ***"The 32 Most Effective SAT Math Strategies."***

* **Algebraic solution:** We do a simple substitution and use the appropriate law of exponents.

$$w = m^2 + m = (t^3)^2 + t^3 = t^6 + t^3$$

This is choice (E).

For a review of the **Basic Laws of Exponents**, see the end of the solution to Problem 8 in Section 8 of Test 1 (p. 35). In particular, look at the fifth law in that table to see why the last equality is true.

For definitions of the **integers** and **positive integers** see the end of the solution to Problem 11 in Section 3 of Test 1 (pp. 14-15).

15. FUNCTIONS

* $6\Delta = (6 - 1)(6 + 1) = (5)(7) = 35$ and $5\Delta = (5 - 1)(5 + 1) = (4)(6) = 24$. Therefore $6\Delta - 5\Delta = 35 - 24 =$ **11**. **Put a nice big, dark circle around 11 so that you can find it easily later.**

Now let's start doing the computations in the answer choices beginning with choice (C).

$4\Delta = (4 - 1)(4 + 1) = (3)(5) = 15$ and $3\Delta = (3 - 1)(3 + 1) = (2)(4) = 8$. Therefore $4\Delta + 3\Delta = 15 + 8 = 23$. This is too large. Thus we can eliminate choices (C), (D), and (E). Let's try choice (B) next.

We already computed $3\Delta = 8$ and $2\Delta = (2 - 1)(2 + 1) = (1)(3) = 3$. Therefore $3\Delta + 2\Delta = 8 + 3 = 11$. So the answer is choice (B).

Remark: You can minimize the amount of time it takes to do these computations by doing everything in your head and just writing down the final answer. For example, for 6Δ you should subtract 6 – 1 to get 5, and then add 6 + 1 to get 7, and then multiply (5)(7) to get 35. Then just write down 35 near 6Δ. Repeat this as you go.

For more information on this technique, see **Strategy 1** in ***"The 32 Most Effective SAT Math Strategies."***

16. ALGEBRA

Solution by starting with choice (C): Let's start with choice (C) and guess that $x = 4$, $y = 2$. Then $\frac{x^2}{y} = \frac{4^2}{2} = \frac{16}{2} = 8$ which is an integer, but $\frac{x}{y} = \frac{4}{2} = 2$ is also an integer. So we can eliminate choice (C).

Let's try choice (D) next and guess that $x = 6$, $y = 4$. It then follows that $\frac{x^2}{y} = \frac{6^2}{4} = \frac{36}{4} = 9$ which is an integer, and $\frac{x}{y} = \frac{6}{4} = 1.5$ which is not an integer. Therefore the answer is choice (D).

For more information on this technique, see **Strategy 1** in ***"The 32 Most Effective SAT Math Strategies."***

*** Quick Method:** It's a bit quicker to compute $\frac{x}{y}$ in each answer choice and cross out any that are integers.

(A) 1
(B) 1.5
(C) 2
(D) 1.5
(E) 3

So we can eliminate choices (A), (C), and (E).

We now compute $\frac{x^2}{y}$ for choices (B) and (D) and we get

(B) $\frac{9}{4}$
(D) $\frac{36}{4} = 9$

We see that (B) does not yield an integer, whereas (D) does. So the answer is choice (D).

Remark: With this method you can get the solution in under 10 seconds as long as you do these computations quickly (but carefully) in your head.

See the solution to Problem 11 in Section 3 of Test 1 (pp. 14-15) for the definition of an **integer**.

17. GEOMETRY

Recall that $|a|$ means the **absolute value** of a. It takes whatever number is between the two lines and makes it nonnegative. For some examples, $|3| = 3$, $|-5| = 5$, $|0| = 0$.

* **Quick graphical solution:** Graphically, taking an absolute value leaves points above the x-axis exactly where they are, and takes points below the x-axis and reflects them across the x-axis (to place them above the x-axis). Now simply note that the graph in choice (B) is the only one that leaves the points above the x-axis exactly where they are. So the answer is choice (B).

Solution by plugging in points: Let's plug in a 0 for x. It then follows that $y = |-2x + 6| = |6| = 6$. So the point (0, 6) is on the graph. Therefore we can eliminate choices (A) and (E).

Let's plug in a 3 for x next. Then $y = |-2x + 6| = |-6 + 6| = |0| = 0$. So the point (3, 0) is on the graph. This eliminates choice (D) as well.

We're down to choices (B) and (E). Let's plug in a 1 for x next. It then follows that $y = |-2x + 6| = |-2 + 6| = |4| = 4$. So the point (1, 4) is on the graph. This eliminates choice (E).

Therefore the answer is choice (B).

For more information on this technique, see **Strategy 5** in ***"The 32 Most Effective SAT Math Strategies."***

Solution using your graphing calculator: Press the Y= button and type the following for Y_1.

$$Y_1 = \text{abs}(-2x+6)$$

Note that you can find "abs(" by pressing MATH, scrolling right to NUM, and then pressing ENTER (or 1).

Now press ZOOM 6 to graph this, and you will see immediately that the answer is choice (B).

18. GEOMETRY

* The dimensions of such a box would be d, d and h. So the volume would be $V = d^2h$, choice (B).

Further explanation: A circle of diameter d fits snuggly inside a square of side length d as shown in the figure below.

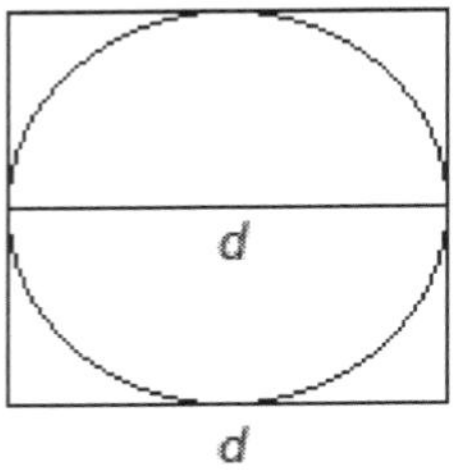

This square has area $A = d^2$.

Now extend this square upwards h units to generate a box that snuggly fits the cylinder.

19. ALGEBRA

Let's begin by translating the sentences into equations. "The square of x is equal to 4 times the square of y" translates to $x^2 = 4y^2$, and "x is 1 more than twice y" translates to $x = 2y + 1$." From here we have several options.

Solution by starting with choice (C): Let's start with choice (C) and guess that $x = -\frac{1}{4}$. Then from the second equation we have

$$-\frac{1}{4} = 2y + 1$$
$$-\frac{1}{4} - 1 = 2y$$
$$-\frac{5}{4} = 2y$$
$$-\frac{5}{8} = y$$

We now check $x = -\frac{1}{4}$, $y = -\frac{5}{8}$ into the first equation

$$x^2 = 4y^2$$
$$(-\frac{1}{4})^2 = 4(-\frac{5}{8})^2$$
$$\frac{1}{16} = 4(\frac{25}{64}) = \frac{25}{16}$$

This is false, so we can eliminate choice (C).

Let's try choice (D) next and guess that $x = \frac{1}{4}$. Then from the second equation we have

$$\frac{1}{4} = 2y + 1$$
$$\frac{1}{4} - 1 = 2y$$
$$-\frac{3}{4} = 2y$$
$$-\frac{3}{8} = y$$

We now check $x = \frac{1}{4}$, $y = -\frac{3}{8}$ into the first equation

$$x^2 = 4y^2$$
$$(\frac{1}{4})^2 = 4(-\frac{3}{8})^2$$
$$\frac{1}{16} = 4(\frac{9}{64}) = \frac{9}{16}$$

This is false, so we can eliminate choice (D).

Let's try choice (E) next and guess that $x = \frac{1}{2}$. Then from the second equation we have

$$\frac{1}{2} = 2y + 1$$
$$\frac{1}{2} - 1 = 2y$$
$$-\frac{1}{2} = 2y$$
$$-\frac{1}{4} = y$$

We now check $x = \frac{1}{2}$, $y = -\frac{1}{4}$ into the first equation

$$x^2 = 4y^2$$
$$(\frac{1}{2})^2 = 4(-\frac{1}{4})^2$$
$$\frac{1}{4} = 4(\frac{1}{16}) = \frac{1}{4}$$

This is true, and so the answer is choice (E).

Algebraic solution 1: We substitute $2y + 1$ in for x in the first equation.

$$x^2 = 4y^2$$
$$(2y + 1)^2 = 4y^2$$
$$(2y + 1)(2y + 1) = 4y^2$$
$$4y^2 + 2y + 2y + 1 = 4y^2$$
$$4y + 1 = 0$$
$$4y = -1$$
$$y = -\frac{1}{4}$$

Now, $x = 2y + 1 = 2(-\frac{1}{4}) + 1 = -\frac{1}{2} + 1 = \frac{1}{2}$, choice (E).

Algebraic solution 2: We solve $x = 2y + 1$ for y first.

$$x = 2y + 1$$
$$x - 1 = 2y$$
$$\frac{x-1}{2} = y$$

We now substitute $\frac{x-1}{2}$ in for y in the first equation.

$$x^2 = 4y^2$$
$$x^2 = 4(\frac{x-1}{2})^2 = \frac{4(x-1)^2}{4} = (x - 1)(x - 1) = x^2 - x - x + 1 = x^2 - 2x + 1$$
$$0 = -2x + 1$$
$$2x = 1$$
$$x = \frac{1}{2}$$

This is answer choice (E).

* **Quickest algebraic solution:** We solve the first equation for x.

$$x^2 = 4y^2$$
$$x = \pm 2y$$

We substitute this into the second equation.

$$x = 2y + 1$$
$$\pm 2y = 2y + 1$$
$$2y = 2y + 1 \text{ or } -2y = 2y + 1$$
$$0 = 1 \text{ or } -4y = 1$$
$$y = -\frac{1}{4}$$

Finally we have $x = 2y + 1 = 2(-\frac{1}{4}) + 1 = -\frac{1}{2} + 1 = \frac{1}{2}$, choice (E).

Note that 0 = 1 is false so that we can disregard this equation.

20. Number Theory

* **Quick solution:** The slope of line ℓ is $\frac{1}{2}$. Since ℓ and q are perpendicular, they have negative reciprocal slopes. Therefore the slope of line q is -2. By also computing the slope of line q directly, we get the following equation.

$$\frac{t-1}{-2} = -2$$
$$t - 1 = 4$$
$$t = 5.$$

Therefore the answer is choice (E).

For more information on this technique, see **Strategy 28** in ***"The 32 Most Effective SAT Math Strategies."***

Note: Slope $= m = \frac{\text{rise}}{\text{run}} = \frac{y_2 - y_1}{x_2 - x_1}$

In this problem the slope of line ℓ is $\frac{1-0}{2-0} = \frac{1}{2}$, and the slope of line q is $\frac{t-1}{0-2}$.

Definitions: Two lines are **perpendicular** if they intersect at right angles. Perpendicular lines have slopes that are negative reciprocals of each other.

As an example, the reciprocal of $\frac{1}{2}$ is 2. The negative reciprocal of $\frac{1}{2}$ is -2.

SECTION 5

1. ALGEBRA

* Since 3(0) = 0, we have that $x = 0$. So $1 + x + x^2 = 1 + 0 + 0^2 = 1$, choice (B).

Remark: To formally solve for x in the equation $3x = 0$, we can divide each side of the equation by 3 to get $x = \frac{0}{3} = 0$.

Note that $\frac{0}{a} = 0$ for any nonzero number a.

2. GEOMETRY

Solution by picking numbers: Let's choose a value for the diameter of circle B, say 2. Then the diameter of circle A is (3)(2) = 6. The radius of circle B is then 1, and the radius of circle A is 3. Therefore the ratio of the radius of circle A to the radius of circle B is 3 : 1, choice (E).

Algebraic solution: Let d be the diameter of circle B. Then the diameter of circle A is $3d$. The radius of circle B is then $\frac{d}{2}$, and the radius of circle A is $\frac{3d}{2}$. Therefore the ratio of the radius of circle A to the radius of circle B is $\frac{3d}{2} \div \frac{d}{2} = \frac{3d}{2} \cdot \frac{2}{d} = \frac{3d}{d} = \frac{3}{1}$. Using the "colon" notation this can be written as 3 : 1, choice (E).

* **Geometric solution:** If the diameter of circle A is 3 times the diameter of circle B, then the radius of circle A is 3 times the radius of circle B. Therefore the ratio of the radius of circle A to the radius of circle B is 3 : 1, choice (E).

For the definitions of **radius** and **diameter** see Problem 8 in Section 3 of Test 1 (p. 13).

3. Number Theory

* **Solution by picking sets:** Let's choose a set N of numbers whose average is 3. A really simple choice is $N = \{3\}$. Then $M = \{6\}$, and the average of the numbers in set M is 6, choice (D).

Note: We could have let N be any set of numbers with average 3. As another example, let $N = \{2, 4\}$. Then $M = \{4, 8\}$, and the average of the numbers in set M is $\frac{4+8}{2} = \frac{12}{2} = 6$.

Here we have used a minor twist on **Strategy 4** in ***"The 32 Most Effective SAT Math Strategies."***

Note: The following solution is included for completeness. Do not worry too much if you cannot understand it.

Complete algebraic solution: Let $N = \{x_1, x_2,..., x_k\}$ be a set with average 3. By converting the average to a sum we see that $x_1 + x_2 + \cdots + x_k = 3k$. Now note that $M = \{2x_1, 2x_2,..., 2x_k\}$, so that the average of the numbers in set M is $\frac{2x_1 + 2x_2 + \cdots + 2x_k}{k} = \frac{2(x_1 + x_2 + \cdots + x_k)}{k} = \frac{2(3k)}{k} = \frac{6k}{k} = 6$, choice (D).

For more information on this technique, see **Strategy 20** in ***"The 32 Most Effective SAT Math Strategies."***

4. Algebra

Solution by picking numbers: Let's choose specific values for P, R and T, say $P = 2$, $R = 3$, and $T = 4$. Then $PRT \times 10^{-2} = 234 \times 10^{-2} = 2.34$ (see note below if you do not know how to compute this). We now substitute our chosen values for P, R, and T into each answer choice.

(A) 0.0234
(B) 0.234
(C) 2.34
(D) 23.4
(E) 23,400

Since choices (A), (B), (D), and (E) came out incorrect, the answer is choice (C).

Note: To compute 234×10^{-2} we can simply type this expression into our calculator as 2.34*10^-2. As an alternative, multiplying by 10^{-2} is equivalent to moving the decimal point to the left 2 places.

For more information on this technique, see **Strategy 4** in ***"The 32 Most Effective SAT Math Strategies."***

* **Quick solution:** As stated in the note above, multiplying by 10^{-2} is equivalent to moving the decimal point to the left 2 places. Therefore the answer is *P.RT*, choice (C).

A quick lesson in multiplying by 10^n where *n* is an integer: If $n \geq 0$, move the decimal point to the right n places. If $n < 0$, move the decimal point to the left n places. Fill in any zeros as is necessary. Here are some examples.

$$234 \times 10^{-2} = 2.34$$
$$234 \times 10^{3} = 234{,}000$$
$$2 \times 10^{-4} = .0002$$
$$2.3 \times 10^{2} = 230$$
$$234 \times 10^{0} = 234$$

Definitions: The **integers** are the counting numbers together with their negatives.

$$\{\ldots,-4, -3, -2, -1, 0, 1, 2, 3, 4,\ldots\}$$

The **digits** are the integers that require only one symbol.

$$\{0, 1, 2, 3, 4, 5, 6, 7, 8, 9\}$$

5. GEOMETRY

Solution by picking numbers: Let's choose values for k and n that make $k + n < k$ true. For example, if we let $k = 2$ and $n = -3$, then we have that $2 + (-3) = -1 < 2$. So we can use these values for k and n. So let's substitute these values for k and n into each answer choice.

(A) $2 > 0$
(B) $2 = 0$
(C) $2 < 0$
(D) $-3 > 0$
(E) $-3 < 0$

Since choices (B), (C), and (D) are false we can eliminate them.

We still need to eliminate one more answer choice. So let's try changing k to $k = -2$, and we'll leave n as $n = -3$. Then we have $-2 + (-3) = -5 < -2$. So we can use these values for k and n. So let's substitute these values for k and n into choices (A) and (E).

(A) $-2 > 0$
(E) $-3 < 0$

Since choice (A) is false we can eliminate it, and the answer is choice (E).

For more information on this technique, see **Strategy 4** in ***"The 32 Most Effective SAT Math Strategies."***

* **Algebraic solution:** We simply subtract k from each side of the inequality.

$$\begin{array}{r} k + n < k \\ \underline{-k \qquad -k} \\ n < 0 \end{array}$$

We see that the answer is choice (E).

6. Geometry

* **Solution using the definition of slope:** Slope = $\frac{\text{rise}}{\text{run}} = \frac{y}{x}$. So we have that $\frac{y}{x} = \frac{7}{16}$. We are also given the $y = 3.5$. So

$$\frac{y}{x} = \frac{7}{16}$$
$$\frac{3.5}{x} = \frac{7}{16}$$
$$7x = 56$$
$$x = 8$$

In going from the second equation to the third equation we cross multiplied. Therefore the answer is choice (A).

Note: Slope = $m = \frac{\text{rise}}{\text{run}} = \frac{y_2 - y_1}{x_2 - x_1}$.

In this problem we only needed to use Slope = $\frac{\text{rise}}{\text{run}}$.

7. Functions

* **Solution by picking a number and graphing:** Let's pick a value for a, say $a = 3$. Then the given graph is for the equation $y = 3x^2 + 2$, and the equation for the graph not shown is $y = x^2 + 2$. Now put both of these into your graphing calculator by pressing the Y= button and typing the following for Y_1 and Y_2.

$$Y_1 = 3X\text{^}2 + 2$$
$$Y_2 = X\text{^}2 + 2$$

Then press ZOOM 6 to graph these in a standard viewing window. Make sure you watch carefully as these are drawn. Y_1 will be drawn first, followed by Y_2. Note that the second one drawn is wider than the first. Therefore the answer is choice (B).

For more information on this technique, see **Strategy 4** in ***"The 32 Most Effective SAT Math Strategies."***

A lesson in transformations for the advanced student: Given a function $f(x)$ and a positive number c, we have the following basic transformations.

$f(x) + c$ vertical shift up c units

$f(x) - c$ vertical shift down c units

$f(x - c)$ horizontal shift right c units

$f(x + c)$ horizontal shift left c units

$-f(x)$ reflection in x-axis

$f(-x)$ reflection in y-axis

$cf(x)$ vertical expansion if $c > 1$, vertical compression if $0 < c < 1$

$f(cx)$ horizontal expansion if $0 < c < 1$, horizontal compression if $c > 1$

In the given question we have a horizontal expansion. To see this is a bit tricky. Let $f(x) = ax^2 + 2$. Then the second equation is

$$y = \frac{a}{3}x^2 + 2 = a(\frac{1}{\sqrt{3}}x)^2 + 2 = f(\frac{1}{\sqrt{3}}x)$$

Since $\frac{1}{\sqrt{3}} < 1$ we see that this is a horizontal expansion. In other words, the graph will be wider.

8. Counting

* **Solution using the counting principle:** The counting principle says that when you perform events in succession you multiply the number of possibilities. There are 3 ways to choose a hat. Once the hat is chosen there are now 2 ways to choose a sweater. Finally, after choosing the hat and sweater, there is 1 way to choose a pair of jeans. Thus, there are (3)(2)(1) = 6 possibilities, choice (B).

Solution by making a list: Let's list all the possibilities in a nice way:

RBW   RWB   BRW   BWR   WRB   WBR

In the above list, R stands for red, B for blue, and W for white. The first position is for the hat, the second for the sweater, and the third for the pair of jeans. We see that there are 6 possibilities, choice (B).

For more information on this technique, see **Strategy 21** in ***"The 32 Most Effective SAT Math Strategies."***

A more sophisticated solution using permutations: We can use a permutation. There are ${}_3P_3 = 3! = (1)(2)(3) = \mathbf{6}$ ways to arrange 3 colors. So the answer is choice (B).

For more information on **permutations** see Problem 14 from Section 8 of Test 1 (p. 38)

9. Algebra

Solution by guessing: Let's take a guess that the number is 5. Then twice the number is 10. When we increase this by 5 we get 10 + 5 = 15. This is a bit too big.

So let's guess that the number is a bit smaller, say 4. Then twice the number is 8. When we increase this by 5 we get 8 + 5 = 13. This is a bit too small.

So let's try 4.5 next. Then twice the number is 9. When we increase this by 5 we get 9 + 5 = 14. This is correct so that the number is in fact **4.5**.

For more information on this technique, see **Strategy 3** in ***"The 32 Most Effective SAT Math Strategies."***

* **Algebraic solution:** Let x be the number. Then $2x + 5 = 14$. Subtracting 5 from each side of the equation yields $2x = 9$. Dividing each side of the equation by 2 gives us $x =$ **9/2** or **4.5**.

Remark: We can also combine these two methods by first writing out the equation $2x + 5 = 14$, and then plugging guesses in for x in this equation. Note that $2(4.5) + 5 = 9 + 5 = 14$.

10. GEOMETRY

* This is a standard SAT problem involving two parallel lines cut by a transversal. In this situation angles that are adjacent to each other add up to 180 degrees. So we have

$$x + y = 180$$
$$x + 3x = 180$$
$$4x = 180$$
$$x = \frac{180}{4} = 45.$$

Therefore $y = 180 - 45 =$ **135**.

Remarks: (1) In the second equation above we simply replaced y by $3x$.

(2) Note that the transversal k creates 8 angles, four of which have measure x. The other four have measure y. Any two non-congruent angles are supplementary, ie. they add up to 180 degrees. In other words $x + y = 180$.

11. GEOMETRY

* The volume of the box is $V = \ell wh = (4)(4)(8) = 128$. The volume of each CD case is $V = \ell wh = (4)(4)\,(\frac{1}{4}) = 4$. We now simply divide the volume of the box by the volume of a CD case. $\frac{128}{4} =$ **32**.

Remark: We can get the answer quickly by performing one computation in our calculator. Type it in just like this: (4*4*8)/(4*4*1/4) = 32

For more information on this technique, see **Strategy 24** in ***"The 32 Most Effective SAT Math Strategies."***

12. ALGEBRA

Algebraic solution: We will start by cross multiplying.

$$\frac{3x+y}{y} = \frac{6}{5}$$

$$(3x + y)(5) = 6y$$

$$15x + 5y = 6y$$

$$15x = y$$

We can get $\frac{x}{y}$ to one side by performing **cross division.** We do this just like cross multiplication, but we divide instead. Dividing each side of the equation by $15y$ will do the trick (this way we get rid of 15 on the left, and y on the right).

$$\frac{x}{y} = \frac{1}{15}$$

So we can grid in **1/15**, **.066**, or **.067**.

*** Quick, clever solution:** Multiply the numerator and denominator of $\frac{6}{5}$ by 3 to rewrite $\frac{6}{5}$ as $\frac{18}{15}$. So we have

$$\frac{3x+y}{y} = \frac{18}{15}$$

Now let $y = 15$, so that we have

$$3x + y = 18$$

$$3x + 15 = 18$$

$$3x = 3$$

$$x = 1$$

It follows that $\frac{x}{y}$ = **1/15**.

Remark: It was not necessary to rewrite $\frac{6}{5}$ as $\frac{18}{15}$ in the above solution. It just makes the computations easier. If we set $y = 5$, and $3x + y = 6$, we get $3x + 5 = 6$, so that $3x = 1$, and $x = \frac{1}{3}$. So $\frac{x}{y} = \frac{1}{3} \div 5 = \frac{1}{3} \cdot \frac{1}{5}$ = **1/15**.

13. Statistics

* The TOTAL increase in profit for the three stores combined is 26,250 – 21,000 = 5250. Since there are three stores, the average increase in profit is $\frac{5250}{3}$ = **1750**.

14. Functions

Solution by guessing: Let's try to guess a value for a, say $a = 3$. Then we have that $f(3) = |3(3) - 17| = |9 - 17| = |-8| = 8$. In this case $f(3) > 3$ so that this value of a does NOT work.

Let's try $a = 5$ next. Then $f(5) = |3(5) - 17| = |15 - 17| = |-2| = 2$. In this case, $f(5) < 5$. So one possible answer is $a =$ **5**.

Remark: The best guesses in this problem would be values of a such that $3a$ is near 17. In fact, a really good guess would be $a = \frac{17}{3}$. In this case we have $f(\frac{17}{3}) = |3(\frac{17}{3}) - 17| = |17 - 17| = |0| = 0$ which is less than $\frac{17}{3}$. So another solution to this problem is $a =$ **17/3**.

For more information on this technique, see **Strategy 3** in ***"The 32 Most Effective SAT Math Strategies."***

* **Quick solution:** Just solve the equation $3a = 17$. So a = **17/3** (see the remark above for a full explanation of why this works).

Algebraic solution: Let's solve the inequality $f(a) < a$, i.e. $|3a - 17| < a$. This is equivalent to the following inequality without absolute values.

$$-a < 3a - 17 < a$$

This is actually two distinct inequalities. Let's solve each one separately.

$-a < 3a - 17$	$3a - 17 < a$
$0 < 4a - 17$	$2a - 17 < 0$
$17 < 4a$	$2a < 17$
$\frac{17}{4} < a$	$a < \frac{17}{2}$
$4.25 < a$	$a < 8.5$

Putting these two inequalities together we have $4.25 < a < 8.5$. So there are many different answers we can grid in.

For example, we can grid in **5**. We can also grid in **7.23**, etc.

Remark: I wouldn't recommend the full algebraic solution on the SAT since it is quite time consuming. You could however combine the two strategies to get a single answer more quickly. For example, you can just solve the inequality $3a - 17 < a$ to get $a < 8.5$ (see above), and then guess $a = 8$. Let's check this. $f(8) = |3(8) - 17| = |24 - 17| = |7| = 7$. So $f(8) < 8$, and one possible answer is **8**.

15. Counting

* **Solution by guessing:** Let's guess that Ari needs to take 5 more red pieces. Then Ari takes $13 - 5 = 8$ green pieces. So Ari now has $3 + 5 = 8$ red pieces, and $4 + 8 = 12$ green pieces. So 5 is too small.

Let's next guess that Ari needs to take 7 more red pieces. Then Ari takes $13 - 7 = 6$ green pieces. So Ari has $3 + 7 = 10$ red pieces, and $4 + 6 = 10$ green pieces. So 7 is still just a bit too small.

8 should do it! Let's check. We guess that Ari needs to take 8 more red pieces. Then Ari takes $13 - 8 = 5$ green pieces. So Ari now has $3 + 8 = 11$ red pieces, and $4 + 5 = 9$ green pieces. So the answer is **8**.

Important note: It is not enough that the number 8 works. It is just as important that we saw that the number 7 did NOT work.

For more information on this technique, see **Strategy 3** in ***"The 32 Most Effective SAT Math Strategies."***

16. Number Theory

Solution by listing: Let's simply list all the "tri-factorable" positive integers that are less than 1000.

$(1)(2)(3) = 6$
$(2)(3)(4) = 24$
$(3)(4)(5) = 60$
$(4)(5)(6) = 120$
$(5)(6)(7) = 210$
$(6)(7)(8) = 336$
$(7)(8)(9) = 504$
$(8)(9)(10) = 720$
$(9)(10)(11) = 990$
$(10)(11)(12) = 1320$, **too big**!

So the tri-factorable integers less than 1000 are 6, 24, 60, 120, 210, 336, 504, 720, and 990. There are **9**.

For more information on this technique, see **Strategy 21** in ***"The 32 Most Effective SAT Math Strategies."***

*** Quick solution:** We really only need to find the largest product of three consecutive integers that gives a number less than 1000.

(10)(11)(12) = 1320, **too big**!
(9)(10)(11) = 990

So we can see if the first factor is an integer between 1 and 9, inclusive, then we get a"tri-factorable" positive integer less than 1000. So the answer is **9**.

For definitions of the **integers** and **positive integers** see the end of the solution to Problem 11 in Section 3 of Test 1 (pp. 14-15).

Consecutive integers are integers that follow each other in order. The difference between consecutive integers is 1. Here are two examples.

1, 2, 3	these are three consecutive integers
-3, -2, -1, 0, 1	these are five consecutive integers

In general, if x is an integer, then x, $x + 1$, $x + 2$, $x + 3$, ... are consecutive integers.

17. ALGEBRA

Solution by guessing: Let's try t = 30 minutes. Carrier A charges \$1 for the first 20 minutes and \$.07 per minute for the last 10 minutes. So in total carrier A charges 1 + .07(10) = 1 + .7 = \$1.70. Carrier B charges .06(30) = \$1.80.

Let's try t = 35 next. Then carrier A charges 1 + .07(15) = 1 + 1.05 = \$2.05. Carrier B charges .06(35) = \$2.10.

Since the price difference has decreased by half, it looks like t = 40 should work. Let's check. Carrier A charges 1 + .07(20) = 1 + 1.4 = \$2.40. Carrier B charges .06(40) = \$2.40. This is a match. So the answer is t = **40**.

For more information on this technique, see **Strategy 3** in ***"The 32 Most Effective SAT Math Strategies."***

* **Algebraic solution:** Even though the algebraic solution is quicker, this may be confusing to many students. Unless you are very skilled at changing word problems into algebraic equations, I recommend you stick with the previous solution.

If $t > 20$, then the cost of a telephone call using carrier A for t minutes is $1 + .07(t - 20)$. The cost of using carrier B for t minutes is $.06t$. We set these equal to each other and solve for t.

$$1 + .07(t - 20) = .06t$$
$$1 + .07t - 1.4 = .06t$$
$$.07t - .4 = .06t$$
$$.01t - .4 = 0$$
$$.01t = .4$$
$$t = \frac{.4}{.01} = \mathbf{40}$$

18. Geometry

* The length of one side of a small square is k. Therefore the perimeter of the figure is $16k$. The area of one small square is k^2. Since there are 10 small squares in the figure, the total area is $10k^2$. We are given that the perimeter is equal to the area. So we solve the following equation for k.

$$10k^2 = 16k$$
$$10k^2 - 16k = 0$$
$$2k(5k - 8) = 0$$
$$2k = 0 \text{ or } 5k - 8 = 0$$
$$k = 0 \text{ or } 5k = 8$$
$$k = 0 \text{ or } k = \frac{8}{5}$$

We reject $k = 0$ (since the length of the side of a square must be positive). The answer is therefore $k =$ **8/5** or **1.6**.

Formula: If s is the length of the side of a square, then the area of the square is $A = s^2$.

SECTION 8

1. NUMBER THEORY

*** Solution by division:** $\frac{15}{90} = \frac{1}{6}$, choice (B).

Remarks: (1) To get the **fraction** of the film that has been completed we divide the **number** of minutes that have passed by the **total** number of minutes in the film.

(2) You can do the computation in your calculator very quickly. Just type 15 / 90 MATH ENTER ENTER. This sequence of buttons will compute $\frac{15}{90}$ as a decimal, and then convert the decimal back to a reduced fraction.

(3) You can also reduce the fraction $\frac{15}{90}$ on your fingers by simply counting how many times 15 goes into 90.

15, 30, 45, 60, 75, 90

That's 6 times. So 15 goes into 15 once, and 15 goes into 90 six times. Therefore the fraction reduces to $\frac{1}{6}$.

2. GEOMETRY

*** Solution by using the fact that the figure is drawn to scale:** It does not say that the figure is not drawn to scale. So we may assume it is. $\overline{JK}$ looks the longest so that the answer is choice (D).

For more information on this technique, see **Strategy 6** in ***"The 32 Most Effective SAT Math Strategies."***

Geometric solution: In a right triangle the hypotenuse is always the longest side. Since $\overline{JK}$ is the hypotenuse of right triangle *JHK*, it is easy to see that $\overline{JK}$ has the greatest length, choice (D).

Some details: (1) In triangle *JHL*, $\overline{JL}$ is the hypotenuse so that $\overline{JL}$ has length greater than the lengths of $\overline{HJ}$ and $\overline{HL}$. So we can eliminate choices (A) and (C).

(2) In triangle *JHK*, $\overline{JK}$ is the hypotenuse so that $\overline{JK}$ has length greater than the length of $\overline{HK}$. So we can eliminate choice (B)

(3) *JK* > *JL* because point *K* is farther from point *H* than point *L*. So we can eliminate choice (E).

3. Functions

Clever solution: Since the function is linear, "**equal jumps in *n* lead to equal jumps in *f*(*n*).**" Note that in the table all the jumps in *n* are equal. Indeed, *n* keeps increasing by 1 unit. Therefore all the jumps in *f*(*n*) must be equal. The jump from 7 to 13 is 13 – 7 = 6. Similarly, the jump from 13 to 19 is 19 – 13 = 6. So to get *p* we can simply add 6 to 19. The answer is therefore 19 + 6 = 25, choice (C).

Note: By a **jump** in *n* we mean the difference between two *n*-values. For example the jump in *n* when *n* goes from 2 to 6 is 4. I will abbreviate this as an "*n*-jump." For example, the *n*-jump from *n* = 1 to *n* = 5 is 5 – 1 = 4.

Other ways to get *p*: Once we see that the *n*-jumps are all the same, there are several ways to get *p*.

(1) Find the *f*(*n*)-jump and add to 19 as was done in the clever solution above: 19 + 6 = 25.

(2) Find the *f*(*n*)-jump and subtract from 31: 31 – 6 = 25.

(3) Simply take the average of 19 and 31: $\frac{19+31}{2} = \frac{50}{2} = 25$.

(4) We can even take the average of 13 and 37: $\frac{13+37}{2} = \frac{50}{2} = 25$.

* **Quickest solution:** Since the *n*-jumps in the table are all equal so are the *f*(*n*)-jumps. Using 7 and 13, we see the *f*(*n*)-jumps are all 13 – 7 = 6. So *p* = 19 + 6 = 25 (here I used method (1) above, but any of the other three methods would also be okay).

Solution using the slope formula: Let's compute the slope of the line. We first need two points. We can take any two, say (1, 7) and (2, 13). Therefore the slope of the line is $m = \frac{13-7}{2-1} = \frac{6}{1} = 6$. We can also use the points (3, 19) and (4, *p*) to compute the slope. So the slope of the line is $m = \frac{p-19}{4-3} = p - 19$. So we have *p* – 19 = 6, and *p* = 6 + 19 = 25, choice (C).

For more information on this technique, see **Strategy 28** in ***"The 32 Most Effective SAT Math Strategies."***

For more information on slope see the notes at the end of Problem 12 in Section 3 of Test 1 (pp. 15-17).

4. ALGEBRA

Solution by plugging in a number: Let's choose a value for n, for example $n = 7$. Then Maly has built houses for 7 years. Twice this would be 14 years, and 5 years less than twice Maly's would be $14 - 5 = \mathbf{9}$. Put a nice big, dark circle around this number. Now substitute 7 for n into each answer choice.

(A) 2
(B) 12
(C) 9
(D) 19
(E) -9

Since (A), (B), (D), and (E) are incorrect we can eliminate them. Therefore the answer is choice (C).

Important note: (C) is **not** the correct answer simply because it is equal to 9. It is correct because all four of the other choices are **not** 9. **You absolutely must check all five choices!**

For more information on this technique, see **Strategy 4** in ***"The 32 Most Effective SAT Math Strategies."***

* **Algebraic solution:** 5 less than twice as long as Maly is 5 less than twice n. This is 5 less than $2n$ which is $2n - 5$, choice (C).

Remark: "a less than b" means $b - a$. The word "twice" means to multiply by 2. The word "is" means =.

Caution: $a - b$ is not the same as $b - a$. So remember in the expression "a less than b," the numbers reverse positions when we write the algebraic equivalent.

5. Geometry

* Angles *APB* and *BPD* form a **linear pair**. This means that they are **supplementary**, that is their measures add up to 180 degrees. So the measure of angle *BPD* is 180 – 80 = 100 degrees. Since $\overline{PC}$ **bisects** angle *BPD*, it follows that the measure of angle *CPD* is $\frac{1}{2}(100) = 50$ degrees, choice (B).

Definitions: Two angles form a **linear pair** if they are **adjacent** and **supplementary.**

Two angles are **supplementary** if their measures add up to 180 degrees.

A line, line segment, or ray **bisects** an angle if it divides the angle into two angles of equal measure.

6. Number Theory

Solution by picking numbers: Let's let x be a specific odd integer, say $x = 5$. The next odd integer greater than 5 is 7. So we will eliminate any answer choice that is not 7. When we replace x by 5, the answer choices turn into the following:

(A) 4
(B) 6
(C) 7
(D) 8
(E) $2(5) - 1 = 10 - 1 = 9$

Since (C) is the only choice that has become 7, we conclude that choice (C) is the answer.

Important note: (C) is **not** the correct answer simply because it is equal to 7. It is correct because all four of the other choices are **not** 7.

For more information on this technique, see **Strategy 4** in ***"The 32 Most Effective SAT Math Strategies."***

* **Advanced Method:** If x is odd, then $x + 1$ is even, and $x + 2$ is odd. Thus, the answer is choice (C).

7. Geometry

Solution by picking numbers: Let's choose values for a and b, for example, $a = 3$ and $b = -2$. So to get to point P we move right 3 and down 2. We would be at the same distance from O if we move left 3 and down 2. This would give the point **(-3,-2)**. Put a nice big, dark circle around this point. Now substitute 3 in for a and -2 in for b in each answer choice.

(A) (-3,-2)
(B) (3,2)
(C) (2,-3)
(D) (2,3)
(E) (-2,3)

Since (B), (C), (D), and (E) are incorrect we can eliminate them. Therefore the answer is choice (A).

Important note: (A) is **not** the correct answer simply because it is equal to (-3,-2). It is correct because all four of the other choices are **not** equal to (-3,-2). **You absolutely must check all five choices!**

Remark: Be very careful substituting a and b into the answer choices here. It is very easy to make mistakes when substituting negative numbers into expressions that already have minus signs. Also, remember that the negative of a negative number is positive.

For more information on this technique, see **Strategy 4** in ***"The 32 Most Effective SAT Math Strategies."***

*** Geometric solution:** We simplify reflect point P across the y-axis. To do this we negate the x-coordinate of the point to get $(-a,b)$, choice (A).

8. Probability

***Quickest solution:** Let w, r, and b be the number of wood, red, and blue beads, respectively. The last sentence tells us that $r = 12$. The sentence before this one implies that there are 3 times as many red beads as blue beads. So $b = 4$, and therefore there are $12 + 4 = 16$ glass beads. Since the number of glass beads is 4 times the number of wood beads, it follows that $w = 4$. Thus, the total is $16 + 4 = 20$, choice (A).

Notes: (1) Notice that we used the information given in the reverse order. That is we started with the information from the last sentence of the paragraph and worked our way backwards.

(2) On the SAT probabilities will generally be equally likely. This means that saying "the probability that a red glass bead will be chosen is three times the probability that a blue glass bead will be chosen" is the same as saying $r = 3b$.

Algebraic solution: Let w, r, and b be the number of wood, red, and blue beads respectively. Since the number of glass beads is 4 times the number of wood beads, we have $r + b = 4w$ (the red and blue beads are the glass ones). Note (2) above gives the equation $r = 3b$. We are given that there are 12 red glass beads, so that $r = 12$. Since $r = 3b$, we have that $12 = 3b$, so that $b = \frac{12}{3} = 4$. Since $r + b = 4w$, $r = 12$, and $b = 4$, we have that $12 + 4 = 4w$, or $4w = 16$. So $w = 4$. The total number of beads is then $w + r + b = 4 + 12 + 4 = 20$, choice (A).

9. FUNCTIONS

Full solution: When you reflect a graph about the x-axis, the x-axis is acting like a mirror. Points on the x-axis must stay where they are, points above the x-axis are reflected below the x-axis, and points below the x-axis are reflected above the x-axis. Therefore the answer is choice (A).

*** Quick solution:** Let's just focus on a single point – the y-intercept (this is the point on the graph that is on the y-axis). Notice that the y-intercept is above the x-axis. So when we reflect the graph in the x-axis, the y-intercept must wind up below the x-axis. Only choice (A) has a negative y-intercept. So the answer is choice (A).

Very minor technical point: Technically the y-intercept is the point $(0, b)$ for some b. So when I say a negative y-intercept, I mean a point of the form $(0, b)$ where $b < 0$.

10. ALGEBRA

*** Solution by guessing:** The two equations suggest that we should find values of x and y such that $x + y = 10$ and $x - y = 4$ (by taking square roots). A little bit of trial and error show that $x = 7$ and $y = 3$ $(7 + 3 = 10$ and $7 - 3 = 4)$. So $xy = (7)(3) = 21$, choice (C).

For more information on this technique, see **Strategy 3** in ***"The 32 Most Effective SAT Math Strategies."***

Remarks: (1) We can formally solve the system of equations above by using the elimination method as follows.

$$\begin{array}{c} x + y = 10 \\ \underline{x - y = 4} \\ 2x = 14 \\ x = 7 \end{array}$$

Note that I added the first two equations to get the third equation. Now substitute $x = 7$ into either of the original equations to get $y = 3$.

(2) I have applied the square root property incorrectly in the solution above. If $(x + y)^2 = 100$, then the square root property says that $x + y = 10$ **or** $x + y = -10$. Similarly, $x - y = 4$ **or** $x - y = -4$. We wind up with four different systems of equations. Each of these systems yield different x and y values, but the product xy is always the same. For example, if we choose $x + y = -10$ and $x - y = 4$, we get $x = -3$, $y = -7$, and therefore we have $xy = (-3)(-7) = 21$, as before.

Exercise: Solve all four systems of equation that you get from applying the square root property correctly, and show that in all cases $xy = 21$.

Note: The remarks above lead to various algebraic solutions to this problem. Below is one more algebraic solution of a different nature.

Algebraic solution: We FOIL the left hand side of each equation.

$$(x + y)^2 = (x + y)(x + y) = x^2 + 2xy + y^2 = 100$$
$$(x - y)^2 = (x - y)(x - y) = x^2 - 2xy + y^2 = 16$$

Now if we subtract the bottom equation from the top equation we get $4xy = 84$ or $xy = \frac{84}{4} = 21$, choice (C).

11. Algebra

Solution by plugging in points: Using choice (C) as a guide let's plug in -1 for x. We get $-1 \leq 4(-1) - 5 = -4 - 5 = -9$. This is false. So we can eliminate choices (C) and (E). Let's plug in 1 for x next (using choice (A) as a guide). We get $-1 \leq 4(1) - 5 = 4 - 5 = -1$. This is true. So we can eliminate choices (B) and (D). The answer is therefore choice (A).

For more information on this technique, see **Strategy 5** in ***"The 32 Most Effective SAT Math Strategies."***

* **Algebraic solution:** We solve the inequality for x.

$$-1 \leq 4x - 5$$
$$4 \leq 4x$$
$$1 \leq x$$

The last inequality is equivalent to $x \geq 1$. The graph of this inequality is in choice (A).

12. GEOMETRY

* Since it does not say that the figure is not drawn to scale we can assume it is. Visually it is not hard to see that we can rotate rectangle *PQRS* inside the circle so that the vertices stay on the circle. Therefore there are infinitely many such rectangles. In particular, there are more than four, choice (E).

Note: Another way to see this is by physically rotating the paper a bit and noticing that the circle remains the same, but the rectangle is now in a new position.

Geometric solution with specific numbers: Let's let minor arc *PQ* measure 150 degrees. Since segment *PQ* is congruent to segment *SR*, minor arc *SR* also has 150 degrees. Since a circle has 360 degrees, there are 60 degrees left that must be split between arc *QR* and arc *PS*. So arc *QR* and arc *PS* each have measure 30 degrees.

Now, choose any point on the circle and label it *P'*, move 150 degrees clockwise along the circumference of the circle plot a point and label it *Q'*. Then continue 30 degrees clockwise and label a point on the circle *R'*. Finally, move 150 more degrees clockwise and label a point *S'*. Rectangle *P'Q'R'S'* is congruent to rectangle *PQRS* and therefore also has perimeter 12.

Since we can perform this procedure beginning at any point on the circle, we see that there are infinitely many such rectangles. In particular, there are more than four, choice (E).

Note: We have used the fact that if two minor arcs are equal in measure, their corresponding chords are equal in measure, and vice versa.

13. ALGEBRA

Solution by picking numbers: Since k appears in the answer choices I might initially attempt to pick a value for k. But in this problem it is much easier to start with a value for n. Let's let $n = 3$. Then $2^n = 2^3 = 8$, and $2^{n+1} = 2^4 = 16$. So $k = 2^n + 2^{n+1} = 8 + 16 = 24$. Also, $2^{n+2} = 2^5 = 32$. Put a nice big, dark circle around the number **32**. Now substitute 24 in for k in each answer choice.

(A) $(24 - 1)/2 = 23/2 = 11.5$
(B) $(4)(24)/3 = 32$
(C) $2(24) = 48$
(D) $2(24) + 1 = 48 + 1 = 49$
(E) $24^2 = 576$

Since (A), (C), (D), and (E) are incorrect we can eliminate them. Therefore the answer is choice (B).

Important note: (B) is **not** the correct answer simply because it is equal to 32. It is correct because all four of the other choices are **not** equal to 32. **You absolutely must check all five choices!**

For more information on this technique, see **Strategy 4** in ***"The 32 Most Effective SAT Math Strategies."***

*** Algebraic solution:** This is tricky.

$$k = 2^n + 2^{n+1} = 2^n(1 + 2) = 3(2^n).$$

Dividing each side by 3 we get $2^n = \frac{k}{3}$. We now multiply each side of the equation by 2^2 to get

$$2^n 2^2 = \frac{(2^2)k}{3}$$
$$2^{n+2} = \frac{4k}{3}$$

This is choice (B).

Questions: Do you see how the factoring was done in the first equation above? Why were we allowed to pull out 2^n? Why were we left with 1 and 2 respectively? If you were able to do this on your own, then your algebra skills are probably very strong. As a hint to answering these questions, note that $2^{n+1} = 2^n \cdot 2^1 = 2^n \cdot 2$.

For a review of the **Basic Laws of Exponents**, see the end of the solution to Problem 8 in Section 8 of Test 1 (p. 35). For definitions of the **integers** and **positive integers** see the end of the solution to Problem 11 in Section 3 of Test 1 (pp. 14-15).

14. Geometry

* Since $AB > AC$, the opposite angles to these sides share the same relationship. That is $z > y$. Therefore $y = z$ is false, choice (E).

For more information on this technique, see **Strategy 26** in ***"The 32 Most Effective SAT Math Strategies."***

15. Data Analysis

* Tom's hotel room expense is 20% of the total, or (.2)(240) = \$48. Since Tom shared the cost of the room equally with 3 **other** people, a total of 4 people paid for the room. Therefore the total cost of the hotel room was 4(48) = \$192, choice (D).

Remark: A common mistake would be to multiply 48 by 3 instead of 4. This became a Level 5 problem because so many students made this mistake on an experimental section of the SAT.

16. Number Theory

* We will systematically try values for n, and draw a picture of the situation to determine the corresponding value for k.

Here is the picture for $n = 3$.

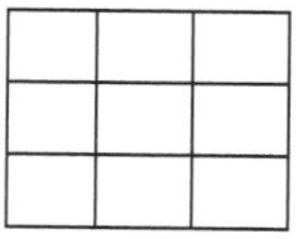

Note that $k = 9 - 1 = 8$.

Here is the picture for $n = 4$.

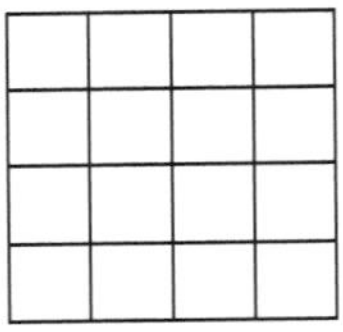

Note that $k = 16 - 4 = 12$.

Here is the picture for $n = 5$.

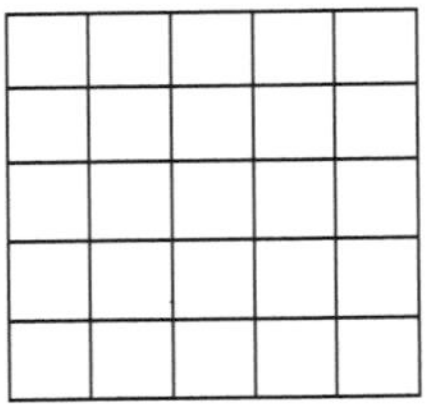

Note that $k = 25 - 9 = 16$.

So the pattern appears to be 8, 12, 16, 20, 24, 28,... Make sure that you keep drawing pictures until this is clear to you. So we see that the answer must be divisible by 4.

Beginning with choice (C) we have $\frac{34}{4} = 285$. So choice (C) is not the answer.

We can eliminate choice (B) because it ends in an odd digit.

Trying choice (E) we have $\frac{52}{4} = 13$. Thus 52 is divisible by 4, and choice (E) is the answer.

For more information on this technique, see **Strategy 17** in ***"The 32 Most Effective SAT Math Strategies."*** Also relevant to this problem are **Strategies 1 and 9.**

For the advanced student: Let's prove that for each n, the corresponding k is divisible by 4.

For fixed n, the total number of squares is n^2, and the number of squares **not** on the boundary is $(n - 2)^2 = n^2 - 4n + 4$. Thus, the number of squares on the boundary is

$$k = n^2 - (n^2 - 4n + 4) = n^2 - n^2 + 4n - 4 = 4n - 4 = 4(n - 1)$$

which is divisible by 4.

Blue Book Test 3 Fully Explained Solutions

Section 2

1. Algebra

Solution by starting with choice (C): We begin by looking at choice (C), and we take a guess that $x = 12$. Then from the first equation we have that $y = x - 5 = 12 - 5 = 7$. The left hand side of the second equation is then $20y - 5y = 20(7) - 5(7) = 140 - 35 = 105$. This is not equal to 15. The value we chose for x was too big. We can therefore eliminate choices (C), (D), and (E).

Let's try choice (A) next, so that we are guessing that $x = 6$. Then from the first equation we have that $y = x - 5 = 6 - 5 = 1$. The left hand side of the second equation is then $20y - 5y = 20(1) - 5(1) = 20 - 5 = 15$. This is correct so that the answer is choice (A).

For more information on this technique, see **Strategy 1** in ***"The 32 Most Effective SAT Math Strategies."***

* **Algebraic solution:** We first solve the second equation for y.

$$20y - 5y = 15$$
$$15y = 15$$
$$y = 1$$

We now substitute $y = 1$ into the first equation and solve for x.

$$y = x - 5$$
$$1 = x - 5$$

We now add 5 to each side of this equation to get $x = 6$. Therefore the answer is choice (A).

Remark: Here is the computation in detail referred to in the second to last sentence above.

$$\begin{array}{r} 1 = x - 5 \\ +5 \quad\quad +5 \\ \hline 6 = x \end{array}$$

2. PROBABILITY

* The number of yellow buttons in the bag is

$$9 - 4 - 3 = 2.$$

Since there are a total of 9 buttons in the bag, the probability of drawing a yellow button from the bag is $\frac{2}{9}$, choice (C).

Remark: Here we have used the **Simple Probability Principle** which says the following. To compute a simple probability where all outcomes are equally likely, divide the number of "successes" by the total number of outcomes.

In this problem there is an equal likelihood of choosing any specific button. The probability is therefore computed by dividing the number of yellow buttons by the total number of buttons.

3. GEOMETRY

* Focus on the missing triangle on the upper left of the figure. Notice that choice (B) has this missing triangle. The answer is choice (B).

4. DATA ANALYSIS

* In a circle graph 25% is represented by a sector with a central angle of 90 degrees, or equivalently one quarter of the circle. The sectors representing pecan, peach, mint and strawberry all have central angles that are less than 90 degrees. So the answer is Four, choice (D).

5. GEOMETRY

Since there are 180 degrees in a triangle, it follows that the other interior angle has a measure of 180 – 37 – 58 = 85 degrees. Now we use that fact that the measure of an exterior angle of a triangle is the sum of the measures of the two opposite interior angles of the triangle.

So we have

$$x = 58 + 37 = 95$$
$$y = 58 + 85 = 143$$
$$z = 37 + 85 = 122$$

So, $x + y + z = 95 + 143 + 122 = 360$, choice (E).

For more information on this technique, see **Strategy 30** in ***"The 32 Most Effective SAT Math Strategies."***

Alternative: We could also find x, y, and z by using the fact that each exterior angle to the triangle is **supplementary** with each adjacent interior angle of the triangle. So we have

$$x = 180 - 85 = 95$$
$$y = 180 - 37 = 143$$
$$z = 180 - 58 = 122$$

* **Quick trick:** A moment's thought will reveal that when we add x, y and z, we are adding each angle of the triangle twice. Since there are 180 degrees in a triangle, the answer is $2 \cdot 180 = 360$, choice (E).

So, the answer to this problem is independent of what any of the interior angles are actually equal to. In fact, none of those angles needed to be given at all.

6. ALGEBRA

Solution by guessing: Let's start with a "random" guess for x, say $x = 1$. So let's plug 1 in for x in the given equation.

$$6x + 4 = 7$$
$$6(1) + 4 = 7$$
$$6 + 4 = 7$$
$$10 = 7$$

Our guess was too big. So let's take a smaller guess like 0.

$$6x + 4 = 7$$
$$6(0) + 4 = 7$$
$$0 + 4 = 7$$
$$4 = 7$$

This guess was too small. Let's try $x = .5$.

$$6x + 4 = 7$$
$$6(.5) + 4 = 7$$
$$3 + 4 = 7$$
$$7 = 7$$

So $x = .5$, and $6x - 4 = 6(.5) - 4 = 3 - 4 = -1$, choice (B).

For more information on this technique, see **Strategy 3** in ***"The 32 Most Effective SAT Math Strategies."***

Algebraic solution: An algebraic solution is a much better choice in this example.

$$6x + 4 = 7$$
$$6x = 3$$
$$6x - 4 = -1$$

Thus, the answer is choice (B).

Remark: Note that we did not need to get x by itself, since $6x$ appeared in both the equation and the expression. We can think of $6x$ as a **block**.

See **Strategy 19** in ***"The 32 Most Effective SAT Math Strategies"*** for more about blocks.

*** Quicker algebraic solution:** We can actually do the algebra in a single step by subtracting 8 from each side of the equation.

$$6x + 4 = 7$$
$$6x - 4 = -1$$

Thus, the answer is choice (B).

7. ALGEBRA

*** Solution by picking numbers and using the fact that the figure is drawn to scale:** We can assume that the figure is drawn to scale (since it does not say that it isn't drawn to scale). So arcs AB, BC, CD, DE, and EA all have the same measure. Let's pick a number for the length of each of these arcs, say 1. Then arc ABC has length 2, and arc AEC has length 3. The requested ratio is therefore 2 to 3, choice (B).

For more information on this technique, see **Strategies 4 and 6** in ***"The 32 Most Effective SAT Math Strategies."***

Solution using the fact that the figure is drawn to scale: We can assume that the figure is drawn to scale (since it does not say that it isn't drawn to scale). So arcs *AB*, *BC*, *CD*, *DE*, and *EA* all have the same measure. Let's call this measure *x*. Then arc *ABC* has length 2*x*, and arc *AEC* has length 3*x*. The requested ratio is therefore $\frac{2x}{3x} = \frac{2}{3}$. Putting this in the form of the answer choices, the answer is 2 to 3, choice (B).

For more information on this technique, see **Strategy 6** in ***"The 32 Most Effective SAT Math Strategies."***

Remark: If two chords have eual length, then the arcs they intercept have equal length as well. In this question, the pentagon is equilateral so that all five sides have the same length. Therefore all five intercepted arcs have the same length.

Definitions: A **polygon** is a two-dimensional geometric figure formed of three or more straight sides.

A polygon is **equilateral** if all of its sides have equal length.

A **pentagon** is a 5-sided polygon.

8. Number Theory

* $(\frac{-1}{2})^2$ = .25. This is the coordinate of point D. So the answer is choice (D).

Remarks:

(1) You can compute $(\frac{-1}{2})^2$ quickly in your calculator. Just type it in exactly as you see it making sure that you include the parentheses.

(2) A common mistake would be to get $\frac{-1}{4}$ as the answer. This is incorrect. Remember that to square a number means to multiply that number by itself. So $(\frac{-1}{2})^2 = (\frac{-1}{2})(\frac{-1}{2}) = \frac{1}{4}$.

(3) When you multiply two negative numbers the result is always positive.

9. Algebra

Solution by picking numbers: Let's choose values for t and w, say $t = 5$ and $w = 2$. Note that $t > w$. We also need to choose a value for s. Let's choose $s = 3$. Then the sum of s and t is $3 + 5 = 8$, and the sum of s and w is $s + w = 3 + 2 = 5$. So the answer is $8 - 5 = 3$. **Put a nice big, dark circle around 3 so that you can find it easily later.** Substituting $t = 5$, $w = 2$, and $s = 3$ into each answer choice gives the following:

(A) $3 - 5 = -2$
(B) $2(3) - 2 = 6 - 2 = 4$
(C) $5 - 2 = 3$
(D) $5 + 2 = 7$
(E) $2(3) - 5 - 2 = 6 - 5 - 2 = 1 - 2 = -1$

Since (A), (B), (D), and (E) each came out incorrect, the answer is choice (C).

Important note: (C) is **not** the correct answer simply because it is equal to 3. It is correct because all four of the other choices are **not** 3. **You absolutely must check all five choices!**

For more information on this technique, see **Strategy 4** in ***"The 32 Most Effective SAT Math Strategies."***

* **Algebraic solution:** $(s + t) - (s + w) = s + t - s - w = t - w$, choice (C).

Common Error: Many students tend to distribute the minus sign incorrectly. The following is incorrect.

$$(s + t) - (s + w) = s + t - s + w = t + w$$

This is actually answer choice (D) which is incorrect. DO NOT fall into this trap!

10. Functions

* We are being asked to compute $P(16) - P(4)$. Now

$$P(4) = 3000 \cdot 2^{4/4} = 3000 \cdot 2^1 = 3000 \cdot 2 = 6000$$
$$P(16) = 3000 \cdot 2^{16/4} = 3000 \cdot 2^4 = 3000 \cdot 16 = 48{,}000$$

So $P(16) - P(4) = 48{,}000 - 6000 = 42{,}000$, choice (D).

Remark: We can do these computations very quickly and easily in our calculator. For example, to compute *P*(4) simply type 3000*2^(4/4) into your calculator. Remember that exponents need to be in parentheses.

11. Statistics

Solution by picking numbers: Let's choose values for s and t, say $s = 5$ and $t = 7$ (See note below for an explanation of this choice). Then we have $s + t = 5 + 7 = 12$, choice (E).

Notes:

(1) $s = 5$ and $t = 7$ is a natural choice because 3 and 7 are at the same distance from 5. Note that $\frac{3+5+7}{3} = \frac{15}{3} = 5$.

(2) There are infinitely many choices for s and t, but all such choices will lead to the same sum. For example we can choose s = 1 and t =11. Indeed, in this case $\frac{3+1+11}{3} = \frac{15}{3} = 5$, and $s + t = 1 + 11 = 12$.

For more information on this technique, see **Strategy 4** in ***"The 32 Most Effective SAT Math Strategies."***

*** Solution by changing averages to sums:** We change the average to a sum using the formula

$$\text{Sum} = \text{Average} \cdot \text{Number}$$

So $3 + s + t = (5)(3)$, or equivalently $3 + s + t = 15$. Subtracting 3 from each side of this equation yields $s + t = 12$, choice (E).

12. Number Theory

* There are 5 + 2 = 7 elements common to sets A and B, choice (D).

Let's find the number of elements in some other regions for extra practice.

	Region	Number of Elements
1	A	$3+4+5+2=14$
2	B	$7+6+5+2=20$
3	C	$8+4+2+6=20$
4	Only A	3
5	Only B	7
6	Only C	8
7	Common to A and C	$4+2=6$
8	Common to B and C	$2+6=8$
9	Common to A, B and C	2
10	A and B but not C	5
11	A and C but not B	4
12	B and C but not A	6

Note: The intersection of sets A and B consists of 2 regions. They are labeled by numbers 9 and 10 in the table.

Definition: The set of elements common to A and B is sometimes called the **intersection** of A and B. The intersection of A and B can be written as $A \cap B$.

13. Percents

* 40 percent of 800 is $(.4)(800) = 320$. So 320 of the students accepted so far are male. Half of 1000 is 500. So $500 - 320 = 180$ more male students must be accepted, choice (D).

Notes:

(1) You can change a percent to a decimal by moving the decimal point over two places to the left. In this case $40\% = .4$.

(2) The word "of" indicates multiplication is to be performed. So 40 percent **of** 800 is $.4 \cdot 800 = 320$.

(3) It is not necessary to compute the number of female students that have been accepted. Additional information has been given in this problem to try to slow you down.

14. ALGEBRA

* **Solution by starting with choice (C):** Let's guess that $t = 3$. Since $t > k$ and $t + k > 4$, it follows that $k = 2$. So $t^2 - k^2 = 3^2 - 2^2 = 9 - 4 = 5$. Since 5 is less than 6, this works, and the answer is choice (C).

For more information on this technique, see **Strategy 1** in ***"The 32 Most Effective SAT Math Strategies."***

15. PERCENTS

* "$\frac{1}{2}$ of 23 percent of 618" = $(\frac{1}{2})(\frac{23}{100})(618) = (\frac{23}{100})(309)$. This is 23 percent of 309, choice (A).

Note: If you choose to write 23 percent as a decimal instead of as a fraction, the computation looks like this.

$$(\frac{1}{2})(.23)(618) = (.23)(309).$$

16. FUNCTIONS

* $g(2) = f(3\cdot 2 + 1) = f(7) = -5$, choice (A).

Remarks: (1) To compute $g(2)$ we substitute a 2 in for x. This explains the first equality above.

(2) We see that $f(7) = -5$ by looking at the table. When x is 7, $f(x)$ is -5.

17. GEOMETRY

* Note that if we flip the bottom half of the figure horizontally, the area we are looking for remains unchanged. We get the following picture.

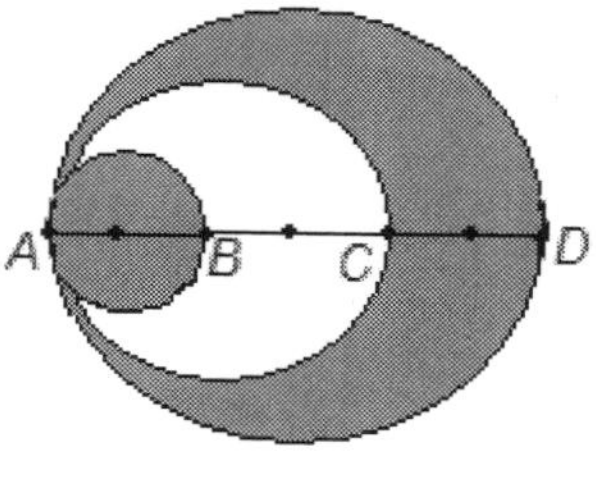

* We first find the radii of each of the three circles. The diameter of the small circle is 2, and so its radius is 1. The diameter of the medium-sized circle is 4, and so its radius is 2. The diameter of the largest circle is 6, and so its radius is 3. We can now find the area of the shaded region as follows.

$$\begin{aligned}\text{Area} &= \text{Area of big circle} - \text{Area of medium circle} + \text{Area of small circle} \\ &= \pi(3)^2 - \pi(2)^2 + \pi(1)^2 = 9\pi - 4\pi + \pi = 6\pi\text{, choice (C).}\end{aligned}$$

For more information on this technique, see **Strategy 23** in ***"The 32 Most Effective SAT Math Strategies."***

18. COUNTING

* We need to count the number of ways to choose 2 points from 6. This is the combination ${}_6C_2 = 15$, choice (A).

Combinations: ${}_6C_2$ means the number of **combinations** of 6 things taken 2 at a time. In a combination order does not matter (as opposed to the **permutation** ${}_6P_2$ where the order does matter).

$${}_6P_2 = \frac{6!}{4!} = 30$$
$${}_6C_2 = \frac{6!}{4!2!} = 15$$

In general, if n is an integer, then $n! = 1 \cdot 2 \cdot 3 \cdots n$
If n and k are integers, then ${}_nP_r = \frac{n!}{(n-r)!}$ and ${}_nC_r = \frac{n!}{r!(n-r)!}$

On the SAT you do **not** need to know these formulas. You can do these computations very quickly on your graphing calculator. For example, to compute ${}_6C_2$, type 6 into your calculator, then in the **Math** menu scroll over to **Prb** and select **nCr** (or press **3**). Then type 2 and hit **Enter**. You will get an answer of **15**.

19. FUNCTIONS

* When $a = b$, we have $f(a + b) = f(a) + f(b) = f(a) + f(a) = 2f(a)$. Therefore $f(a + b) = 2f(a)$ and I is true.

Also, $f(b) + f(b) = f(b + b) = f(2b) = f(2a)$. So we have that $f(b) + f(b) = f(2a)$ and III is true.

So the answer is either choice (C) or (E). Since it seems unlikely that II should be true, a good guess would be choice (C).

Let's show that II does not need to be true by providing a counterexample.

Let $f(x) = x$. Then $f(x + y) = x + y = f(x) + f(y)$. So we see that this function f has the given property. Let $a = b = 1$. Then $f(a + b) = f(1 + 1) = f(2) = 2$, and $[f(1)]^2 = 1^2 = 1$. So $f(a + b) \neq [f(a)]^2$.

Therefore the answer is choice (C).

20. Algebra

Solution by picking numbers: Let's choose values for x and y, say $x = 4$ and $y = 1000$. Note that the area is $xy = 4000$ so that the given condition is satisfied. Also, the total length of the rope is $1000 + 4(4) =$ **1016** meters. **Put a nice, big, dark circle around the number 1016.** Now substitute 1000 in for y in each answer choice and eliminate any answer that does not come out to 1016.

(A) $1000 + 4000/1000 = 1004$
(B) $1000 + 16{,}000/1000 = 1016$
(C) $1000 + 16{,}000/3000 \sim 1005.3333$
(D) $3000 + 8000/3000 \sim 3002.6667$
(E) $3000 + 16{,}000/3000 \sim 3005.3333$

Since choices (A), (C), (D), and (E) came out incorrect, the answer is choice (B).

For more information on this technique, see **Strategy 4** in ***"The 32 Most Effective SAT Math Strategies."***

*** Algebraic solution:** We are given that $A = xy = 4000$. So $x = \frac{4000}{y}$. The total length of the rope is $y + 4x = y + 4(\frac{4000}{y}) = y + \frac{16{,}000}{y}$, choice (B).

SECTION 5

1. STATISTICS

* Fred and Norman own a total of 128 – 44 = 84 comic books. The average is then $\frac{84}{2} = 42$, choice (A).

2. GEOMETRY

* **Solution using the fact that the figure is drawn to scale:** We can assume that the figure is drawn to scale (since it does not say that it isn't drawn to scale). Since we go right 6 units to get to (6,0), we go up 6 units to get to point *P*. So the coordinates of point *P* are (0,6), choice (B).

For more information on this technique, see **Strategy 6** in ***"The 32 Most Effective SAT Math Strategies."***

3. ALGEBRA

Solution by picking numbers: Let's choose a value for n, say $n = 4$. The total charge to use the copy machine is then \$1 +\$ 0.40 = **\$1.40**. **Put a nice, big, dark circle around the number 1.40.** Now substitute 4 in for n in each answer choice and eliminate any answer that does not come out to 1.40.

(A) 0.90(4) = 3.6
(B) 1.10(4) = 4.4
(C) 1.00 + 10(4) = 41
(D) 1.00 + 0.10(4) = 1.4
(E) 1.00 + 0.10 + 4 = 5.1

Since choices (A), (B), (C), and (E) came out incorrect, the answer is choice (D).

For more information on this technique, see **Strategy 4** in ***"The 32 Most Effective SAT Math Strategies."***

* **Algebraic solution:** The total charge is \$1.00 for the service fee, plus \$0.10n for the copies. This is $1.00 + 0.10n$ dollars, choice (D).

4. Algebra

* aa has value 2. ab, ac, and ba have value 1. bc has value 0.

So, the sum of the values of the six pairs is $2 + 1 + 1 + 0 + 2 + 1 = 7$, choice (B).

5. Geometry

Solution using a 45, 45, 90 triangle: Since all sides of a square have equal length, an isosceles right triangle is formed. An isosceles right triangle is the same as a 45, 45, 90 triangle. So we can get the length of a side of the triangle just by looking at the formula for a 45, 45, 90 right triangle. Here $s = \frac{4}{\sqrt{2}}$. The area of the square is then $A = s^2 = \left(\frac{4}{\sqrt{2}}\right)^2 = 8$, choice (A).

Solution using the Pythagorean Theorem: If we let s be the length of a side of the square, then by the Pythagorean Theorem

$$s^2 + s^2 = 4^2$$
$$2s^2 = 16$$
$$s^2 = 8$$

So $A = s^2 = 8$, choice (A).

Note: We did not need to finish solving for s here because we are looking for the area of the square which is $A = s^2$.

* **Using an area formula:** The area of a square is $\boldsymbol{A = \frac{d^2}{2}}$ where d is the length of the diagonal of the square. Therefore in this problem

$$A = \frac{d^2}{2} = \frac{4^2}{2} = \frac{16}{2} = 8, \text{ choice (A).}$$

6. Algebra

* Since x is inversely proportional to y, the product of x and y is constant. To make things as simple as possible let's assume that the constant is 1. So we have $xy = 1$. Now let's solve for $\frac{1}{x^2}$.

$$xy = 1$$
$$x = \frac{1}{y}$$
$$\frac{1}{x} = y$$
$$\frac{1}{x^2} = (\frac{1}{x})^2 = y^2$$

So $\frac{1}{x^2}$ is directly proportional to y^2, choice (E).

Remarks: (1) x inversely proportional to y means $xy = k$ for some constant k. In most SAT problems we can get away with always setting k equal to 1.

(2) y directly proportional to x means $y = kx$ for some constant k. So y^2 directly proportional to $\frac{1}{x^2}$ means $y^2 = k(\frac{1}{x^2})$ for some constant k. In the above solution k turned out to be 1.

(3) k is called the **constant of proportionality**.

Solution without choosing a value for k:

$$xy = k$$
$$x = \frac{k}{y}$$
$$\frac{1}{x} = (\frac{1}{k})y$$
$$\frac{1}{x^2} = (\frac{1}{k^2})y^2$$

So $\frac{1}{x^2}$ is directly proportional to y^2 with constant of proportionality $\frac{1}{k^2}$. Therefore the answer is choice (E).

7. GEOMETRY

* We draw a picture.

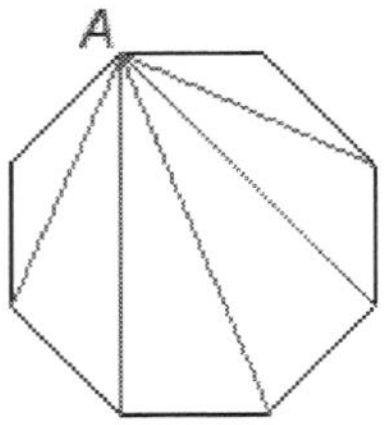

Observe that there are Six triangles, choice (C).

For more information on this technique, see **Strategy 9** in ***"The 32 Most Effective SAT Math Strategies."***

8. ALGEBRA

Solution by plugging in numbers: Let's plug in some simple values for x.

$x = 0$: $8k = m$

$x = 8$: $0 = 64 - 40k + m$

Substituting $8k$ for m in the second equation yields $0 = 64 - 32k$, so that $32k = 64$, and $k = 2$. Finally, $m = 8k = 8 \cdot 2 =$ **16**.

Solution by equating like terms: Multiply out the left hand side (FOIL) to get

$$x^2 - kx - 8x + 8k = x^2 - (k + 8)x + 8k$$

Setting the coefficient of x on the left equal to the coefficient of x on the right yields $-(k + 8) = -5k$, or $k + 8 = 5k$, or $4k = 8$. So $k = 2$. Equating the constant terms on left and right yields $8k = m$. Substituting 2 in for k gives $m = 8 \cdot 2 = 16$, choice (B).

*** Quickest solution:** The left hand side is 0 when $x = 8$ and $x = k$. The coefficient of x is the negative of the sum of these roots, so $5k = k + 8$, or $4k = 8$. So $k = 2$. The constant term is the product of these roots, so that $m = 8k = 8 \cdot 2 = 16$, choice (B).

Note: For the previous solution we used the following general theory:

Let $\boldsymbol{r}$ and $\boldsymbol{s}$ be the roots of the quadratic equation $\boldsymbol{x^2 + bx + c = 0}$. Then

$$\boldsymbol{b = -(r + s)} \quad \text{and} \quad \boldsymbol{c = rs}.$$

9. ALGEBRA

Solution by setting up a ratio: We begin by identifying 2 key words. Let's choose "miles" and "hours."

miles	62	x
hours	4	3

We now find x by cross multiplying and dividing.

$$\frac{62}{4} = \frac{x}{3}$$

$$186 = 4x$$

$$x = \frac{186}{4} = \mathbf{46.5} \text{ (or } \mathbf{93/2}\text{)}.$$

For more information on this technique, see **Strategy 14** in ***"The 32 Most Effective SAT Math Strategies."***

Alternate solution: Using $d = r{\cdot}t$ (distance = rate · time), we have

$$62 = r{\cdot}4$$

$$r = \frac{62}{4} = 15.5 \text{ mph}$$

Using $d = r{\cdot}t$ again, we have $d = 15.5{\cdot}3 = \mathbf{46.5}$.

*** Quick computation:** 62 miles in 4 hours is 15.5 miles per hour (divide 62 by 4 in your calculator). Thus, the bird travelled 3·15.5 = **46.5** miles in 3 hours.

10. Geometry

* $PQ + PR + PS + PT = 1 + 1 + 1 + 1 = \mathbf{4}$.

Note: Each of the line segments in the sum is a radius of the circle.

Here is a picture.

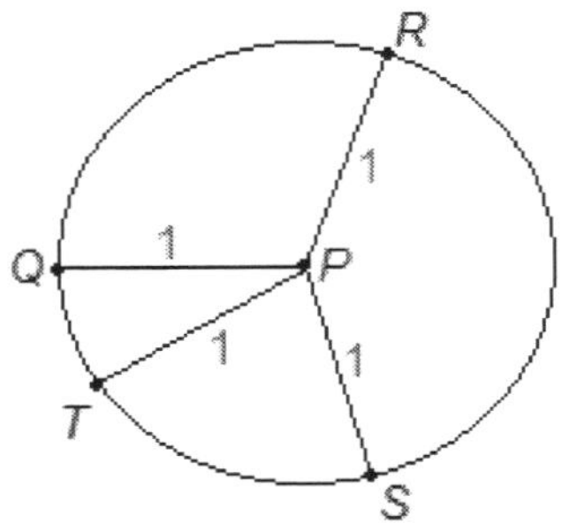

11. Number Theory

Solution by picking a number: Let's choose a value for b, say $b = 1$. Then the equation becomes $10^a = 10{,}000$. Some simple guesses for a in your calculator will lead to the solution $a = \mathbf{4}$.

For more information on this technique, see **Strategies 3 and 4** in ***"The 32 Most Effective SAT Math Strategies."***

* Since 10,000 has four zeroes, $10{,}000 = 10^4$. So $ab = 4$. Thus, we can choose $a = 1$, $b = 4$. In particular, $a = \mathbf{1}$ works.

Remark: The factors of 4 are **1**, **2**, and **4**. So these are all possible values for a.

12. GEOMETRY

* We substitute $x = 5$ and $y = -1$ into the equation to get

$$2(5) - 3(-1) = c$$
$$10 + 3 = c$$
$$13 = c.$$

So c = **13**.

Remark: A point has the form (a,b) where a is the x-coordinate of the point and b is the y-coordinate of the point.

13. DATA ANALYSIS

* **Solution by brute force:** Let's just list the results for each year.

Year	Absolute Value of Difference
1990	600 – 600 = 0
1991	700 – 650 = 50
1992	800 – 650 = 150
1993	850 – 800 = 50
1994	750 – 650 = 100
1995	800 – 750 = 50
1996	900 – 850 = 50
1997	1150 – 1100 = 50
1998	1100 – 1050 = 50
1999	1000 – 1000 = 0

From the table we see that the answer is **1992**.

Remarks: (1) Note that to do these computations we subtracted the x- and y-coordinates of each point. We always wrote the larger number first. We can do this because we are looking for the **absolute value** of the difference.

(2) This method is quite time consuming. That said, if you do not see another way to solve a problem you may want to begin solving it by brute force as was done here. Try to look for patterns as you do each computation. This may enable you to switch to a quicker method (such as the one below).

* **Quick solution**: The absolute value of the difference will be greatest the further away the point is from the line $y = x$. This is the perfect diagonal line that passes through the lower left corner and upper right corner of the grid (these are the points (0,0) and (1200,1200)). Now just note that **1992** is furthest from this line.

14. Algebra

* Let x be the number. Then $5x = x + 5$. So $4x = 5$, and therefore $x =$ **5/4** or **1.25**.

Remarks: Five times a number can be written symbolically as $5x$, where x is the number. Similarly, the number added to five can be written symbolically as $x + 5$. The expression "is the same as" can be replaced with an equal sign.

15. Geometry

* **Solution by drawing pictures:** The given picture is just too confusing to look at. Let's draw our own pictures to scale containing just some of the given information.

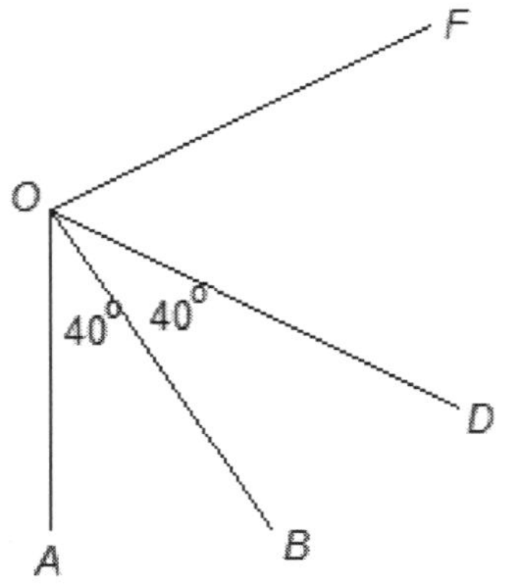

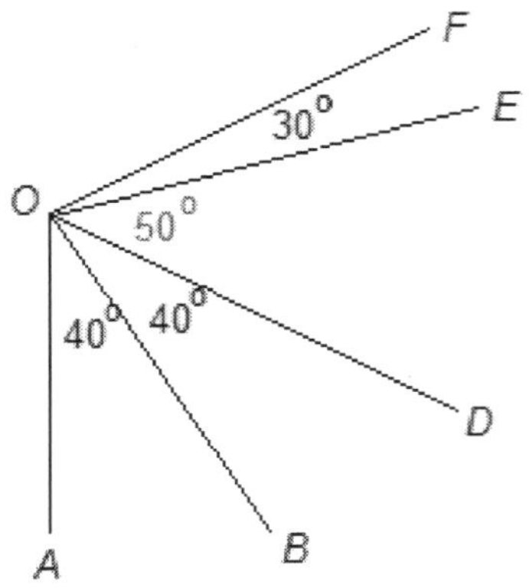

In the first figure on the left we have drawn angle *AOF* bisected by $\overline{OD}$, and we also drew $\overline{OB}$ bisecting angle *AOD*. We are given that angle *AOB* has measure 40 degrees. Since $\overline{OB}$ bisects angle *AOD*, the measure of angle *BOD* also has measure 40 degrees.

In the figure on the right we have added $\overline{OE}$ to the picture. We are given that angle *EOF* has measure 30 degrees. Since $\overline{OD}$ bisects angle *AOF*, and angle *AOD* has measure 40 + 40 = 80 degrees, so does angle *DOF*. So angle *DOE* has measure 80 – 30 = 50 degrees.

It follows that angle *BOE* has measure 40 + 50 = **90** degrees.

Note: We left $\overline{OC}$ out of our pictures completely. We did not need the information about this segment at all in our solution.

For more information on this technique, see **Strategy 9** in ***"The 32 Most Effective SAT Math Strategies."***

16. Number Theory

* 1 appears 1 time, 2 appears 2 times, and so on until we get to 11 which appears 11 times. Finally we stop at the first instance of 12. So we have $n = 1 + 2 + 3 + \ldots + 11 + 1 =$ **67**.

Remark: There are several ways of computing this sum. Here are a few.

(1) Do it directly in your calculator.

(2) Let's formally write out the sum of the numbers from 1 through 11 forwards and backwards, and then add term by term.

$$\begin{array}{c} 1 + 2 + 3 + \ldots + 11 \\ \underline{11 + 10 + 9 + \ldots + 1} \\ 12 + 12 + 12 + \ldots + 12 \end{array}$$

We are adding 12 to itself 11 times, so that 2(1 +...+ 11) = (12)(11) = 132. So $1 + 2 + 3 + \ldots + 11 = \frac{132}{2} = 66$. Finally we add 1 to get **67**.

(3) Use the arithmetic series formula $\boldsymbol{A_n = m \cdot n}$ where m is the number of terms and n is the average of the first and last term. This formula gives $11 \cdot \frac{(1+11)}{2} + 1 =$ **67**.

(4) Use the sum feature on your calculator.

For definitions of the **integers** and **positive integers** see the end of the solution to Problem 11 in Section 3 of Test 1 (pp. 14-15).

17. Number Theory

* **Solution by using a ratio:** We need to replace each 4 inches along the paper strip by 5 inches. So we set up the following ratio.

length along strip	4	80
length in bold	5	x

We now find x by cross multiplying and dividing.

$$\frac{4}{5} = \frac{80}{x}$$

$$4x = 400$$

$$x = \frac{400}{4} = \mathbf{100}.$$

For more information on this technique, see **Strategy 14** in ***"The 32 Most Effective SAT Math Strategies."***

18. Geometry

* Since the area of the square is 64, then using the formula $A = s^2$, we have that $s = \sqrt{A} = \sqrt{64} = 8$. It follows that the point R is (4,8). Since R is also on the graph of $y = ax^2$, we have $8 = a(4)^2 = 16a$. So $a = \frac{8}{16}$ = **1/2** or **.5**.

Notes: (1) Note that $OS = 4$ because it is half the length of the square.

(2) To plot point R we move right 4 and up 8. Thus, point R is (4,8).

SECTION 8

1. ALGEBRA

Solution by guessing: Let's guess that the number is 40. Then $\frac{3}{4}\cdot 40 = 30$ which is too big. So let's try 20 next. Then $\frac{3}{4}\cdot 20 = 15$ which is too small. Let's try 24. Then $\frac{3}{4}\cdot 24 = 18$ which is correct. So the number is 24, and $\frac{1}{4}$ of the number is $\frac{1}{4}\cdot 24 = 6$, choice (C).

Notes: (1) We only guessed numbers that were divisible by 4, and we could have used our calculator for each of the above computations.

(2) The word "of" means to multiply.

For more information on this technique, see **Strategy 3** in ***"The 32 Most Effective SAT Math Strategies."***

Algebraic solution: Let x be the number. Then $\frac{3}{4}\cdot x = 18$. So, $x = \frac{4}{3}\cdot 18 = 24$. Finally, $\frac{1}{4}\cdot 24 = 6$, choice (C).

* **Quick algebraic solution:** From the equation $\frac{3}{4}\cdot x = 18$, we can simply divide each side by 3 to get $\frac{1}{4}\cdot x = 6$, choice (C).

2. ALGEBRA AND FUNCTIONS

* 5* = 5(5 – 1) = 5(4) = 20, choice (B).

3. DATA ANALYSIS

* We simply look at where the solid line intersects the dotted line. This happens at an age of 45, choice (D).

Note: If we were asked for the best estimate of the diameter of the eye pupil for which the average diameter of the eye pupil during the day will equal the average diameter of the eye pupil at night, then the answer would be 4.

4. Number Theory

Toni spent 2 hours per day commuting for 5 days, for a total of $2 \cdot 5 = 10$ hours. In 5 days there are a total of $24 \cdot 5 = 120$ hours. So the fraction of the total number of hours in these five days that she spent commuting is $\frac{10}{120} = \frac{1}{12}$, choice (A)

Remark: The fraction $\frac{10}{120}$ can be reduced in your calculator by dividing 10 by 120, and then pressing MATH ENTER ENTER.

* **Quicker solution**: We really only need to look at one day: $\frac{2}{24} = \frac{1}{12}$, choice (A).

5. Algebra

* $(x + 1)^2 = (\sqrt{3})^2 = 3$, choice (C).

6. Geometry

* The sides of a triangle satisfy the same comparative relationships as their opposite angles. For example, the angle with the largest measure is opposite the longest side. Since 10 is the largest side length, x is the largest degree measure. Since 8 is the smallest side length, t is the smallest degree measure. This puts r right in the middle, So $t < r < x$. This is choice (A).

For more information on this technique, see **Strategy 26** in ***"The 32 Most Effective SAT Math Strategies."***

7. Algebra

Solution by starting with choice (C): Let's start with choice (C) and guess that $y = 1$. Then $|6 - 5y| = |6 - 5 \cdot 1| = |6 - 5| = |1| = 1$. Since 1 is not greater than 20 we can eliminate choice (C). A moment's thought may lead you to suspect choice (A) (if you do not see this it is okay – just keep trying the answer choices until you get to it). Now, setting $y = -3$ gives us $|6 - 5y| = |6 - 5(-3)| = |6 + 15| = |21| = 21$. Since 21 is greater than 20, the answer is choice (A).

For more information on this technique, see **Strategy 1** in **"The 32 Most Effective SAT Math Strategies."**

*** Partial algebraic solution:** We can try to simply eliminate the absolute values and solve the resulting inequality.

$$6 - 5y > 20$$
$$-5y > 14$$
$$y < -\frac{14}{5} = -2.8$$

Since $-3 < -2.8$, the answer is choice (A).

Note: The inequality changed direction in the last step because we divided each side of the inequality by a negative number.

Complete algebraic solution: The given absolute value inequality is equivalent to $6 - 5y < -20$ or $6 - 5y > 20$. Let's solve these two inequalities simultaneously.

$$6 - 5y < -20 \quad \text{or} \quad 6 - 5y > 20$$
$$-5y < -26 \quad \text{or} \quad -5y > 14$$
$$y > \frac{26}{5} = 5.2 \quad \text{or} \quad y < -\frac{14}{5} = -2.8$$

So $y < -2.8$ or $y > 5.2$. Since $-3 < -2.8$, the answer is choice (A).

8. GEOMETRY

***Quickest solution:** Triangle *ABC* is a 3-4-5 right triangle. If we double the length of each side we get a perimeter of 6 + 8 + 10 = 24, choice (D).

Notes: (1) 3, 4, 5 and 5, 12, 13 are the two most common **Pythagorean triples**. These sets of numbers satisfy the Pythagorean Theorem.

(2) If you do not remember the Pythagorean triples it is no big deal. Just use the Pythagorean Theorem. If c is the length of the hypotenuse of the given triangle, we have that $c^2 = 3^2 + 4^2 = 9 + 16 = 25$. So $c = 5$.

9. DATA ANALYSIS

* We simply compute each of the 5 ratios using our calculator.

(A) 4000/1400 ~ 2.857
(B) 3300/1300 ~ 2.538
(C) 3618/1012 ~ 3.575
(D) 2268/1242 ~ 1.826
(E) 2100/762 ~ 2.756

The greatest number is in choice (C).

10. Geometry

* We first compute the slope of line ℓ. We use the points (0,1) and (3,0) and compute $\frac{rise}{run} = \frac{-1}{3}$ (to get from (0,1) to (3,0) we go down 1, right 3). Since line *n* is perpendicular to line ℓ, the slope of line *n* is the negative reciprocal of the slope of line ℓ. So the answer is $\frac{3}{1} = 3$, choice (E).

Remark: We can also find the slope of line ℓ by using the slope formula $m = \frac{y_2 - y_1}{x_2 - x_1} = \frac{0-1}{3-0} = \frac{-1}{3}$.

11. Algebra

Algebraic solution:

$$2x + 5 = 3kx + 5$$
$$2x = 3kx$$
$$2 = 3k$$
$$\frac{2}{3} = k$$

So, the answer is choice (E).

Remarks: (1) Since the original equation has 5 on each side, we can begin by simply striking off 5 from each side.

(2) We can assume that $x \neq 0$ since the equation is true for ALL values of *x*. Thus, in the second step we can divide out the *x* on each side.

12. Number Theory

* At most one of the integers can be zero. So if none of the integers were positive, then at least 10 would be negative, and then clearly the integers couldn't add to zero. So certainly at least one integer must be positive.

If ten of the integers were not positive, then let the eleventh integer be the negative of the sum of the other ten. Then the sum of the eleven integers would be zero.

So the answer is One, choice (B).

Example: Here is a concrete example of a list of eleven different integers whose sum is zero with exactly one integer positive.

-9, -8, -7, -6, -5, -4, -3, -2, -1, 0, 45

13. COUNTING

*** Solution by listing:** Let's list all the possibilities

$$10+5+1+1$$
$$10+1+1+1+1+1+1+1$$
$$5+5+5+1+1$$
$$5+5+1+1+1+1+1+1+1$$
$$5+1+1+1+1+1+1+1+1+1+1+1+1$$
$$1+1+1+1+1+1+1+1+1+1+1+1+1+1+1+1+1$$

We see that there are Six possibilities, choice (E).

Remark: To save time you may want to abbreviate the list. For example,

one 10, one 5, two 1's
three 5's, 2 ones
one 5, twelve 1's
one 10, seven 1's
two 5's, 7 ones
seventeen 1's

For more information on this technique, see **Strategy 21** in ***"The 32 Most Effective SAT Math Strategies."***

14. FUNCTIONS

Solution by plugging in points: Note that if $f(x) = 0$, then $2f(x) = 2(0) = 0$ also. Graphically, this means that $y = f(x)$ and $y = 2f(x)$ have the same x-intercepts. So we can eliminate choices (A) and (C).

Now let's focus on any point, say the point (3,1). Note that this point is on the original graph. Equivalently, $f(3) = 1$. So $2f(3) = 2(1) = 2$. Therefore the point (3,2) is on the graph of $y = 2f(x)$. Of the remaining three answer choices, only the graph in answer choice (D) satisfies this requirement. So the answer is choice (D).

For more information on this technique, see **Strategy 5** in ***"The 32 Most Effective SAT Math Strategies."***

* **Solution using a transformation:** The graph of $y = 2f(x)$ is a vertical expansion of the graph of $y = f(x)$ by a factor of 2. This is choice (D).

For a lesson on **transformations** see the end of the solution to Problem 7 in Section 5 of Test 2 (p. 62).

15. Number Theory

* Let's write out a few terms of this sequence: 2, -4, 8, -16, 32, -64, 128

Note that the first, third and fifth terms are the only odd number terms less than 100. Also note that **every** even numbered term is less than 100. This gives a total of 3 + 25 = 28 terms, choice (C).

16. Geometry

* The diameter of the sphere is the long diagonal of the cube.

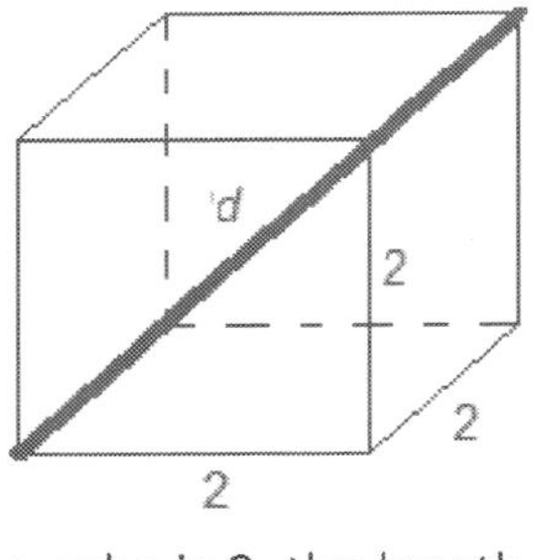

* Since the volume of the cube is 8, the length of a side of the cube is 2 (we get this by taking the cube root of 8). We now use the **Generalized Pythagorean Theorem.**

The diameter of the sphere is then given by

$$d^2 = a^2 + b^2 + c^2 = 2^2 + 2^2 + 2^2 = 4 + 4 + 4 = 4 \cdot 3.$$

So $d = 2\sqrt{3}$, choice (D).

Note: The **Generalized Pythagorean Theorem** says that the length d of the long diagonal of a rectangular solid is given by $d^2 = a^2 + b^2 + c^2$ where a, b and c are the length, width and height of the rectangular solid.

Blue Book Test 4 Fully Explained Solutions

Section 3

1. Algebra

Solution by starting with choice (E): We begin by looking at choice (E), and we plug $b = 3$ into the given inequality. We get $3(3) + 1 = 10$. Since 10 is **not** less than 10, the answer is choice (E).

Remarks: (1) The symbol "<" is read as "less than." The smaller number is on the left.

(2) We began with choice (E) instead of choice (C) here because the inequality in the question indicates that the largest number should be the one to fail.

For more information on this technique, see **Strategy 2** in ***"The 32 Most Effective SAT Math Strategies."***

* **Algebraic solution:** We solve the inequality for b.

$$3b + 1 < 10$$
$$3b < 9$$
$$b < 3$$

In particular, b cannot be 3, choice (E).

2. Algebra

Solution by starting with choice (C): Let's start with choice (C) so that we are guessing that $x = 4$. Then $2^{4x} = 2^{4\cdot4} = 2^{16} = 65{,}536$. This is too big. So we can eliminate choices (C), (D), and (E).

Let's try choice (A) next so that $x = 1$. Then $2^{4x} = 2^4 = 16$. This is correct so that the answer is choice (A).

For more information on this technique, see **Strategy 1** in ***"The 32 Most Effective SAT Math Strategies."***

* **Algebraic solution:** $16 = 2^4$. So we have $2^{4x} = 2^4$. So $4x = 4$, and therefore $x = 1$, choice (A).

3. Number Theory

* **Solution by plugging in a number:** Let's choose a value for r, say $r = 3$. Then $r - 2 = 3 - 2 = 1$, and $r + 5 = 3 + 5 = 8$. Since 8 is 7 greater than 1, the answer is choice (E).

Note: $8 - 1 = 7$.

For more information on this technique, see **Strategy 4** in ***"The 32 Most Effective SAT Math Strategies."***

Algebraic solution: $(r + 5) - (r - 2) = r + 5 - r + 2 = 7$, choice (E).

Warning: A common mistake is to distribute the subtraction symbol incorrectly. The following computation is **wrong**.

$$(r + 5) - (r - 2) = r + 5 - r - 2$$

This incorrect computation might lead one to choose choice (B) which is wrong.

4. Geometry

* The given picture is of a box with length 4, width 3, and height 2. When we unfold the box we get a rectangle with length 4 and width 3 in the middle, and four other rectangles attached to each side. Only choice (E) has the proper dimensions for the center rectangle.

The answer is choice (E).

Exercise: Find a small cardboard box and unfold the flaps. Compare this actual unfolded box with the pictures in the answer choices.

5. Geometry

* Let's simply trace all the paths.

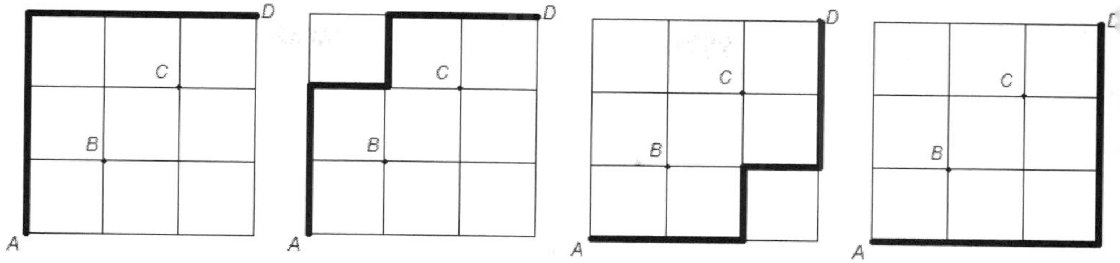

We see that there are four different paths, choice (B).

6. ALGEBRA

Solution by guessing: Let's start with a guess for n, say $n = 100$. Then $\frac{3}{7}$ of n is $\frac{3}{7} \cdot 100 \sim 42.86$. This is a bit too big.

So let's try $n = 95$ next. Then $\frac{3}{7}$ of n is $\frac{3}{7} \cdot 95 \sim 40.71$. This is too small.

Let's try $n = 98$. Then $\frac{3}{7}$ of n is $\frac{3}{7} \cdot 98 = 42$. This is correct. So $n = 98$.

Now, $\frac{5}{7}$ of n is $\frac{5}{7} \cdot 98 = 70$, choice (A).

For more information on this technique, see **Strategy 3** in ***"The 32 Most Effective SAT Math Strategies."***

Algebraic solution: We multiply each side of the given equation by $\frac{7}{3}$.

$$\frac{3}{7}n = 42$$
$$(\tfrac{7}{3})(\tfrac{3}{7}n) = 42(\tfrac{7}{3})$$
$$n = 98.$$

Now, $\frac{5}{7}$ of n is $\frac{5}{7} \cdot 98 = 70$, choice (A).

*** Quickest algebraic solution:** We multiply each side of the given equation by $\frac{5}{3}$.

$$\frac{3}{7}n = 42$$
$$(\tfrac{5}{3})(\tfrac{3}{7}n) = 42(\tfrac{5}{3})$$
$$\frac{5}{7}n = 70.$$

Therefore the answer is choice (A).

7. PROBABILITY

* Let's split each of the rectangles D, E, and F into two equal pieces.

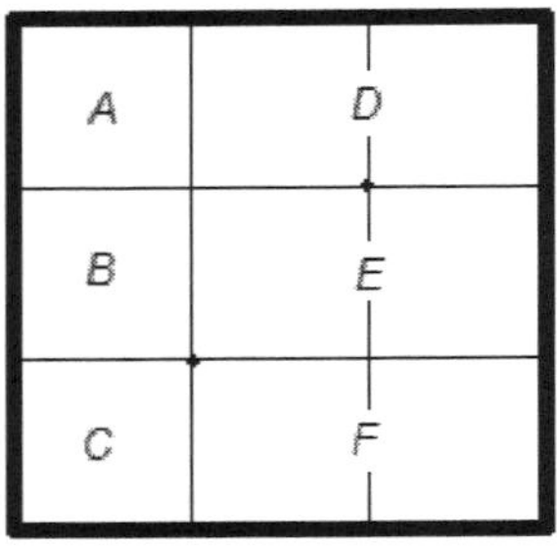

The probability that the marble will fall into any one of the 9 squares in the figure above is $\frac{1}{9}$. Therefore the probability that the marble will fall into compartment F is $\frac{2}{9}$, choice (E).

Remark: Here we have used the **Simple Probability Principle** which says that to compute a simple probability where all outcomes are equally likely, divide the number of "successes" by the total number of outcomes.

For more information on this technique, see **Strategy 9** in ***"The 32 Most Effective SAT Math Strategies."***

8. NUMBER THEORY

Solution by picking numbers: Let's choose values for a and b, say $a = 1$ and $b = 3$. Note that we have chosen a and b to be odd. Now let's check each Roman numeral.

I. $(a + 1)b = 2 \cdot 3 = 6$
II. $(a + 1) + b = 2 + 3 = 5$
III. $(a + 1) - b = 2 - 3 = -1$

Note that II and III are odd, but I is not. The answer is in fact choice (E).

Remark: Technically all we did here was eliminate I. But if you understand how evens and odds work with respect to addition and multiplication, then you understand that it is sufficient to use any odd numbers for a and b.

The following describes what happens when you add and multiply various combinations of even and odd integers.

$$\begin{array}{ll} e + e = e & ee = e \\ e + o = o & eo = e \\ o + e = o & oe = e \\ o + o = e & oo = o \end{array}$$

For example, the sum of an even and an odd integer is odd ($e + o = o$).

* **Quick solution:** Since a is odd, $a + 1$ is even. Therefore $(a + 1)b$ is even, $(a + 1) + b$ is odd, and $(a + 1) - b$ is odd using the rules in the above remark. So the answer is choice (E).

9. Counting

* There are 98 zeros after the 98th one, there are 99 zeros after the 99th one, and there are 100 zeros after 100th one. So the total number of zeros is 98 + 99 + 100 = 297, choice (D).

Warning: Do not accidently add 101 more zeros. These occur **after** the 101st one, but we are stopping **at** the 101st one.

10. Functions

* $f(2) = \frac{3-2(2)^2}{2} = \frac{3-2(4)}{2} = \frac{3-8}{2} = -\frac{5}{2}$, choice (D).

Remarks: (1) To compute $f(2)$ we substitute a 2 in for x. This explains the first equality above.

(2) You can also do the above computation in your calculator and then change the answer back to a fraction. Simply type (3 – 2*2^2)/2 MATH ENTER ENTER.

11. Geometry

Solution by picking numbers: Let's choose values for x and y, say $x = 91$ and $y = 89$. Note that x and y must be chosen so that $x + y = 180$. Also note that we have chosen x so that $x > 90$. Since $y < 90$, we can eliminate choices (B), (C), (D) and (E). The answer is therefore choice (A).

Notes: (1) $\perp$ is an abbreviation for "is perpendicular to," and $\parallel$ is an abbreviation for "is parallel to."

(2) In order for $n \perp m$ to be true, y would have to equal 90. This is why we can eliminate choice (D).

(3) Since $\ell \perp n$, in order for $\ell \parallel m$ to be true, m would also have to be perpendicular to n. This is why we can eliminate choice (E).

For more information on this technique, see **Strategy 4** in ***"The 32 Most Effective SAT Math Strategies."***

12. Geometry

* A point on the x-axis has a y-coordinate of 0. So the point has the form $(a,0)$. So we plug in a for x and 0 for y in the given equation.

$$\begin{aligned} y &= 5x - 10 \\ 0 &= 5a - 10 \\ 10 &= 5a \\ 2 &= a \end{aligned}$$

So the answer is 2, choice (D).

13. Statistics

* Let's list the temperatures in increasing order (without t).

27, 33, 40, 44, 50, 68

In order for the median to be 40, we need to put an additional number to the left of 40 while keeping the numbers in increasing order. So t must be less than or equal to 40. Therefore t CANNOT be 42, choice (E).

14. Geometry

* Let's draw in a side on the bottom of the figure.

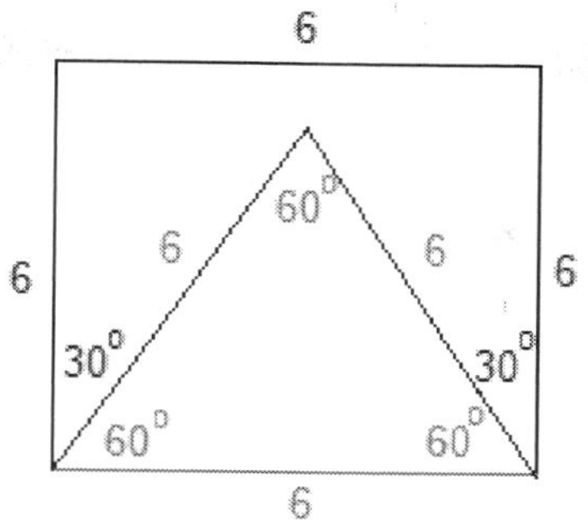

Note that a triangle is formed inside a square. Since the measure of each angle of a square is 90 degrees, we get that each of the angles on the bottom of the triangle has a measure of 60 degrees. It follows that the third angle has measure 180 – 60 – 60 = 60 degrees, and therefore the triangle is equilateral.

Since a square has 4 congruent sides, the length of the new side on the bottom is 6. Since the triangle is equilateral, each side of the triangle has length 6.

The perimeter of the original figure is then $6 \cdot 5 = 30$, choice (D).

Warning: Do not accidentally add an extra 6 for the bottom side of the square. That side was not part of the original figure.

15. Number Theory

* The prime factorization of 38 is $2 \cdot 19$. So $m = 19$. The prime factorization of 100 is $2^2 \cdot 5^2$. So $n = 5$. Therefore $m + n = 19 + 5 = 24$, choice (C).

Here is a quick lesson in **prime factorization** for those of you that have forgotten.

The Fundamental Theorem of Arithmetic: Every integer greater than 1 can be written "uniquely" as a product of primes.

The word "uniquely" is written in quotes because prime factorizations are only unique if we agree to write the primes in increasing order.

For example, 38 can be written as $2 \cdot 19$ or as $19 \cdot 2$. But these two factorizations are the same except that we changed the order of the factors.

To make things as simple as possible we always agree to use the **canonical representation**. The word "canonical" is just a fancy name for "natural," and the most natural way to write a prime factorization is in increasing order of primes. So the canonical representation of 38 is $2 \cdot 19$.

As another example, the canonical representation of 100 is $2 \cdot 2 \cdot 5 \cdot 5$. We can tidy this up a bit by rewriting $2 \cdot 2$ as 2^2 and $5 \cdot 5$ as 5^2. So the canonical representation of 100 is $2^2 \cdot 5^2$.

If you are new to factoring, you may find it helpful to draw a factor tree. For example here is a factor tree for 100:

100
↙↘
[2] 50
↙↘
[2] 25
↙↘
[5] [5]

To draw this tree we started by writing 100 as the product $2 \cdot 50$. We put a box around 2 because 2 is prime, and does not need to be factored anymore. We then proceeded to factor 50 as $2 \cdot 25$. We put a box around 2, again because 2 is prime. Finally, we factor 25 as $5 \cdot 5$. We put a box around each 5 because 5 is prime. We now see that we are done, and the prime factorization can be found by multiplying all of the boxed numbers together. Remember that we will usually want the canonical representation, so write the final product in increasing order of primes.

By the Fundamental Theorem of Arithmetic above it does not matter how we factor the number – we will always get the same canonical form. For example, here is a different factor tree for 100:

100
↙↘
4 25
↙↘ ↙↘
[2] [2] [5] [5]

16. Geometry

Let's draw a picture.

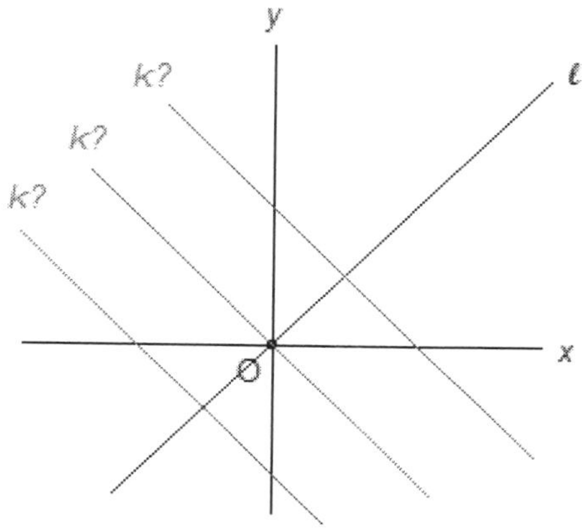

In the above figure we have drawn line ℓ together with three possibilities for line k. Note that only one of the lines passes through (0,0). This eliminates choice (A). None of these lines have positive slope. This eliminates choice (B). The top line has a positive y-intercept. This eliminates choice (E). The bottom line has a negative x-intercept. This eliminates choice (D). Therefore the answer is choice (C).

For more information on this technique, see **Strategy 9** in ***"The 32 Most Effective SAT Math Strategies."***

*** Quick solution:** Perpendicular lines have slopes that are negative reciprocals of each other. Since line ℓ has a positive slope, it follows that line k has a negative slope, choice (C).

17. Algebra and Functions

$$1 \Uparrow 2 = \frac{1+2}{1-2} = \frac{3}{-1} = -3 \qquad \text{and} \qquad 2 \Uparrow x = \frac{2+x}{2-x}$$

So we have $-3 = \frac{2+x}{2-x}$. There are several ways to finish from here.

Starting with choice (C): Let's start with choice (C) and guess that $x = 2$. This would make the denominator on the right 0, so we can eliminate choice (C).

Let's try (B) next and guess that $x = 3$. Then we have $\frac{2+x}{2-x} = \frac{2+3}{2-3} = \frac{5}{-1} = -5$ which is not equal to -3. Let's try (A) and guess that $x = 4$. Then we have $\frac{2+x}{2-x} = \frac{2+4}{2-4} = \frac{6}{-2} = -3$. This is correct, so the answer is choice (A).

For more information on this technique, see **Strategy 1** in ***"The 32 Most Effective SAT Math Strategies."***

*** Algebraic solution:** We begin by cross multiplying.

$$\frac{-3}{1} = \frac{2+x}{2-x}$$

$$-3(2 - x) = 1(2 + x)$$

$$-6 + 3x = 2 + x$$

$$2x = 8$$

Therefore $x = 4$, choice (A).

Notes: (1) In going from the first to the second step we cross multiplied.

(2) In going from the second to the third step we distributed the -3 on the left hand side of the equation. Note that $(-3)(-x) = +3x$.

(3) In going from the third to the fourth step we subtracted x from each side of the equation **and** added 6 to each side of the equation.

(4) In going from the fourth to the fifth step we simply divided each side of the equation by 2.

18. Algebra

Solution by picking numbers: Let's choose values for x, z, and n Let's say $x = 10$, $z = 4$, and $n = 3$. So the customer buys the first shirt for 10 dollars, and the next two shirts for 6 dollars each for a total cost of **22** dollars. **Put a nice big, dark circle around the number 22 so you can find it easily later.** Now let's substitute our chosen values for x, z, and n into each answer choice and use our calculator.

(A) $10 + (3 - 1)(10 - 4) = 22$
(B) $10 + 3(10 - 4) = 28$
(C) $3(10 - 4) = 18$

(D) $\frac{10 + (10 - 4)}{3} \sim 5.3333$

(E) $(10 - 4) + \frac{10-4}{3} = 8$

Since choices (B), (C), (D), and (E) came out incorrect, the answer is choice (A).

Remark: Since $x - z$ appears so often in the answer choices you may want to compute $x - z = 4$ and substitute this in everywhere $x - z$ appears.

For more information on this technique, see **Strategy 4** in ***"The 32 Most Effective SAT Math Strategies."***

*** Algebraic solution:** After buying 1 shirt for x dollars, the customer will buy $n - 1$ more for $x - z$ dollars. This gives a total of $x + (n - 1)(x - z)$ dollars, choice (A).

19. GEOMETRY

We begin by setting up a ratio to find the circumference of the circle.

$$\frac{30}{360} = \frac{6\pi}{C}$$

We cross multiply to get $30C = 2160\pi$. So $C = \frac{2160\pi}{30} = 72\pi$.

Next we find the radius of the circle using the formula $C = 2\pi r$. So we have $2\pi r = 72\pi$ and so $r = 36$.

Now, the area of the circle is $\pi(36)^2 = 1296\pi$.

Finally, we set up another ratio to find the area a of the sector.

$$\frac{30}{360} = \frac{a}{1296\pi}$$

We cross multiply to get $38{,}880\pi = 360a$. Therefore $a = \frac{38{,}880\pi}{360} = 108\pi$, choice (A).

Quicker solution: Since 30 degrees is $\frac{1}{12}$ of the circle, the circumference of the circle is $12(6\pi) = 72\pi$. So the radius is $\frac{72\pi}{2\pi} = 36$. The area of the whole circle is then $\pi(36)^2 = 1296\pi$. Finally, we see that the area of the sector is $\frac{1296\pi}{12} = 108\pi$, choice (A).

* **Quick computation:** We multiply 6 by 6, square the result, then divide by 12 to get $\frac{(6\cdot6)^2}{12} = 108$. So the answer is choice (A).

Remark: It may take some thought to see why that quick computation works. Compare this last solution to the previous one to see where these numbers come from and why π isn't involved in the computation.

20. Percents

Solution by picking numbers: Let's choose a value for n, say $n = 100$. Then there are 100 men enrolled and 175 women enrolled for a total of 275. So the fraction of men enrolled is $\frac{100}{275} \sim .3636$. We change this number to a percent by moving the decimal to the right 2 places to get approximately **36.36**%. **Put a nice big, dark circle around the number 36.36 so you can find it easily later.** Now let's substitute our chosen value of $n = 100$ into each answer choice and use our calculator.

(A) $\frac{100}{175} \sim .5714$

(B) $\frac{100}{275} \sim .3636$

(C) $\frac{100}{100(275)} \sim .0036$

(D) $\frac{100(100)}{175} \sim .0057$

(E) $\frac{100(100)}{275} \sim 36.36$

Since choices (A), (B), (C), and (D) came out incorrect, the answer is choice (E).

For more information on this technique, see **Strategy 4** in ***"The 32 Most Effective SAT Math Strategies."***

* **Algebraic solution:** There are n men enrolled and $n + 75$ women enrolled for a total of $n + n + 75 = 2n + 75$. The fraction of men enrolled is then $\frac{n}{2n+75}$, and we change this to a percent by multiplying by 100. We get $\frac{100n}{2n+75}$%, choice (E).

SECTION 6

1. ALGEBRA AND FUNCTIONS

Solution by starting with choice (C): Begin by looking at choice (C). We substitute 9 in for ◊ in the given equation.

$$\frac{3+9}{2} = 7\frac{1}{2}$$
$$\frac{12}{2} = 7\frac{1}{2}$$
$$6 = 7\frac{1}{2}$$

The equation is false. So we can eliminate choices (A), (B), and (C). Let's try choice (D) next. We substitute 12 in for ◊.

$$\frac{3+12}{2} = 7\frac{1}{2}$$
$$\frac{15}{2} = 7\frac{1}{2}$$
$$7\frac{1}{2} = 7\frac{1}{2}$$

Thus, the answer is choice (D).

*** Algebraic solution:**

$$\frac{3+\lozenge}{2} = 7\frac{1}{2}$$
$$3+\lozenge = 15$$
$$\lozenge = 12$$

This is choice (D).

2. GEOMETRY

* Angles 2, 4, 6, and 8 all have equal measure. Therefore the sum of the measures of angles 2 and 4 is equal to the sum of the measures of angles 6 and 8, choice (D).

Remarks: (1) Angles 2 and 4 are **vertical angles**. Vertical angles have equal measure. Angles 6 and 8 are also vertical angles.

(2) When parallel lines are cut by a **transversal**, each pair of **alternate interior angles** formed has the same measure. Angles 4 and 6 are alternate interior angles and therefore they have equal measure.

3. Data Analysis

* Let's fill in the more of the table.

	Employed	Unemployed	Total
Men	27,000		
Women	21,000	**500**	21,500
Total	48,000	2500	50,500

Note that we got 2500 from the computation 50,500 – 48,000 = 2500, and we got 21,000 from 48,000 – 27,000 = 21,000. Finally, we get the number we're looking for from 21,500 – 21,000 = 500, choice (A).

4. Functions

* We are being asked to compute $A(15) = 4 \cdot 15 - 30 = 60 - 30 = 30$. So the net amount they raised is \$30, choice (E).

5. Algebra

Solution by picking numbers: Let's choose values for x, r, v, and k that satisfy the given conditions, say $x = 4$, $r = 3$, $v = 12$, $k =$ **4**. **Put a nice big, dark circle around k = 4 so you can find it easily later.** Now substitute 4 in for x in each answer choice.

(A) 1

(B) $\frac{1}{4}$

(C) $4 - 1 = 3$

(D) 4

(E) $4 + 1 = 5$

Since choices (A), (B), (C), and (E) came out incorrect, the answer is choice (D).

For more information on this technique, see **Strategy 4** in ***"The 32 Most Effective SAT Math Strategies."***

* **Algebraic solution:** Since xr and kr are both equal to v, they are equal to each other. So $kr = xr$. Since $rv \neq 0$, $r \neq 0$. So we can divide each side of the last equation by r to get $k = x$, choice (D).

6. Number Theory

* **Solution by guessing:** Let's choose values for the number of white eggs and the number of brown eggs so that the ratio is $\frac{2}{3}$.

White eggs	Brown eggs	Total
2	3	5
4	6	10
6	9	15
8	12	20

At this point we see that the number of eggs in the basket must be a multiple of 5. Since 12 is **not** a multiple of 5, the answer is choice (B).

For more information on this technique, see **Strategy 4** in ***"The 32 Most Effective SAT Math Strategies."***

* **Formal solution:** We can represent the number of white eggs by $2x$ and the number of brown eggs by $3x$ where x is an integer. It follows that the total number of eggs in the basket is $2x + 3x = 5x$. So the number of eggs in the basket is a multiple of 5. Since 12 is **not** a multiple of 5, the answer is choice (B)

7. Algebra

* $\sqrt{18} = \sqrt{9 \cdot 2} = \sqrt{9}\sqrt{2} = 3\sqrt{2}$. So $18\sqrt{18} = 18 \cdot 3\sqrt{2} = 54\sqrt{2}$. Thus, $r = 54$ and $t = 2$. Therefore $rt = 54 \cdot 2 = 108$, choice (C).

8. Geometry

Solution by picking numbers: Let's choose values for a and b using the picture to give reasonable estimates (it does not say "figure not drawn to scale"). Let's try $a = 70$ and $b = 50$. Using the fact that each triangle has 180 degrees, we will find c.

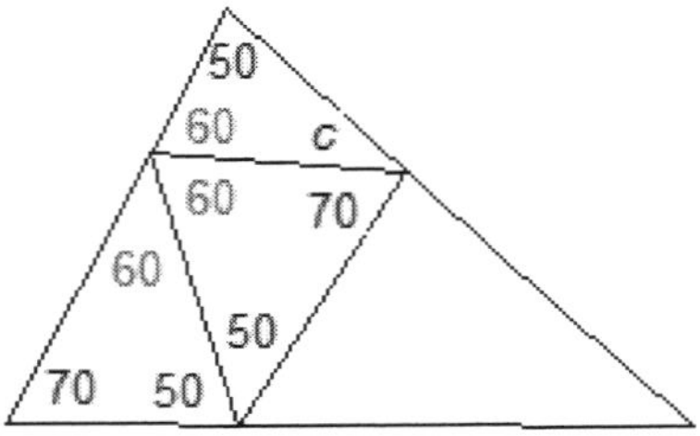

To see where the bottom two 60's come from, simply note that we have 180 – 70 – 50 = 60. For the topmost 60, note that 180 – 60 – 60 = 60. Finally, c = 180 – 60 – 50 = **70**. **Put a nice big, dark circle around 70 so you can find it easily later.** Now substitute 70 in for a and 50 in for b in each answer choice.

(A) 70 + 3(50) – 180 = 40

(B) 2(70) + 2(50) – 180 = 60

(C) 180 – 70 – 50 = 60

(D) 360 – 70 – 50 = 240

(E) 360 – 2(70) – 3(50) = 70

Since choices (A), (B), (C), and (D) came out incorrect, the answer is choice (E).

For more information on this technique, see **Strategies 4 and 5** in ***"The 32 Most Effective SAT Math Strategies."***

Algebraic solution: I **do not** recommend solving this problem algebraically, but I am including this solution for completeness.

Let's look at the picture carefully.

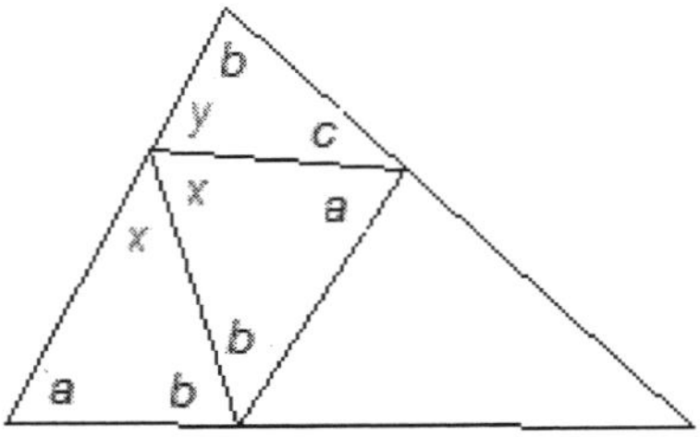

Since a triangle has 180 degrees, $x = 180 - a - b$. Also, since the angles labeled x, x, and y form a straight line, we have

$$y = 180 - 2x = 180 - 2(180 - a - b) = 180 - 360 + 2a + 2b = 2a + 2b - 180.$$

Finally, we have

$$c = 180 - b - y = 180 - b - (2a + 2b - 180) = 180 - b - 2a - 2b + 180$$
$$= 360 - 2a - 3b.$$

This is choice (E).

***Quick solution:** Let's remove the blank triangle on the right from the picture to form the following quadrilateral.

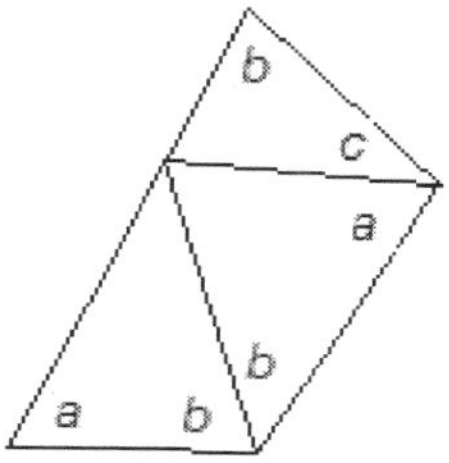

Now, the angle measures of a quadrilateral add up to 360 degrees so that $b + a + b + b + a + c = 360$. That is $2a + 3b + c = 360$, and so we have $c = 360 - 2a - 3b$, choice (E).

9. Algebra

* $4t^3 = 4 \cdot 351 =$ **1404**.

Remark: There is no need to find t in this question.

10. Geometry

* We take the average of the two numbers by adding them up and then dividing by 2. $\frac{53+62}{2} = \frac{115}{2} =$ **57.5**.

11. Geometry

* Since two angles of the triangle have the same measure, the triangle is **isosceles**. Therefore two of the sides have the same length. So the third side of the triangle must have a length of either 50 or 30. To make the perimeter as small as possible, let the third side have length 30. Then the perimeter of the triangle will be $50 + 30 + 30 =$ **110**.

Definition: An **isosceles** triangle is a triangle with 2 congruent sides. Note that the angles opposite these 2 sides are also congruent.

Conversely, if a triangle has 2 congruent angles, then the sides opposite these angles are congruent, and so the triangle is isosceles.

12. ALGEBRA

* We have

$$x^2 - y^2 = (x + y)(x - y)$$
$$77 = 11(x - y)$$

So $x - y = \frac{77}{11} = 7$.

We now add.

$$\begin{array}{r} x + y = 11 \\ \underline{x - y = 7} \\ 2x = 18 \\ x = \mathbf{9} \end{array}$$

For more information on this technique, see **Strategy 16** in ***"The 32 Most Effective SAT Math Strategies."***

13. GEOMETRY

* Let's choose a degree measure between 20 and 30 degrees. Let's use 24 degrees, Since there are 360 degrees in a circle, we divide $\frac{360}{24} = \mathbf{15}$.

Complete solution: $\frac{360}{20} = 18$ and $\frac{360}{30} = 12$. So we can grid in any integer strictly between 12 and 18.

The complete list of possible answers is **13**, **14**, **15**, **16**, **17**.

14. ALGEBRA

Solution by guessing: Let's take a guess for a, say $a = 2$. Then the first 5 terms of the sequence are 2, 6, 18, 54, and 162. The sum of these terms is 2 + 6 + 18 + 54 + 162 = 242. This is too small.

Let's guess $a = 5$ next. Then the first 5 terms of the sequence are 5, 15, 45, 135, and 405. The sum is 5 + 15 + 45 + 135 + 405 = 605. This is correct. So the answer is **5**.

* **Algebraic solution:** The first 5 terms of the sequence are a, $3a$, $9a$, $27a$, and $81a$. The sum is $a + 3a + 9a + 27a + 81a = 121a$. So we just need to solve the equation $121a = 605$. So $a = \frac{605}{121} = \mathbf{5}$.

15. Geometry

* **Solution by picking numbers** Let's let $QS = 1$, $QV = 3$, $PT = 3$, and $PR = 4$. It follows that $SV = 3 - 1 = 2$.

Now, $\frac{area\ \Delta PST}{area\ \Delta PQR} = \frac{\frac{1}{2}(PT)(SV)}{\frac{1}{2}(PR)(QV)} = \frac{\frac{1}{2}(3)(2)}{\frac{1}{2}(4)(3)}$ = **1/2** or **.5**.

16. Functions

* $h(2m) = 14 + \frac{(2m)^2}{4} = 14 + \frac{4m^2}{4} = 14 + m^2$. So we have $14 + m^2 = 9m$. We can now either try to guess values for m that satisfy this equation, or we can solve the equation for m algebraically. Here is the algebraic solution.

$$14 + m^2 = 9m$$
$$m^2 - 9m + 14 = 0$$
$$(m - 2)(m - 7) = 0$$

So m = **2** or **7**.

17. Number Theory

* Each Type A clock chimes 8 times at 8:00, 1 time at 7:30 and 1 time at 8:30 for a total of 10 chimes. Since there are 10 Type A clocks, we get $10 \cdot 10 = 100$ chimes altogether from Type A clocks.

Each Type B clock chimes 8 times at 8:00. Since there are 5 Type B clocks, we get $5 \cdot 8 = 40$ chimes altogether from Type B clocks.

Each Type C clock chimes 1 time at 8:00, 1 time at 7:30, and 1 time at 8:30 for a total of 3 chimes. As there are 3 Type C clocks, we get $3 \cdot 3 = 9$ chimes altogether from Type C clocks.

So in total, the number of chimes is 100 + 40 + 9 = **149**.

18. Counting

* We will use the **counting principle** which says that if one event is followed by a second independent event, the number of possibilities is multiplied.

Since the shaded card cannot be placed at an end, there are 4 possibilities for the leftmost position. Once a card has been placed in the leftmost position, there are then 3 possibilities for the rightmost position. For the remaining positions, the shaded card can now be used. So once 2 cards have been placed on the ends, there are 3 possibilities for the second position, 2 possibilities for the middle position, and finally 1 possibility for the fourth position.

Using the counting principle we get $4 \cdot 3 \cdot 3 \cdot 2 \cdot 1 =$ **72** arrangements.

Note: We considered the "special cases" first. Here the two ends are the special cases because at the ends there is a restriction on what can be placed. Handling the special cases first in counting problems often leads to the simplest solution.

Common error: Many students will try the following computation:

$$4 \cdot 4 \cdot 3 \cdot 2 \cdot 1 = 96.$$

This is not right. The first 4 is correct, but the second 4 is not. If you want to do the second position next, you would have to consider 2 cases: the case where the shaded card is placed there and the case where the shaded card is not placed there. This would have to be repeated for each position leading to a tedious amount of computation. Here is the correct computation if you were to solve the problem this way.

$$4 \cdot 1 \cdot 3 \cdot 2 \cdot 1 + 4 \cdot 3 \cdot 1 \cdot 2 \cdot 1 + 4 \cdot 3 \cdot 2 \cdot 1 \cdot 1 = 24 + 24 + 24 = \mathbf{72}.$$

The advanced student might want to attempt to understand how this last computation works.

Section 9

1. Algebra

Solution by starting with choice (C): Let's start with choice (C) and guess that there are 8 girls on the bus. Then there are also 8 boys on the bus. After the first stop, 4 boys get off the bus leaving 4 boys and 8 girls. Since there are twice as many girls as boys on the bus, this is correct. So the answer is choice (C).

For more information on this technique, see **Strategy 1** in ***"The 32 Most Effective SAT Math Strategies."***

Algebraic solution: Let x be the number of girls on the bus. After the first stop, there are x girls on the bus and $x - 4$ boys on the bus. Since there are twice as many girls as boys on the bus, we have $x = 2(x - 4) = 2x - 8$. So $x = 8$, choice (C).

A detailed look at that last computation: To solve that last equation we subtract x from each side of the equation and then add 8 to each side of the equation. Here are the details.

$$\begin{array}{rcl} x &=& 2x - 8 \\ \underline{-x} && \underline{-x\quad} \\ 0 &=& x - 8 \\ \underline{+8} && \underline{\quad +8} \\ 8 &=& x \end{array}$$

2. Geometry

* If a linear function has a negative slope, its graph moves downwards as you trace it from left to right. This eliminates choices (A) and (B).

If the graph of a function has a positive y-intercept, it passes through the y-axis above the x-axis.

So the answer is choice (D).

For more information on slope see the notes at the end of Problem 12 in Section 12 of Test 1 (pp. 15-17).

3. Data Analysis

* We simply divide 1.89 by 6 to get $\frac{1.89}{6}$ = .315. The closest approximation is given in choice (B).

4. Data Analysis

* 21 donuts will cost the least if you purchase a box of 12, a box of 6, and 3 single donuts. The total is 3.59 + 1.89 + 3(.40) = 6.68, choice (B).

Remark: We did assume here that you save money by purchasing a larger box. This is a pretty safe assumption, but let's just check to be safe.

We already noted in question 3 that if you purchase a box of 6, you are paying $0.315 per donut. If you purchase a box of 12, the cost per donut is $\frac{3.59}{12}$ ~.299. So we have confirmed that the larger the box you purchase, the more money you save.

5. Functions

* 5 is the *x*-value and *h*(5) is the corresponding *y*-value. To find *h*(5) on the graph, first find 5 on the *x*-axis with your finger. Then move your finger straight up until you hit the graph. *h*(5) is the *y*-coordinate of that point which is about 3, choice (C).

Remarks: (1) *h*(5) = 3 is equivalent to "the point (5,3) is on the graph of the function *h*."

(2) If you still have trouble seeing the *y*-coordinate of the point, try the following. After finding 5 on the *x*-axis with your finger and moving your finger straight up until you hit the graph, proceed by moving your finger straight to the left until you hit the *y*-axis. Note that your finger winds up midway between 2 and 4. So *h*(5) = 3.

6. Geometry

First note that the measures of the three angles must add up to 360 degrees. We can now proceed in two ways.

Method 1- Starting with choice (C): Let's start with choice (C) and guess that $x = 40$. Then we have $2(40) + 3(40) + 4(40) = 80 + 120 + 160 = 360$. This is correct so that the answer is choice (C).

For more information on this technique, see **Strategy 1** in ***"The 32 Most Effective SAT Math Strategies."***

* **Method 2 – Algebraic solution:** $2x + 3x + 4x = 9x$. So we have $9x = 360$, and therefore $x = \frac{360}{9} = 40$, choice (C).

7. Algebra

* Since $\sqrt{9} = 3$, it follows that $9^{-1/2} = \frac{1}{9^{\frac{1}{2}}} = \frac{1}{\sqrt{9}} = \frac{1}{3}$. So $x = 9$. Also $2^4 = 16$ and $4 > 2$. So $y = 2$ and $z = 4$. Finally, $x + z = 9 + 4 = 13$, choice (D).

Negative and Fractional Exponents

Law	Example
$x^{-1} = 1/x$	$3^{-1} = 1/3$
$x^{-a} = 1/x^a$	$9^{-2} = 1/81$
$x^{1/n} = \sqrt[n]{x}$	$x^{1/3} = \sqrt[3]{x}$
$x^{m/n} = \sqrt[n]{x^m} = (\sqrt[n]{x})^m$	$x^{9/2} = \sqrt{x^9} = (\sqrt{x})^9$

8. Geometry

* A circle is symmetric about its center. So two points on the circle will have the same y-coordinate if their x-coordinates are at the same distance from 4. The following are pairs of points at the same distance from 4.

3 and 5	These are 1 unit away from 4.
2 and 6	These are 2 units away from 4.

And we can stop here since 2 and 6 is answer choice (C).

9. Number Theory

* **Solution by starting with choice (C):** Let's start with choice (C) and guess that $p = 4$. Then $2p + 7 = 2 \cdot 4 + 7 = 15$. The remainder when 15 is divided by 5 is 0 (note that 5 goes into 15 three times with 0 left over). This is not right.

Let's try choice (B) next and guess that $p = 3$. Then $2p + 7 = 2\cdot3 + 7 = 13$. The remainder when 13 is divided by 5 is 3 (note that 5 goes into 13 two times with 3 left over). This is correct. So the answer is choice (B).

For more information on this technique, see **Strategy 1** in ***"The 32 Most Effective SAT Math Strategies."***

10. COUNTING

* Since Stacy is the 12th tallest student, there are 11 students taller than Stacy. Similarly, since Stacy is the 12th shortest student, there are 11 students shorter than Stacy. Therefore there are 11 + 11 + 1 = 23 students in the class, choice (B).

Remarks: (1) We added 11 students that are taller than Stacy, plus 11 students that are shorter than Stacy, plus 1 more for Stacy herself.

(2) If it helps you can form a list as follows.

/ / / / / / / / / / / S / / / / / / / / / / /

This list was formed by starting with S in the middle for Stacy, then putting 11 slashes to the right of Stacy for the taller students, and then putting 11 slashes to the left of Stacy for the shorter students. Now just count all the marks (including the S).

(3) Here is another possible way to write the list.

1 2 3 4 5 6 7 8 9 10 11 12 11 10 9 8 7 6 5 4 3 2 1

11. ALGEBRA

* **Quick solution:** Since c is negative, the graph of g has a negative y-intercept. This means that the graph hits the y-axis below the x-axis. This only happens in choice (A).

Notes: (1) The **general form** for the quadratic function $\boldsymbol{g}$ is

$$\boldsymbol{g(x) = ax^2 + bx + c}.$$

The graph of this function is a parabola. This parabola opens upwards if $a > 0$ and downwards if $a < 0$.

So in this example, since a is negative, we can eliminate choices (D) and (E). (We didn't need to do this in the quick solution above.)

(2) Note that $g(0) = a(0)^2 + b(0) + c = c$. In other words, the point $(0,c)$ is on the graph of g. In the solution above we used this fact alone to answer this question very quickly.

Graphing calculator solution with picking numbers: Choose values for a, b, and c that are consistent with the given information, say $a = -2$, $b = 3$, and $c = -4$. In your graphing calculator press Y=, and then type

-2X^2 + 3X – 4

Now press ZOOM 6 to put the graph in a standard window.

You will get a graph that most closely resembles the graph in choice (A).

For more information on this technique, see **Strategy 4** in ***"The 32 Most Effective SAT Math Strategies."***

12. GEOMETRY

*** Solution by picking numbers:** Let's add some information to the picture.

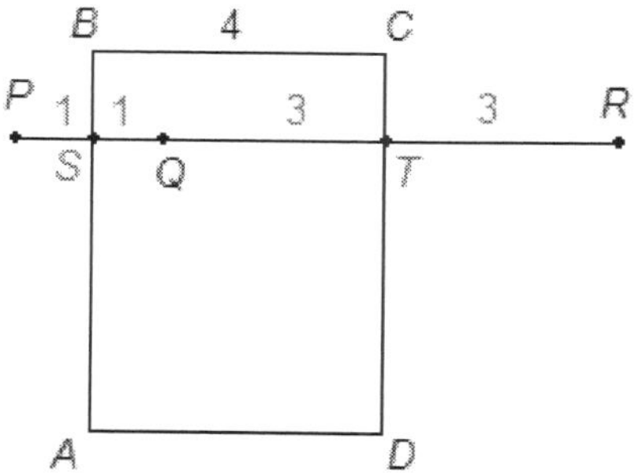

Note that we added points S and T to the picture to make the explanation easier to follow. $BC = 4$ was added to the picture, but $AB = 6$ was not because this is extra information that is not needed to solve the problem.

We chose values for SQ and QT of 1 and 3, respectively (we could have chosen any two numbers that add to 4). By the symmetry given in the question, it follows that $PS = 1$ and $TR = 3$. Finally, we have that $PR = 1 + 1 + 3 + 3 = 8$, choice (B).

For more information on this technique, see **Strategies 4** and **9** in ***"The 32 Most Effective SAT Math Strategies."***

Formal solution: The following picture gives a more formal solution.

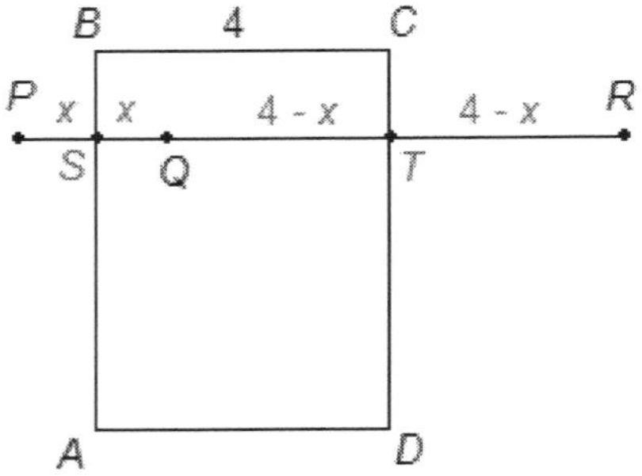

Now, we have that $PR = x + x + (4 - x) + (4 - x) = 8$, choice (B).

13. PERCENTS

*** Solution by picking a number:** Since this is a percent problem, let's start with a price of \$100. When we increase the price by 10%, the new price becomes \$110. When we decrease this price by 25% we get a final price of \$82.50 (see remark below). Since we began with \$100, the answer is 82.5%, choice (C).

Remark: We can decrease 110 by 25% in two ways.

Method 1: Take 25% of 110 and then subtract this number from 110.

$$110 - .25(110) = 82.5$$

Method 2: Take 75% of 110.

$$.75(110) = 82.5$$

Algebraic solution (not recommended): Let x be the initial price of the telephone. We increase the price by 10% by multiplying by 1.1. We then decrease the price by 25% by multiplying by .75. So we get

$$.75(1.1x) = .825x.$$

As a percent , .825 is 82.5%, choice (C).

For more information on converting between decimals and percents see the notes at the end of Problem 5 in Section 3 of Test 1 (p. 12).

14. Algebra

* **Algebraic solution:** We are given that $4w = w + 4$. Subtracting w from each side of this equation gives $3w = 4$, choice (E).

Warning: There is no need to solve for w here. In fact, doing so might lead you to choose choice (C) which is incorrect.

15. Geometry

* If the shortest side is x, then the other two sides are $x + 2$ and $x + 4$. We now use the Pythagorean Theorem $c^2 = a^2 + b^2$. In this question that becomes $(x + 4)^2 = x^2 + (x + 2)^2$. This is the same as choice (C).

Remarks: (1) The Pythagorean Theorem is one of the formulas given at the beginning of each math section of the SAT.

(2) In the formula for the Pythagorean Theorem, c is the length of the hypotenuse of the right triangle. The hypotenuse is always the longest side which is why it is equal to $x + 4$ in this problem.

Consecutive even integers are even integers that follow each other in order. The difference between consecutive even integers is 2. Here are two examples.

2, 4, 6	these are three consecutive even integers
-6, -4, -2, 0, 2	these are five consecutive even integers

In general, if x is an even integer, then x, $x + 2$, $x + 4$, $x + 6$,... are consecutive even integers.

16. Number Theory

* Let's start by trying a value for x, say $x = 2$ (note that x is an integer greater than 1). Then $y = 2 + \frac{1}{2} = 2.5$. Note that $y \neq x$, so we cannot eliminate I. Since 2.5 is not an integer, II is false. Since $xy = (2)(2.5) = 5$ and $x^2 = 4$, we have $xy > x^2$, and we cannot eliminate III. So the answer is either (A), (B), or (D). For I note that since x is greater than 1, y is a little more than x. In particular, y is not equal to x. So I must be true. For III, we have $xy = x(x + \frac{1}{x}) = x^2 + 1$ which is greater than x^2. So III must be true. Therefore the answer is choice (D).

Blue Book Test 5 Fully Explained Solutions

Section 2

1. Algebra

Solution by starting with choice (C): We begin by looking at choice (C), and we plug $x = 3$ into the given equation. We get $3(3) + 9 = 5(3) + 1$, or equivalently $18 = 16$. This is incorrect, so we can eliminate choice (C).

Let's try choice (D) next, and plug $x = 4$ into the equation. This time we get $3(4) + 9 = 5(4) + 1$, or equivalently $21 = 21$. This is correct, so the answer is choice (D).

For more information on this technique, see **Strategy 1** in ***"The 32 Most Effective SAT Math Strategies."***

* **Algebraic solution:** We solve the equation for x.

$$3x + 9 = 5x + 1$$
$$8 = 2x$$
$$4 = x$$

So the answer is choice (D).

A detailed look at the computations: To get from the first equation to the second equation above subtract $3x$ from each side of the equation and then subtract 1 from each side of the equation. Here are the details.

$$\begin{array}{rcl} 3x + 9 &=& 5x + 1 \\ \underline{-3x } && \underline{-3x } \\ 9 &=& 2x + 1 \\ \underline{-1} && \underline{-1} \\ 8 &=& 2x \end{array}$$

To get from the second equation to the third equation we simply divide each side of the equation by 2.

2. Number Theory

* **Solution by guessing:** Let's guess that we multiply each term by 2. Since $7 \cdot 2 = 14$, we see that we would then have to add 1 to get to 15.

So we are guessing that we must multiply each term by 2 and then add 1 to get to the next term. Let's check this for the remaining terms.

$$15 \cdot 2 + 1 = 31 \qquad\qquad 31 \cdot 2 + 1 = 63.$$

This is correct. So $m = 2$, choice (B).

For more information on this technique, see **Strategy 3** in ***"The 32 Most Effective SAT Math Strategies."***

Algebraic solution: We solve the following system of equations for m.

$$\begin{array}{c} 15m + p = 31 \\ \underline{7m + p = 15} \\ 8m = 16 \end{array}$$

The last equation came from subtracting the second from the first.

We now divide each side of this last equation by 8 to get $m = \frac{16}{8} = 2$, choice (B).

For more information on this technique, see **Strategy 16** in ***"The 32 Most Effective SAT Math Strategies."***

3. Counting

* **Solution by listing:** Let's list all the possible color/size combinations.

RS	RM	RL	RE
WS	WM	WL	WE
BS	BM	BL	BE

So there are 12 combinations, choice (B).

Note: When writing our list we just used the first letter of each color followed by the first letter of each size. This will save a lot of time compared to writing out each of the words over and over again.

For more information on this technique, see **Strategy 21** in ***"The 32 Most Effective SAT Math Strategies."***

*** Solution using the counting principle:** The **counting principle** says that if one event is followed by a second independent event, the number of possibilities is multiplied. There are 3 ways to choose a color. Once a color has been chosen, there are 4 ways to choose a size. Therefore there are (3)(4) = 12 combinations, choice (B).

Important note: Do not let the word "combinations" in the problem itself trick you. This is **not** a combination in the mathematical sense.

4. FUNCTIONS

Solution by starting with choice (C): Let's start with choice (C) and try the function $f(x) = \frac{4}{x}$. Then $f(-3) = \frac{4}{-3} = \frac{-4}{3}$ and $f(3) = \frac{4}{3}$. So $f(-3) < f(3)$ and we can eliminate choice (C).

Let's try choice (D) next so that $f(x) = 4 - x^3$. Then $f(-3) = 4 - (-3)^3 = 31$ and $f(3) = 4 - 3^3 = -23$. So $f(-3) > f(3)$. Therefore the answer is choice (D).

*** Solution by a quick process of elimination:** Choices (A), (B) and (E) only have even powers of *x*. Therefore you get the same value whether you plug in a positive or negative number. In particular, we will have that $f(-3) = f(3)$. So we can eliminate choices (A), (B), and (E).

In choice (C), substituting a negative number in for *x* will produce a negative result and substituting in a positive number for *x* will produce a positive result. So $f(-3) < f(3)$, and we can eliminate choice (C).

There is only one answer choice left, choice (D).

Remark: The functions in choices (A), (B), and (E) are **even** functions, and the function in choice (C) is an **odd** function.

See p. 59 in ***"The 32 Most Effective SAT Math Strategies"* for more information on even and odd functions.**

5. ALGEBRA

Let *y* be the force required to stretch the spring beyond its natural length, and let *x* be the length the spring is being stretched.

Solution 1: Since *y* is proportional to *x*, $y = kx$ for some constant *k*. We are given that $y = 15$ when $x = 8$, so that $15 = k(8)$, or $k = \frac{15}{8}$. So $y = \frac{15x}{8}$.

When $x = 20$, we have $y = \frac{15(20)}{8} = 37.5$, choice (E).

* **Solution 2:** Since y is proportional to x, $\frac{y}{x}$ is a constant. So we get the following ratio: $\frac{15}{8} = \frac{y}{20}$. Cross multiplying gives $300 = 8y$, so that $y = 37.5$, choice (E).

Solution 3: The graph *of* $y = f(x)$ is a line passing through the points (0, 0) and (8, 15). The slope of this line is $\frac{15-0}{8-0} = \frac{15}{8}$. Writing the equation of the line in slope-intercept form we have $y = \frac{15}{8}x$. As in solution 1, when $x = 20$, we have $y = \frac{15(20)}{8} = 37.5$, choice (E).

Here is a quick lesson in **direct variation:**

The following are all equivalent ways of saying the same thing:
(1) y varies directly as x
(2) y is directly proportional to x
(3) $y = kx$ for some constant k
(4) $\frac{y}{x}$ is constant
(5) the graph of $y = f(x)$ is a nonvertical line through the origin.

For example, in the equation $y = 5x$, y varies directly as x. Here is a partial table of values for this equation.

x	1	2	3	4
y	5	10	15	20

Note that we can tell that this table represents a direct relationship between x and y because $\frac{5}{1} = \frac{10}{2} = \frac{15}{3} = \frac{20}{4}$. Here the **constant of variation** is 5. Here is a graph of the equation.

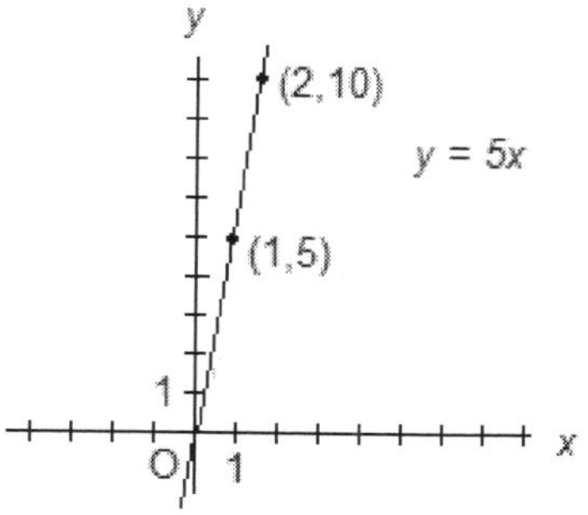

Note that we can tell that this graph represents a direct relationship between x and y because it is a nonvertical line through the origin. The constant of variation is the slope of the line, in this case $m = 5$.

6. GEOMETRY

* Let's draw a picture.

It is now pretty easy to see that $YZ = \frac{1}{2}XZ$, and that $2XY = XZ$ so that I and III are true. Since III is true, clearly II is false. So the answer is choice (E).

For more information on this technique, see **Strategy 9** in ***"The 32 Most Effective SAT Math Strategies."***

Solution by picking numbers: If you are having trouble understanding the above solution, you may want to choose a specific value for *XY*, say *XY* = 1. It then follows that *YZ* = 1 and *XZ* = 2. We then have the following.

I.	$1 = \frac{1}{2} \cdot 2$	This is true.
II.	$\frac{1}{2} \cdot 2 = 2 \cdot 1$	This is false.
III.	$2 \cdot 1 = 2$	This is true.

This seems to indicate that the answer is choice (E), which in fact it is.

Remark: Remember that we can usually only use the technique of picking numbers to eliminate answer choices. So technically, in the last solution we really only eliminated answer choices (B) and (D). However, a little thought should convince you that the results are actually independent of the number we decided to choose.

For more information on this technique, see **Strategy 4** in ***"The 32 Most Effective SAT Math Strategies."***

7. ALGEBRA

* **Algebraic solution:** Since $2r$ and $6t$ are equal to the same quantity, it follows that $2r = 6t$. To solve this for r we simply divide each side of this last equation by 2. So $r = \frac{6t}{2} = 3t$, choice (C).

Solution by picking numbers: Let's choose a value for t, say $t = 10$. Then $5s = 6t = 6(10) = 60$. So $s = \frac{60}{5} = 12$. It follows that $2r = 5s = 5(12) = 60$. Therefore $r = \frac{60}{2} = \mathbf{30}$. Put a nice big, dark circle around 30 so you can find it easily later. We now substitute $t = 10$ into each answer choice.

(A) $\frac{12}{25} \cdot 10 = 4.8$

(B) $\frac{6}{5} \cdot 10 = 12$

(C) $3 \cdot 10 = 30$

(D) $15 \cdot 10 = 150$

(E) $30 \cdot 10 = 300$

Since choices (A), (B), (D), and (E) came out incorrect, the answer is choice (C).

For more information on this technique, see **Strategy 4** in ***"The 32 Most Effective SAT Math Strategies."***

8. ALGEBRA

Solution by picking numbers: Let's suppose that there were $k = 37$ passengers, and $n = 4$ buses that each seat a maximum of $x = 10$ passengers. Then 3 of the buses are filled and 1 bus has 3 seats left over. So the given condition is satisfied. Let's now substitute these values into the equations in each answer choice.

(A) $4 \cdot 10 - 3 = 37$	True
(B) $4 \cdot 10 + 3 = 37$	False
(C) $4 + 10 + 3 = 37$	False
(D) $4 \cdot 37 = 10 + 3$	False
(E) $4 \cdot 37 = 10 - 3$	False

Since (B), (C), (D), and (E) came out false, the answer is choice (A).

For more information on this technique, see **Strategy 4** in ***"The 32 Most Effective SAT Math Strategies."***

* **Algebraic solution:** nx is the total number of passengers that n buses can hold. Since one of the buses has 3 empty seats, we subtract 3 from this expression to get the total number of passengers (which is k).

Therefore $nx - 3 = k$, choice (A).

9. GEOMETRY

* This is a standard SAT problem involving two parallel lines cut by a transversal. In this example there are actually two transversals. It's useful to isolate just one of them. We do this below.

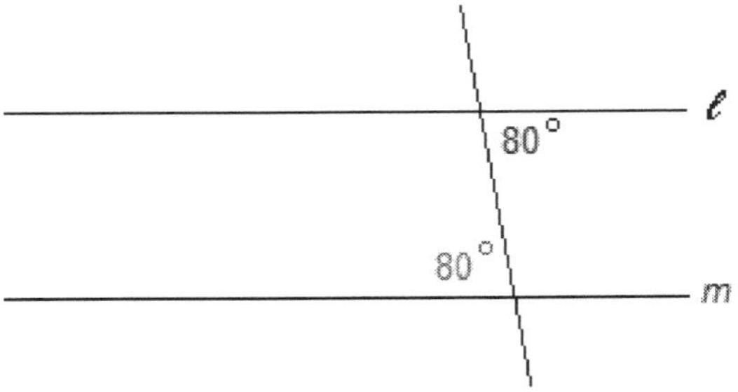

Note that we have extended the ends of the transversal so that the picture is more recognizable. Also, the transversal creates 8 angles, four of which have measure 80 degrees. The other four measure 100 degrees. Any two non-congruent angles are supplementary, ie. they add up to 180 degrees.

Now let's draw the second transversal, and notice that the 80 degree angle is split into two angles of 50 and 30 degrees.

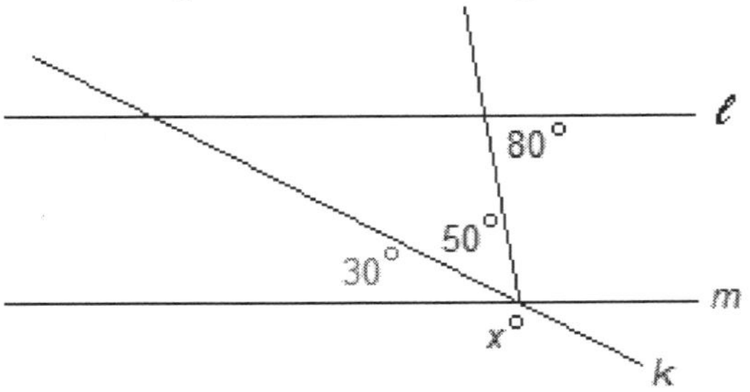

Finally, we have $x = 180 - 30 = 150$, choice (A).

10. ALGEBRA

* It is easy to see that substituting in 0 for x yields 0 on each side of the inequality. So we get $0 < 0$, which is false. So the answer is choice (B).

Remark: If you did not realize immediately that 0 would make the statement false, it's no big deal. Simply start with choice (C) as usual (see problem 1 from this section for example) and use your calculator carefully until you eventually find your way to choice (B) at which point you should still get the correct answer.

11. Geometry

Solution by picking numbers: Let's assume that the back wheel has a diameter of 4. It follows that the new front wheel has a diameter of 2. So the radii of the back and front wheel are 2 and 1, respectively. So the circumference of the back and front wheel are 4π and 2π, respectively. Since the back wheel has twice the circumference of the front wheel, the front wheel will make 2 revolutions for each revolution of the back wheel, choice (C).

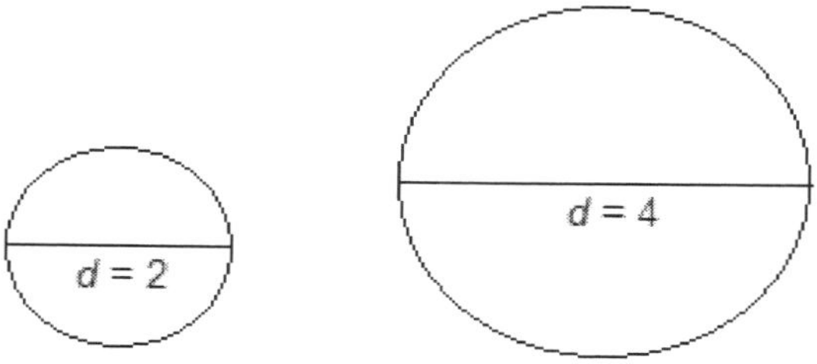

Remarks: (1) A **revolution** is one full rotation. The circumference of the circle gives the length of one revolution of the circle.

(2) The formula for circumference is given at the beginning of each math section of the SAT ($C = 2\pi r$). Note that the circumference formula can also be written as $C = \pi d$.

(3) The number of revolutions is **inversely proportional** to the circumference of the circle. In this example, we have $(1)(4\pi) = (2)(2\pi)$.

* **Quick solution:** Since there is a linear relationship between the circumference of a circle and its diameter ($C = \pi d$), halving the diameter also halves the circumference. Since the front wheel has half the circumference of the back wheel, it will make 2 revolutions for each revolution of the back wheel.

12. Probability

* **Solution by picking numbers:** Let's assume that there are 3 positive numbers. Then there are 5 numbers in total, and so there are 5 – 3 = 2 negative numbers. Thus, $\frac{n}{p} = \frac{2}{3}$, choice (C).

Remark: Here we have used the **Simple Probability Principle** which says the following. To compute a simple probability where all outcomes are equally likely, divide the number of "successes" by the total number of outcomes.

13. Functions

* We are given that $c(20) = 640$. Thus, $640 = \frac{600(20)-200}{20} + k = 590 + k$. Therefore $k = 640 - 590 = 50$, choice (B).

14. Number Theory

* Let's just begin checking if various pairs (x,y) of positive integers satisfy the given inequality.

(1,1)	$2(1) + 3(1) = 5$	Yes.
(1,2)	$2(1) + 3(2) = 8$	No.
(2,1)	$2(2) + 3(1) = 7$	No.

Clearly no other pairs will work. So the answer is One, choice (A).

15. Geometry

* Since triangle ABC has two angles with equal measure, it is an **isosceles** triangle. In particular, the sides opposite these two angles have equal length. So $BC = 8$, and the perimeter of triangle ABC is $8 + 8 + 5 = 21$.

Since triangle DEF has two angles with measure 60 degrees, the third angle also measures 60 degrees, and therefore the triangle is **equilateral**. So all three sides have the same length, and the perimeter of triangle DEF is $5 + 5 + 5 = 15$. Finally, $21 - 15 = 6$, choice (C).

16. Algebra

Solution by picking numbers: Let's choose values for x and y, say $x = 3$ and $y = 5$. Then $y^2 - x^2 = 5^2 - 3^2 = 25 - 9 = \mathbf{16}$. Put a nice big, dark circle around 16 so you can find it easily later. We now substitute $x = 3$ into each answer choice.

(A) 6

(B) 12

(C) 8

(D) 10

(E) 16

Since choices (A), (B), (C), and (D) came out incorrect, the answer is choice (E).

For more information on this technique, see **Strategy 4** in ***"The 32 Most Effective SAT Math Strategies."***

* **Algebraic solution:** Since x and y are consecutive odd integers, it follows that $y = x + 2$. So $y^2 - x^2 = (x + 2)^2 - x^2 = x^2 + 4x + 4 - x^2 = 4x + 4$, choice (E).

Note: $(x + 2)^2 = (x + 2)(x + 2) = x^2 + 2x + 2x + 4 = x^2 + 4x + 4$.

Consecutive odd integers are odd integers that follow each other in order. The difference between consecutive odd integers is 2. Here are two examples.

1, 3, 5	these are three consecutive odd integers
-5, -3, -1, 1, 3	these are five consecutive odd integers

In general, if x is an odd integer, then x, $x + 2$, $x + 4$, $x + 6$,... are consecutive odd integers.

17. GEOMETRY

* Let's put the given line into slope-intercept form by subtracting $4x$ from each side of the equation. We get $y = -4x + k$, and we see that the slope of this line is -4. Since line ℓ is perpendicular to this line, line ℓ has a slope of $\frac{1}{4}$. Since line ℓ passes through the origin (the point (0,0)), it follows that the equation of line ℓ is $y = \frac{1}{4}x$. Since the point $(t,t + 1)$ is on line ℓ, we have $t + 1 = \frac{1}{4}t$. We need to solve this last equation for t.

$$t + 1 = \frac{1}{4}t$$
$$4t + 4 = t$$
$$3t + 4 = 0$$
$$3t = -4$$
$$t = \frac{-4}{3}$$

Therefore the answer is choice (A).

For more information on this technique, see **Strategy 28** in ***"The 32 Most Effective SAT Math Strategies."***

18. Statistics

*** Solution by changing averages to sums:** We use the formula

Sum = Average · Number.

Since the Average of x and y is k, and the Number of things we are averaging is 2, the Sum of x and y is $x + y = 2k$. So the average of x, y, and z is $\frac{x+y+z}{3} = \frac{2k+z}{3}$, choice (A).

For more information on this technique, see **Strategy 20** in ***"The 32 Most Effective SAT Math Strategies."***

Solution by picking numbers: Let's choose values for x, y, and z. Let's let $x = 1$, $y = 3$, and $z = 8$. It follows that $k = 2$, and the average of x, y, and z is **4**. Put a nice big, dark circle around 4 so you can find it easily later. We now substitute $k = 2$ and $z = 8$ into each answer choice.

(A) $\frac{2 \cdot 2+8}{3} = 4$

(B) $\frac{2 \cdot 2+8}{2} = 6$

(C) $\frac{2+8}{3} \sim 3.3333$

(D) $\frac{2+8}{2} = 5$

(E) $\frac{2(2+8)}{3} \sim 6.6667$

Since choices (B), (C), (D), and (E) came out incorrect, the answer is choice (A).

For more information on this technique, see **Strategy 4** in ***"The 32 Most Effective SAT Math Strategies."***

19. Geometry

* We are given that the triangle has a side of length 2. So $XY = 2$. Since the triangle is equilateral, the altitude YW is also a median. So $XW = 1$

and therefore triangle XYW is a 30, 60, 90 triangle. So $YW = \sqrt{3}$. Note that $\overline{YW}$ is a diameter of the circle so that the radius of the circle has length $r = \frac{\sqrt{3}}{2}$. So the area of the circle is $A = \pi r^2 = \pi(\frac{\sqrt{3}}{2})^2 = \frac{3\pi}{4}$, choice (C).

Remarks: (1) In general, for an **isosceles** triangle, the **median**, **altitude**, and **angle bisector** from the vertex opposite the two congruent angles are all equal. In particular, for an **equilateral** triangle, these three segments are all equal no matter which vertex you choose to draw the segment from.

(2). When you draw the altitude (or equivalently median or angle bisector) from any vertex to the opposite base in an equilateral triangle, two 30, 60, 90 triangles are formed. The formula for a 30, 60, 90 triangle is given in the beginning of each math section of the SAT.

Definitions: A **triangle** is a two-dimensional geometric figure with three sides and three angles. The sum of the degree measures of all three angles of a triangle is 180.

A triangle is **isosceles** if it has two sides of equal length. Equivalently, an isosceles triangle has two angles of equal measure.

A triangle is **equilateral** if all three of its sides have equal length. Equivalently, an equilateral triangle has three angles of equal measure (all three angles measure 60 degrees).

Example:

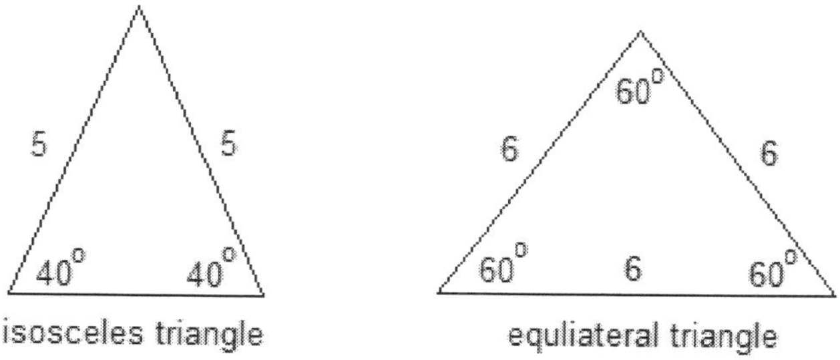

A **median** from the vertex of a triangle to the opposite base divides the base into two congruent segments.

An **altitude** from the vertex of a triangle to the opposite base is perpendicular to the base.

An **angle bisector** from the vertex of a triangle to the opposite base divides the angle at the vertex into two congruent angles.

20. Number Theory

* **Solution by brute force:** Let's just try each positive integer in succession beginning with $k = 4$ (we do not need to try $k = 1, 2$, or 3 because dividing by these numbers can never produce a remainder of 3).

4 goes into 15 3 times with a remainder of 3.
5 goes into 15 3 times with a remainder of 0.
6 goes into 15 2 times with a remainder of 3.
7 goes into 15 2 times with a remainder of 1.
8 goes into 15 1 time with a remainder of 7.
9 goes into 15 1 time with a remainder of 6.
10 goes into 15 1 time with a remainder of 5.
11 goes into 15 1 time with a remainder of 4.
12 goes into 15 1 time with a remainder of 3.
13 goes into 15 1 time with a remainder of 2.
14 goes into 15 1 time with a remainder of 1.
15 goes into 15 1 time with a remainder of 0.
16 goes into 15 0 times with a remainder of 16

From this point forward the remainder will be the same as the divisor, and the divisors will all be greater than 3. So we see that 4, 6, and 12 are the only values for k that give the correct remainder. So the answer is Three, choice (C).

Important: To find a remainder you must perform division **by hand**. Dividing in your calculator does **not** give you a remainder (although you can use the calculator algorithm mentioned below)

Remark: The process above can be streamlined if your pattern recognition skill level is fairly decent. For example, once 8 is eliminated it may occur to you that the remainders will decrease by 1 each time we increase k up until $k = 15$.

Note: See problem 11 in section 3 of Test 1 (pp. 14-15) for a **Calculator Algorithm** for finding remainders.

SECTION 4

1. ALGEBRA

We subtract 6 from each side of the equation to get

$$s + t - 6 = 3 - 6 = -3.$$

This is choice (A).

* This problem has a **block** of $s + t$. We can replace $s + t$ on the right by 3 to get $s + t - 6 = 3 - 6 = -3$, choice (A).

For more information on this technique, see **Strategy 19** in ***"The 32 Most Effective SAT Math Strategies."***

2. GEOMETRY

* **Solution by starting with choice (C):** The distance from C to Q is CQ which is the length of a side of the cube. The distance from C to P is CP which is the length of a long diagonal of the cube. So $CP > CQ$. In particular C is **not** the same distance from P as it is from Q. So the answer is choice (C).

Remarks: (1) A long diagonal of a cube has the longest length of any segment between two points on the cube.

(2) The length of the long diagonal of a rectangular solid can be found by using the **Generalized Pythagorean Theorem**.

$$d^2 = a^2 + b^2 + c^2$$

where a, b and c are the length, width and height of the rectangular solid.

(3) If it helps you, you can choose a specific value for the length of a side of the cube, say $CQ = 1$. Then $(CP)^2 = 1^2 + 1^2 + 1^2 = 3$, and thus, $CP = \sqrt{3}$ which is bigger than 1.

3. Data Analysis

* If you are having trouble estimating the given percentages in the the circle graph, the following picture may help.

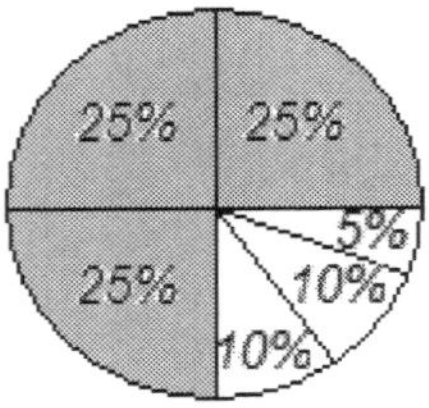

Note that 78% is just a bit more than the shaded area in the above picture. So we can eliminate choices (A), (B), and (E). Since "News Groups" and "Other" are supposed to have the same area we can eliminate choice (C). Therefore the answer is choice (D).

4. Number Theory

* **Solution by guessing:** The fraction $\frac{3}{4}$ can be written as

$$\frac{6}{8}, \frac{9}{12}, \frac{12}{16}, \frac{15}{20}, \frac{18}{24}, \ldots$$

by multiplying the numerator and denominator by 2, 3, 4, 5, 6, etc.

The fraction $\frac{15}{20}$ has a numerator which is 5 less than its denominator. So the answer is 20, choice (D).

For more information on this technique, see **Strategy 3** in ***"The 32 Most Effective SAT Math Strategies."***

Solution by starting with choice (C): Let's start with choice (C) and guess that the denominator of the fraction is 16. Since (4)(4) = 16, it follows that the numerator of the fraction is (3)(4) = 12. But 16 – 12 = 4. This is a bit too small.

Let's try choice (D) next and guess that the denominator of the fraction is 20. Since (4)(5) = 20, it follows that the numerator of the fraction is (3)(5) = 15. Since 20 – 15 = 5, the answer is choice (D).

For more information on this technique, see **Strategy 1** in ***"The 32 Most Effective SAT Math Strategies."***

Algebraic solution: The numerator of the fraction is $3x$, the denominator of the fraction is $4x$, so that $4x - 3x = 5$. So $x = 5$, and therefore the denominator of the fraction is $4x = 4(5) = 20$, choice (D).

5. GEOMETRY

* The length of the base of the triangle is $b = 5k - 2k = 3k$, and the height of the triangle is $h = 6 - 2 = 4$. So the area of the triangle is

$$A = \frac{1}{2}bh = \frac{1}{2}(3k)(4) = 6k.$$

We are also given that the area of the triangle is 18. So $6k = 18$, and therefore $k = \frac{18}{6} = 3$, choice (E).

Remarks: (1) The formula for the area of a triangle is given at the beginning of each math section of the SAT.

(2) To get the length of the interval from a to c we simply subtract $c - a$. We have done this twice here, once to find the length of the base of the triangle and once to find the height.

6. ALGEBRA

Solution by picking numbers: Let's choose a value for m, say $m = 1$. Then $10k^{-1} = 100$. So $k^{-1} = 10$, and $k = .1$.Note also that $m^{-1} = \mathbf{1}$. Put a nice big, dark circle around **1** so you can find it easily later. We now substitute $k = .1$ into each answer choice.

(A) $\frac{.1}{10} = .01$

(B) $\frac{.1}{90} \sim .0011$

(C) $\frac{\sqrt{.1}}{10} \sim .0316$

(D) $\frac{1}{10 \cdot .1} = 1$

(E) $\frac{1}{90 \cdot .1} \sim .1111$

Since choices (A), (B), (C), and (E) came out incorrect, the answer is choice (D).

For more information on this technique, see **Strategy 4** in ***"The 32 Most Effective SAT Math Strategies."***

* **Algebraic solution:** We solve for m^{-1}.

$$10m^2k^{-1} = 100m$$
$$10k^{-1} = 100m^{-1}$$
$$\frac{1}{10k} = m^{-1}$$

So the answer is choice (D).

Further explanation: (1) To get from the first equality to the second, we divided each side of the first equation by m^2. Recall that when we divide two expressions with the same base you subtract the exponents. So we have that $\frac{m}{m^2} = m^{-1}$.

(2) To get from the second equality to the third equality, we divided each side of the second equation by 100. We also rewrote k^{-1} as $\frac{1}{k}$.

For a review of the **Laws of Exponents** used here see the end of the solution to Problem 8 in Section 8 of Test 1 (p. 35) and Problem 7 in Section 9 of Test 4 (p. 129).

7. GEOMETRY

* Let's draw a picture.

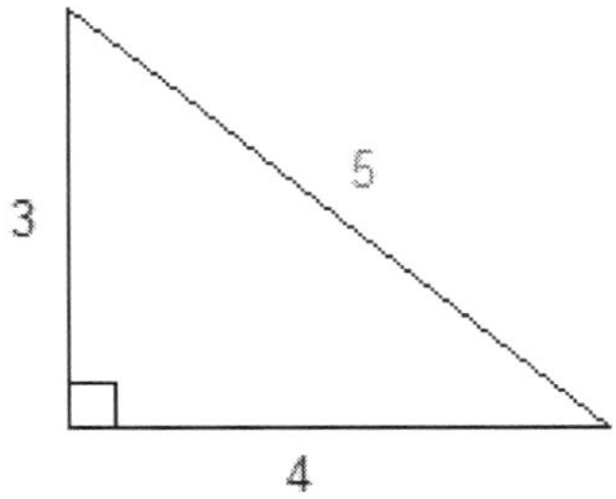

We start with a right triangle with legs of length 3 and 4. It follows that the hypotenuse of the triangle is 5. Note that this picture only shows what happens in 1 hour. Since we want the result after 4 hours, the answer is 5(4) = 20, choice (E).

Remarks: (1) You can get the length of the hypotenuse of this triangle by recognizing the Pythagorean Triple 3, 4, 5 or by using the Pythagorean Theorem.

$$c^2 = a^2 + b^2 = 3^2 + 4^2 = 9 + 16 = 25$$
$$c = 5.$$

(2) As an alternative, we can first multiply each of 3 and 4 by 4 first, and then apply the Pythagorean Theorem.

$$c^2 = a^2 + b^2 = 12^2 + 16^2 = 144 + 256 = 400$$
$$c = 20$$

Here is a picture.

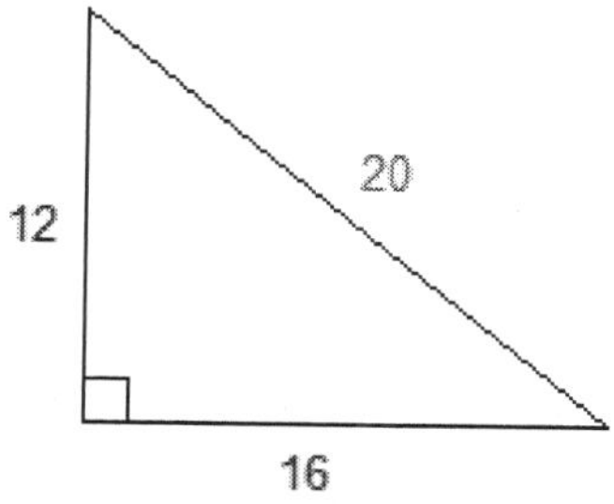

8. FUNCTIONS

* b and 3 are the x-values and $f(b)$ and $f(3)$ are the corresponding y-values (which are given to be equal). To see $f(3)$ on the graph, first find 3 on the x-axis with your finger. Then move your finger straight up until you hit the graph. $f(3)$ is the y-coordinate of that point which is equal to 5. Now move your finger straight to the left until you hit the graph again (this point has the same y-coordinate). Now simply note that the x-coordinate of this point is -1. So $b = -1$, choice (C)

Remarks: (1) $f(3) = 5$ is equivalent to "the point (3,5) is on the graph of the function f." Similarly, $f(b) = 5$ is equivalent to "the point $(b,5)$ is on the graph of the function f."

(2) $f(b) = f(3)$ means that the two points with x-coordinates of b and 3 have the same y-coordinate. In this example, we see that $b = -1$ so that the points (-1,5) and (3,5) are both on the graph of the function f.

9. ALGEBRA

* The family needs (5)(4) = 20 bottles of water. The least number greater than 20 that is divisible by 3 is 21. So the number of packages of water that the family must buy is $\frac{21}{3}$ = **7**.

Remarks: (1) If the family only buys 6 packages of water, they will only have (6)(3) = 18 bottles, and they will be 2 bottles short.

(2) You may be tempted to divide 20 by 3 in your calculator and then round to the nearest integer. In this problem you would actually get the correct answer by doing this. But it is important to realize that this method is WRONG! In a similar question if the decimal approximation rounded down to the nearest integer, you would get the answer wrong by rounding down. You would still have to move up!

10. Algebra

* **Solution by guessing:** We might initially be tempted to try $k = 7$ since $10 - 7 = 3$. But $|7 - 5| = |2| = 2$. Since this is not 8, our guess of 7 is wrong.

Since $10 - 13 = -3$, it looks like $k = 13$. Indeed, $|10 - 13| = |-3| = 3$ and $|13 - 5| = |8| = 8$. So $k =$ **13**.

Algebraic solution: The equation $|10 - k| = 3$ is equivalent to $10 - k = 3$ or $10 - k = -3$. So $k = 7$ or $k = 13$. Now, as in the first solution, substitute 7 and 13 into the second equation and you will see that $k =$ **13**.

Remark: An equation with an absolute value will most likely have two solutions. Don't be tricked into finding just one.

11. Geometry

* The upper rightmost angle (formed by lines ℓ and m) has a measure of $90 - 65 = 25$ degrees. Since ℓ is a straight line, $20 + x + 25 = 180$. So we have $x = 180 - 20 - 25 =$ **135**.

12. Statistics

We simply list 9 consecutive integers with 42 in the middle.

38, 39, 40, 41, 42, 43, 44, 45, 46

Notice that 42 is the median and the greatest of the 9 integers is **46**.

* **Quicker solution:** Since 42 is the median and there are 9 integers all together, there are 4 more integers after 42. Thus, $42 + 4 =$ **46**.

For the definition of the **integers** see the end of the solution to Problem 11 in Section 3 of Test 1 (pp. 14-15). For the definition of **consecutive integers** see the end of the solution to Problem 16 in Section 5 of Test 2 (p. 68). For the definition of **median** see the end of the solution to Problem 12 in Section 2 of Test 2 (pp. 49-50).

13. FUNCTIONS

* $f(p) = p + 1$, and since $2f(p) = 20$, we have $f(p) = 10$. So $p + 1 = 10$, and therefore $p = 9$. Finally, $f(3p) = 3p + 1 = 3(9) + 1 = 27 + 1 =$ **28**.

14. GEOMETRY

* Angle *NML* has measure 180 – 125 = 55. Since *LN* = *LM*, triangle *LNM* is isosceles, and angle *LNM* also has measure 55. So angle *NLM* has measure 180 – 55 – 55 = 70. Thus, angle *KLN* has measure 90 – 70 = 20. So $x = 90 - 20 =$ **70**.

Notes: (1) Here is the picture with all missing angles filled in.

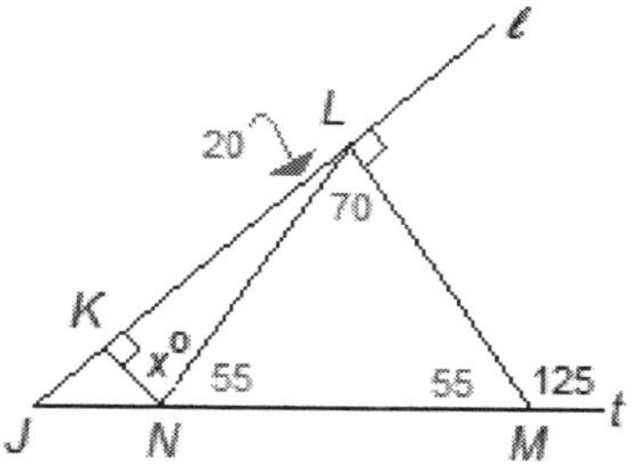

(2) The rightmost 55 degree angle and the 125 degree angle form a **linear pair**. Therefore they are **supplementary** which is why their measures must add to 180 degrees.

(3) Since *LN* = *LM*, the angles opposite these sides must have equal measure.

(4) Angle *KLM* is a right angle. So the measures of angles *KLN* and *NLM* must add to 90 degrees.

15. Number Theory

Solution by drawing a picture: Let's first split the cup into five pieces and fill one fifth with orange juice.

orange

Now we split the cup into 3 parts with vertical lines and evenly distribute the remaining parts with orange, grapefruit and pineapple juice (this is not possible physically, but mathematically it gives us what we want).

orange	grapefruit	pineapple
orange	grapefruit	pineapple
orange	grapefruit	pineapple
orange	grapefruit	pineapple
orange	orange	orange

Now simply observe that 7 out of the 15 parts are labeled "orange." So the answer is **7/15**, **.466**, or **.467**.

Remark: I labeled all of the parts for clarification, but when you actually draw the picture you might just want to shade the orange parts and not bother with the other parts. This will save time. The picture would then look as follows.

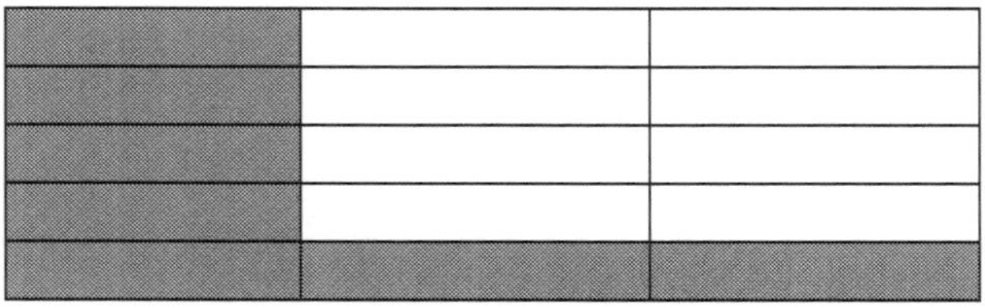

For more information on this technique, see **Strategy 9** in ***"The 32 Most Effective SAT Math Strategies."***

* **Quick computation:** $\frac{1}{5} + (\frac{1}{3})(\frac{4}{5}) \sim .4666666667$. So we can grid in **.466**, **.467**, or **7/15**.

16. PERCENTS

* **Algebraic solution:**

$$a + 2b = 1.25(4b)$$
$$a + 2b = 5b$$
$$a = 3b$$
$$\frac{a}{b} = \mathbf{3}$$

Notes: (1) We changed the percent to a decimal by moving the decimal point over 2 places to the left. If a number does not have a decimal point, there is always a "hidden" decimal point at the end of the number. So 125 percent can be written as the decimal 1.25.

(2) The phrase "is equal to" translates to "=," and the word "of" translates to multiplication.

Solution by picking numbers: Let's choose a value for b, say $b = 25$. Then $2b = 50$, $4b = 100$, and 125 percent of $4b$ is 125. So we have $a + 50 = 125$. Therefore $a = 75$, and $\frac{a}{b} = \frac{75}{25} = \mathbf{3}$.

For more information on this technique, see **Strategy 4** in ***"The 32 Most Effective SAT Math Strategies."***

17. GEOMETRY

* Since there are 9 subintervals between 0 and 1, the length of each of these subintervals is $\frac{1}{9}$. There are 6 subintervals between 0 and $\sqrt{x}$, so that $\sqrt{x} = \frac{6}{9} = \frac{2}{3}$. Therefore, $x = (\frac{2}{3})^2 = \frac{4}{9}$ or **.444**.

Note about intervals and subintervals: If $a < b$, the length of the interval from a to b is $b - a$. If there are n subintervals between a and b, the length of each subinterval is $\frac{b-a}{n}$.

18. GEOMETRY

* **Solution using a right triangle:** Let's plot the two points and form a right triangle.

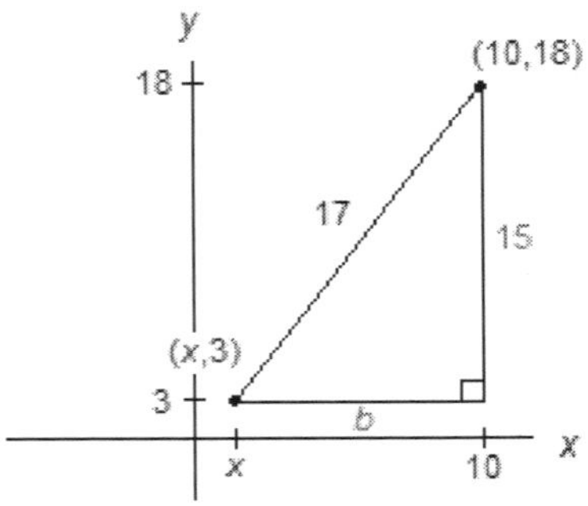

Note that we got the length of the right leg by subtracting 18 – 3 = 15. We now use the Pythagorean Theorem.

$$b^2 + 15^2 = 17^2$$
$$b^2 + 225 = 289$$
$$b^2 = 64$$
$$b = 8$$

It follows that x = **2**.

Remarks: (1) If you recognize the **Pythagorean triple** 8, 15, 17, then you do not need to use the Pythagorean Theorem.

(2) 3, 4, 5 and 5, 12, 13 are the two most common Pythagorean triples. In this problem we used the slightly less common triple 8, 15, 17.

(3) Note that it is possible to draw another picture where x is to the right of 10. In this case we would get the solution x = **18**.

Solution using the distance formula: Students that have taken Precalculus might notice that the distance formula can be used to solve this problem. The distance formula is $\boldsymbol{d = \sqrt{(x_2 - x_1)^2 + (y_2 - y_1)^2}}$

Plugging the numbers from this problem into the distance formula yields

$$17 = \sqrt{(x - 10)^2 + (3 - 18)^2}$$
$$289 = (x - 10)^2 + 225$$
$$64 = (x - 10)^2$$
$$\pm 8 = x - 10$$
$$x = 10 \pm 8$$

So $x = 10 - 8 = 2$ or $x = 10 + 8 = 18$. Therefore the two possible solutions are **2** and **18**.

SECTION 8

1. NUMBER THEORY

* We are looking for a positive even integer less than 5. Such an integer is 4, choice (B)

Remarks: (1) Another positive even integer less than 5 is 2, but that is not an answer choice.

For definitions of the **integers** and **positive integers** see the end of the solution to Problem 11 in Section 3 of Test 1 (pp. 14-15).

The **even integers** are integers that are twice another integer.

$$\{\ldots,-4, -2, 0, 2, 4,\ldots\}$$

Note that 0 is an even integer.

2. ALGEBRA

Solution by starting with choice (C): We start with choice (C) and take a guess that $k = 529$. Then $8 + \sqrt{k} = 8 + \sqrt{529} = 31$. This is too big, so let's try choice (B) and set $k = 49$ to get $8 + \sqrt{k} = 8 + \sqrt{49} = 15$. Since this is correct, the answer is choice (B).

Algebraic solution:

$$8 + \sqrt{k} = 15$$
$$\sqrt{k} = 7$$
$$k = 49$$

This is choice (B).

* **Mental math:** Since $8 + 7 = 15$, we have $\sqrt{k} = 7$. So $k = 49$, choice (B).

3. NUMBER THEORY

* The total number of people polled was $35 + 14 + 1 = 50$, and the number in favor of building a new library was 35. Therefore the fraction of those polled that were in favor of building a new library was $\frac{35}{50} = \frac{7}{10}$, choice (A).

Remark: To reduce the fraction $\frac{35}{50}$ in your calculator, simply divide 35 by 50, then press MATH ENTER ENTER.

4. Geometry

* **Quick solution:** $t + u = 70 + 30 = 100$, choice (C).

Notes: (1) The two unlabeled angles are **vertical angles**. Since vertical angles are congruent, and all triangles have angles whose measures add up to 180 degrees, it follows that $t + u = 70 + 30$.

(2) The unlabeled angles have measure $180 - 70 - 30 = 80$. It follows that $t + u = 180 - 80 = 100$.

5. Data Analysis

* **Quick solution:** Observe that the difference in heights of the bars corresponding to 1984 and 1985 is the biggest. So the answer is (D).

Numerical solution: Let's compute all the changes:

1981 and 1982: $3.75 - 3.50 = .25$
1982 and 1983: $4.25 - 3.50 = .75$
1983 and 1984: $4.75 - 4.25 = .50$
1984 and 1985: $4.75 - 3.75 = 1$
1985 and 1986: $4.50 - 3.75 = .75$

We see that the change between 1984 and 1985 is greatest. This is choice (D).

6. Functions

* k is the x-value and $g(k) = 1$ is the corresponding y-value. Looking at the graph we see that in order for the y value to be 1, the x value can be any number between -1 and 0. In particular, -0.5 is an acceptable value for k, choice (B).

Remarks: $g(-0.5) = 1$ is equivalent to "the point (-0.5,1) is on the graph of the function g."

7. Algebra

* **Solution by guessing:** Let's guess values for a, b, and c, keeping in mind that they have to be positive and different, and they are probably not too large. So let's guess $a = 1$, $b = 2$, $c = 3$. So we type in our calculator $(2^1)(2^2)(2^3)$ and get an output of 64. So we can use these values for a,b, and c.

So we compute $2^1 + 2^2 + 2^3 = 14$, choice (A).

For more information on this technique, see **Strategy 3** in ***"The 32 Most Effective SAT Math Strategies."***

Algebraic solution: $2^a \cdot 2^b \cdot 2^c = 2^{a+b+c}$, and $64 = 2^6$. So $a + b + c = 6$. We see that $a = 1$, $b = 2$, $c = 3$ satisfies this equation.

So, $2^a + 2^b + 2^c = 2^1 + 2^2 + 2^3 = 14$, choice (A).

For a review of the **Laws of Exponents** used here see the end of the solution to Problem 8 in Section 8 of Test 1 (p. 35).

8. Geometry

* Let's draw a picture of the line segment beginning at (-2,-7) and ending at (3,-7).

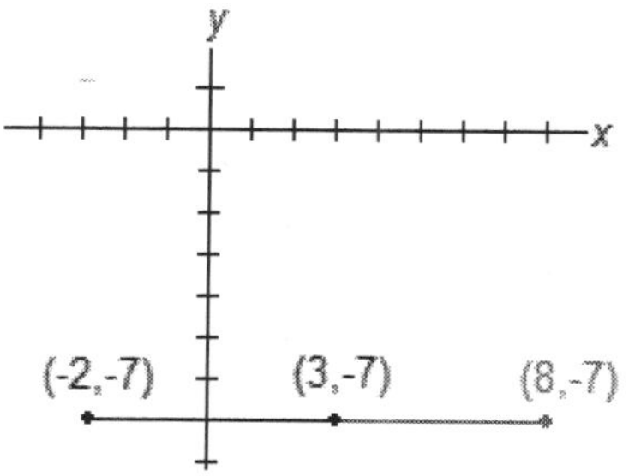

Since we move 5 units to the right to get from (-2,-7) to (3,-7), we simply move 5 more units to the right to get the other endpoint of the diameter. This is the point (8,-7), choice (E).

Remark: The line segment shown in the picture above is a **diameter** of the circle. This is a line segment whose endpoints lie on the circle passing through the center of the circle.

In the figure above, (-2,-7) and (8,-7) lie on the circle, and (3,-7) is the center of the circle.

9. ALGEBRA

* **Solution by starting with choice (C):** We are given that h is between 30 and 50. That is, $30 < h < 50$. Using the answer choices as a guide, and starting with choice (C), let us subtract 30 from each part of this inequality. We have that $30 - 30 = 0$ and $50 - 30 = 20$. Therefore we have $0 < h - 30 < 20$. But we want the number on the far left to be the negative of the number on the far right. So we need to subtract **more**.

So let's look at choice (D) next and subtract 40 from each part of the inequality. We have that $30 - 40 = -10$ and $50 - 40 = 10$. Therefore we have $-10 < h - 30 < 10$. This is equivalent to $|h - 30| < 10$. So the answer is choice (D).

For more information on this technique, see **Strategy 1** in ***"The 32 Most Effective SAT Math Strategies."***

10. GEOMETRY

The first cylinder has a volume of $v = \pi r^2h = \pi(5)^2(4) = 100\pi$. The second cylinder has a volume of $V = \pi r^2h = \pi(5)^2(8) = 200\pi$. This is twice the volume of the first cylinder so that $V = 2v$, choice (B).

Note: The formula $V = \pi r^2h$ for the volume of a cylinder is given at the beginning of each math section of the SAT.

* **Quick solution:** If you double the height of a cylinder, the volume will also be doubled. So the answer is choice (B).

Note: If the radius of the cylinder were doubled, then the volume would **not** be doubled. Observe that $\pi(10)^2(4) = 400\pi$. This is 4 times the volume of the original cylinder. This is because the formula for volume has r^2 in it. So in general, if you double the radius, the volume will be multiplied by $2^2 = 4$.

11. ALGEBRA AND FUNCTIONS

* For each of the three given possible values for n, we need to check if $n < -2 < 0$. Since $-2 < 0$, we simply have to check if $n < -2$. Of the three given numbers only $-3 < -2$. So the answer is choice (A).

12. Percents

*** Solution by picking a number:** Let's choose a value for x. Since this is a percent problem the best choice is probably $x = 100$. Then 20 percent of x is 20. So 20 is 80 percent of y. That is $20 = .8y$. Thus, $y = \frac{20}{.8} = 25$. Since $x = 100$, we see that y is 25 percent of x, choice (B).

Algebraic solution: We are given that $.2x = .8y$. So $y = \frac{.2x}{.8} = .25x$. So y is 25 percent of x, choice (B).

For more information on converting between decimals and percents see the notes at the end of Problem 5 in Section 3 of Test 1 (p. 12).

13. Number Theory

*** Solution by picking numbers:** Let's choose values for x, y and z so that $x + y$ is even and $(x + y)^2 + x + z$ is odd, say $x = 1$, $y = 3$, and $z = 2$. Note that $1 + 3 = 4$ which is even, and $(1 + 3)^2 + 1 + 2 = 19$ which is odd. Now let's determine if each answer choice is true or false.

(A) True
(B) False
(C) True
(D) False
(E) False

So we can eliminate choices (B), (D), and (E).

Now note that $x = 2$, $y = 4$, $z = 1$ also satisfies the given conditions. In this case we can eliminate choice (A) so that the answer is choice (C).

*** Direct solution:** Since $x + y$ is even, $(x + y)^2$ is also even. It follows that $x + z$ is odd. If x and z were both even, then $x + z$ would be even. So one of x or z must be odd. In particular, if z is even, then x is odd, choice (C).

For further explanation see the notes at the end of Problem 8 in Section 3 of Test 4 (pp. 110-111).

14. Algebra

*** Solution by picking a number:** Let's choose a value for x, say $x = .1$. Note that $0 < .1 < 1$. Now let's substitute .1 in for x next to each roman numeral.

I. $.01 > .001$
II. $.1 > .05$
III. $.1 > .001$

All three of these are true, so a good guess at this point would be (E).

To be safe, let's try one more number, say $x = .9$.

I. $.81 > .729$
II. $.9 > .45$
III. $.9 > .729$

Again, all three of these are true giving more evidence that the correct answer is choice (E).

Remark: Although choice (E) is correct, we have not really shown this using this method. We have a lot of evidence to suggest that choice (E) is correct, so that choice (E) is a really good guess. Remember that most of the time picking numbers can only be used to eliminate answers.

* **Precise solution:** For $0 < x < 1$ we have $x > x^2 > x^3 > \ldots$ For $x > 0$ we have $x > \frac{x}{2}$. Therefore the answer is choice (E).

15. Data Analysis

* We are looking for an equation of the line that comes as close as possible to all of the points on the scatterplot. Recall the slope-intercept form of the equation of a line $y = mx + b$ where m is the slope of the line and $(0,b)$ is the y-intercept of the line.

For those of you that do not see how the above equation matches up with the answer choices, let's rewrite the answer choices replacing $t(p)$ with y and p with x.

(A) $y = 44$
(B) $y = 1x + 0$
(C) $y = 44x + 0$
(D) $y = \frac{1}{44}x + 0$
(E) $y = 1x + 44$

Note that the graphs of the equations in choices (B), (C), and (D) are lines that pass through the origin (the point (0,0)). Since none of the points in the scatterplot are anywhere near (0,0) we can eliminate these choices. The graph of the equation in choice (E) has a y-intercept of (0,44) and a slope of 44. So it starts in a good position, but then sharply rises avoiding all the points in the scatterplot.

The graph of the equation in choice (A) is a horizontal line passing through the point (0,44). Clearly this is the best answer choice. So the answer is choice (A).

16. GEOMETRY

*** Solution by picking a number:** Using the fact that opposite sides of a rectangle are congruent, we see that $2L = 3W$ (there are 2 segments of length L along the left edge, and 3 segments of length W along the right edge of the large rectangle).

Let's choose values for L and W so that $2L = 3W$. The easiest such choice is $L = 3$ and $W = 2$. With these choices for L and W, the area of each small rectangle is $LW = (3)(2) = 6$, and the area of the large rectangular region is $(12L)(10L)= (12)(3)(10)(3) = 1080$.

Finally, to compute the number of small rectangles that fit inside the large rectangular region we simply divide the areas: $\frac{1080}{6} = 180$, choice (E).

Here we used **Strategies 4** and **24** in ***"The 32 Most Effective SAT Math Strategies."***

Direct solution: The area of each small rectangle is LW, and the area of the large rectangular region is $(12L)(10L)$.

To compute the number of small rectangles that fit inside the large rectangular region we simply divide the areas:

$$\frac{(12L)(10L)}{LW} = \frac{120L^2}{L(\frac{2L}{3})} = 120 \div \frac{2}{3} = 120 \cdot \frac{3}{2} = 180, \text{ choice (E).}$$

Remark: We used the fact that $2L = 3W$ (see previous solution) to get that $W = \frac{2L}{3}$.

For more information on this technique, see **Strategy 24** in ***"The 32 Most Effective SAT Math Strategies."***

Blue Book Test 6 Fully Explained Solutions

Section 2

1. Algebra

* **Quick computation:** 12 + 4(8) = 44, choice (C).

Notes: One package contains 12 rolls, and the remaining 4 packages contain 8 rolls each. So there are 12 + 8 + 8 + 8 + 8 = 12 + 4(8) rolls all together.

2. Geometry

* Let's draw a picture.

Note that $BC = 30 + 20 = 50$. So $AC = 30 + 50 = 80$, choice (D).

For more information on this technique, see **Strategy 9** in ***"The 32 Most Effective SAT Math Strategies."***

3. Algebra

Solution by picking a number: Let's choose a value for a, say $a = 5$. Then we have $x + 3 = 5$, so that $x = 2$. Thus, $2x + 6 = 2(2) + 6 =$ **10**. Put a nice, big , dark circle around **10**, and plug in a 5 for a in each answer choice.

(A) 8
(B) 11
(C) 10
(D) 13
(E) 16

Since choices (A), (B), (D), and (E) came out incorrect, the answer is choice (C).

For more information on this technique, see **Strategy 4** in ***"The 32 Most Effective SAT Math Strategies."***

* **Algebraic solution:** $2x + 6 = 2(x + 3) = 2a$, choice (C).

4. Data Analysis

Solution by brute force: We compute the positive difference between the x-coordinate and y-coordinate of each point.

(A) $70 - 40 = 30$
(B) $60 - 40 = 20$
(C) $70 - 60 = 10$
(D) $80 - 80 = 0$
(E) $80 - 60 = 20$

Remark: Note that we want the **positive** difference. So for each point we subtracted the smaller number from the larger number (except for D where the x- and y-coordinates of the point were equal).

Note that the greatest positive difference is 30, choice (A).

* **Graphical solution:** Draw the line $y = x$ (this is the line passing through (0,0) and (100,100)). Note that point A is furthest from this line. So the answer is choice (A).

5. Statistics

* Beginning with student A we see the 5 scores on test II were 70, 60, 70, 80, and 60. So the average was $\frac{70+60+70+80+60}{5} = \frac{340}{5} = 68$, choice (C).

6. Number Theory

* **Solution by picking numbers:** Let's estimate the values of the variables in the picture, say $t = -1.2$, $u = -.8$, $v = -.5$, $w = -.2$, $x = .2$, $y = 1.2$, $z = 1.8$. Then $|u + v| = |-.8 + (-.5)| = |-1.3| = 1.3$. This is closest to y, choice (D).

Remark: Under the MATH menu in your TI-84 graphing calculator you can use the ABS(function if you do not want to do the above computation by hand. You can type ABS(-.8+(-.5)) and you will get the output **1.3**.

For more information on this technique, see **Strategy 4** in ***"The 32 Most Effective SAT Math Strategies."***

7. ALGEBRA

* **Calculator solution:** It's easier to input a decimal into your calculator, so let's use our calculator and plug in .5 for x. We type the following in our calculator.

1/.5 + 1/(.5 – 1) ENTER

The output is 0, choice (B).

Alternate calculator solution: This time we leave $\frac{1}{2}$ as a fraction. So we use our calculator and plug in $\frac{1}{2}$ for x. We type the following in our calculator.

1/(1/2) + 1/(1/2 – 1) ENTER

The output is 0, choice (B).

Solution by hand (not recommended):

$$\frac{1}{\frac{1}{2}} + \frac{1}{\frac{1}{2} - 1} = 2 + \frac{1}{-\frac{1}{2}} = 2 - 2 = 0.$$

So the answer is choice (B).

8. GEOMETRY

* Since it does not say "Figure not drawn to scale," we can assume it is. So $ORST$ is a square. Since the y-coordinate of point S is 3, $SR = 3$. Since the figure is a square, $RO = SR = 3$. So to get from O to R we must travel 3 units to the left. Thus, $k = -3$, choice (A).

For more information on this technique, see **Strategy 6** in ***"The 32 Most Effective SAT Math Strategies."***

Technical note: To see that $ORST$ is a square (without using the fact that the figure is drawn to scale), simply note that $ORST$ is a parallelogram with at least one right angle and $RS = ST$.

9. Functions

Solution by plugging in points: Let's start by plugging in 0 for x, and eliminating any answer choice for which $f(x) \neq 1$.

(A) $f(0) = 1$
(B) $f(0) = 2$
(C) $f(0) = -2$
(D) $f(0) = -1$
(E) $f(0) = 1$

We can eliminate choices (B), (C), and (D).

Next let's plug in 1 for x in the choices that have not been eliminated. We will eliminate any answer choice for which $f(x) \neq 2$.

(A) $f(1) = 1^2 + 1 = 1 + 1 = 2$
(E) $f(1) = 2(1)^2 + 1 = 2(1) + 1 = 2 + 1 = 3$

We can eliminate choice (E). Therefore the answer is choice (A).

For more information on this technique, see **Strategy 5** in ***"The 32 Most Effective SAT Math Strategies."***

*** Quick observation:** Note that each number in the second row of the chart is always 1 more than the square of the number above it. So the answer is $f(x) = x^2 + 1$, choice (A).

10. Algebra

Solution by picking numbers: Let's let $x = 3$ and $y = 12$. Then 3 years ago the person was 12 years old. So this person is now 15 years old, and 1 year ago the person was **14**. Put a nice big, dark circle around the number **14** so you can find it easily later. We now substitute $x = 3$, $y = 12$ into each answer choice and eliminate any that do not come out to 14.

(A) $12 - 1 = 11$
(B) $12 - 3 - 1 = 8$
(C) $3 - 12 - 1 = -10$
(D) $12 + 3 + 1 = 16$
(E) $12 + 3 - 1 = 14$

Since choices (A), (B), (C), and (D) came out incorrect, the answer is choice (E).

For more information on this technique, see **Strategy 4** in ***"The 32 Most Effective SAT Math Strategies."***

* **Algebraic solution (not recommended):** Since x years ago the person was y years old, the person is now $y + x$ years old. So 1 year ago the person was $y + x - 1$ years old, choice (E).

11. Number Theory

* Let's attempt to put the letters in alphabetical order in as few steps as possible.

ZWYX XYWZ XWYZ WXYZ

We did it in three steps. So it seems like the answer is choice (B).

Notes: For the first step we reversed the entire sequence. For the second and third steps we interchanged two adjacent letters. It should be clear that if we start with a reversal of the whole sequence, we need two more steps to put the letters in alphabetical order. Getting the W to the other side of the X takes two steps, and reversing the sequence another step. So if we start by moving the W it will still take three steps. If instead we begin by trying to get X to the other side of W, then this will take two steps. We still need to get Y to the other side of the W, and then the Z will still be in the wrong position. So this will take more steps. Similarly if we start by moving Y or Z.

12. Geometry

* We simply divide the volumes to get $\frac{20 \cdot 24 \cdot 32}{4 \cdot 4 \cdot 4} = 240$, choice (D).

Notes: (1) The formula for the volume of a rectangular solid is $V = \ell wh$, where ℓ, w and h are the length, width and height of the rectangular solid respectively. This formula is given at the beginning of each math section on the SAT.

(2) In particular, the volume of a cube is $V = s^3$ where s is the length of a side of the cube.

For more information on this technique, see **Strategy 24** in ***"The 32 Most Effective SAT Math Strategies."***

13. NUMBER THEORY

* **Solution by picking a number:** Let's choose a value for n, say $n = .5$. Then $\sqrt{n} \sim .7071$ and $n^2 = .25$. So $n^2 < n < \sqrt{n}$, choice (E).

Note: Squaring a positive fraction gives a smaller positive fraction. Taking the square root of a positive fraction gives a larger positive fraction. This is the exact opposite of what happens when you apply these operations to numbers greater than 1.

For more information on this technique, see **Strategy 4** in ***"The 32 Most Effective SAT Math Strategies."***

14. GEOMETRY

* We need to compute the slope of $\overline{OC}$. Note that $\overline{OC}$ contains the points (0,0) and (4,3). Plug these two points into the formula for slope to get $m = \frac{3-0}{4-0} = \frac{3}{4}$, choice (C).

Remarks: (1) If the line j passes through the origin (the point (0, 0)) and the point (a, b) with $a \neq 0$, then the slope of line j is simply $\frac{b}{a}$.

(2) In general, the slope of a line is $m = \frac{rise}{run} = \frac{y_2-y_1}{x_2-x_1}$.

(3) We can also get the slope of $\overline{OC}$ by observing that to get from O to C we need to travel up 3, then right 4. So $m = \frac{rise}{run} = \frac{3}{4}$.

15. NUMBER THEORY

* Let's create a table that shows each time given in **both** EST and PST. First we are given that 12:00 PM EST corresponds to 9:00 AM PST.

EST	PST
12:00 PM	9:00 AM

Now note that there is a 3 hour time difference. So 4:00 PM PST corresponds to 7:00 PM EST.

EST	PST
12:00 PM	9:00 AM
7:00 PM	4:00 PM

Also, 12:00 PM PST corresponds to 3:00 PM EST.

EST	PST
12:00 PM	9:00 AM
3:00 PM	12:00 PM
7:00 PM	4:00 PM

From the second table we see that the first trip took 7 hours. Since the second trip began at 3:00 PM EST , it's arrival time was 10:00 PM EST, choice (A).

Note: (1) It would be very difficult to figure this out without converting all times to either EST or PST. Here I chose to convert them all to EST.

(2) For each time in EST, the equivalent in PST is 3 hours earlier.

16. GEOMETRY

* The length and width of the rectangle are 2 and 1, respectively. To see this, note that the left side of the rectangle is a radius of one of the quarter circles, and the bottom of the rectangle consists of 2 radii – one from each quarter circle. It follows that the area of the rectangle is $A = \ell w = (2)(1) = 2$.

The area of a circle of radius 1 is $A = \pi r^2 = \pi(1)^2 = \pi$. So the area of each quarter circle of radius 1 is $\frac{\pi}{4}$. To get the area of the shaded region we subtract.

Area of Rectangle – Area of Quarter Circles

$$2 - 2(\frac{\pi}{4})$$

$$2 - \frac{\pi}{2}$$

Thus, the answer is choice (B).

For more information on this technique, see **Strategy 23** in ***"The 32 Most Effective SAT Math Strategies."***

17. Functions

* **Solution using a basic transformation:** We shift the original graph to the left 2 units. When applying a shift, it usually helps to focus on a single point. Let us focus on the point (1,0). When shifting 2 units to the left, the point (1,0) moves to the point (-1,0). So the answer is choice (C).

For a lesson on **transformations** see the end of the solution to Problem 7 in Section 5 of Test 2 (p. 62).

Solution by tracking a point: Note that the point (1,0) is on the original graph. Equivalently, $f(1) = 0$. Let $g(x) = f(x + 2)$. Note that $g(-1) = f(1) = 0$. In other words, the point (-1,0) is on the new graph. So the only possible answer is choice (C).

18. Geometry

* Since $AB = BC$, the angles opposite these sides have equal measure. We are given that angle ABC has measure 30 degrees. So angles BAC and ACB each have measure $\frac{180 - 30}{2} = 75$ degrees.

Since $DE = EF = DF$, it follows that triangle DEF is equilateral, and therefore each of its angles measure 60 degrees. In particular, the measure of angle EDF is 60 degrees. Since the measure of angle BDE is 50 degrees, the measure of angle ADF is $180 - 60 - 50 = 70$ degrees.

Finally, the measure of angle DFA is $180 - 75 - 70 = 35$ degrees, choice (B).

If you would like to see the solution visually see the picture below.

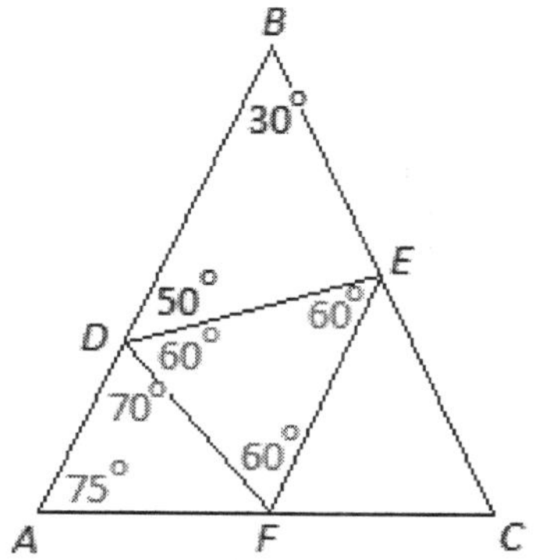

19. ALGEBRA

* Let's eliminate the denominators in each equation by cross multiplying.

(A) $ac = bf$
(B) $fa = bc$ or equivalently $af = bc$
(C) $cb = fa$ or equivalently $af = bc$
(D) $af = bc$
(E) $af = bc$

Now just observe that all of these are the same EXCEPT choice (A).

20. ALGEBRA

* **Solution by picking numbers:** Let's choose values for a and b. We will try $a = 1$, $b = 1$. Then $a \square b = 1 \square 1 = 1(1) - 1 = 1 - 1 = 0$. Thus, the expression in I can be equal to zero. So the answer is (A), (D), or (E). Next, $(a + b) \square b = 2 \square 1 = 2(1) - 1 = 2 - 1 = 1$. So it is still not clear if II can be equal to zero. Finally, $a \square (a + b) = 1 \square 2 = 1(2) - 2 = 2 - 2 = 0$. So the expression in III can be equal to zero. So the answer is choice (E).

Remarks: (1) The choice of using $a = b = 1$ was made by looking at the expression $xy - x$, and observing that $(1)(1) - 1 = 0$.

(2) It turned out to be unnecessary to determine if the expression in II could be zero.

(3) It might be instructive to write out what each of the expressions looks like after applying the operation "□" and then simplifying.

I. $a \square b = ab - b = b(a - 1)$
II. $(a + b) \square b = (a + b)b - b = b(a + b - 1)$
III. $a \square (a + b) = a(a + b) - (a + b) = (a + b)(a - 1)$

Note that I and III both have a factor of $(a - 1)$ which means substituting in $a = 1$ will make these expressions zero.

On the other hand, in order for the expression in II to be zero, either b or $a + b - 1$ must be zero. But b is given to be positive so that $b \neq 0$. Also, if $a + b - 1 = 0$, then $a + b = 1$. But a and b are both positive integers, so that $a + b$ must be at least 2. Therefore, the expression in II cannot be zero.

SECTION 4

1. ALGEBRA

* Since $z = 2$, we have $y = 3z = 3(2) = 6$. Replacing y by 6 in the first equation gives $x - 6 = 8$, or $x = 8 + 6 = 14$, choice (E).

2. NUMBER THEORY

Solution by picking numbers: Let's choose ages for Todd, Marta, and Susan. Let's say that Todd is 20, Marta is 12, and Susan is 25. Note that with these choices Todd is older than Marta and younger than Susan. Now, we have that $t = 20$, $m = 12$, and $s = 25$. Thus, $m < t < s$, choice (A).

Remark: When using the symbol "<," note that the symbol always points toward the smaller number. In this case $12 < 20$ and $20 < 25$.

For more information on this technique, see **Strategy 4** in ***"The 32 Most Effective SAT Math Strategies."***

* **Algebraic solution:** Since Todd is older than Marta, $t > m$. Also, since Todd is younger than Susan, $t < s$. The inequality $t > m$ can also be written $m < t$. Combining $m < t$ with $t < s$ gives $m < t < s$, choice (A).

3. STATISTICS

* We use the basic formula for average.

$$\textbf{Average} = \frac{\textbf{Sum}}{\textbf{Number}}$$

In this problem we are given that the Sum is 5. Since we are averaging 2 numbers, the Number is 2. So the average is $\frac{5}{2}$, choice (B).

For more information on this technique, see **Strategy 20** in ***"The 32 Most Effective SAT Math Strategies."***

Alternate solution: Since the areas of the two regions are equal and the sum of the areas of the regions is 5, each region must have area $\frac{5}{2}$. Therefore the average is also $\frac{5}{2}$, choice (B).

Remarks: (1) When you are averaging numbers that are all equal, the average is just that number. In this case, that number is $\frac{5}{2}$.

(2) If you forget the little fact mentioned in Remark (1), you can just compute the average directly: $\frac{\frac{5}{2}+\frac{5}{2}}{2} = \frac{5}{2}$. This last computation can be done in your TI-84 calculator by typing ((5 / 2) + (5 / 2)) /2, followed by MATH ENTER ENTER (the last combination of buttons will turn the resulting decimal into a fraction).

4. Number Theory

* **Solution by guessing:** Let's guess values for n until we get one of the answer choices. Here are some possible guesses.

$n = 3$ $\quad n^2 + 1 = 3^2 + 1 = 9 + 1 = 10$
$n = 4$ $\quad n^2 + 1 = 4^2 + 1 = 16 + 1 = 17$
$n = 5$ $\quad n^2 + 1 = 5^2 + 1 = 25 + 1 = 26$
$n = 6$ $\quad n^2 + 1 = 6^2 + 1 = 36 + 1 = 37$
$n = 7$ $\quad n^2 + 1 = 7^2 + 1 = 49 + 1 = 50$

Therefore the answer is choice (E).

For more information on this technique, see **Strategy 3** in ***"The 32 Most Effective SAT Math Strategies."***

Direct solution: We are looking for a number that is 1 more than a perfect square. The perfect squares are 1, 4, 9, 16, 25, 36, 49,... So clearly 50 is 1 more than the perfect square 49, choice (E).

5. Geometry

* Note that the triangle is **isosceles**. In particular y is equal to the measure of the unlabeled angle. So $2y = 180 - 40 = 140$, and therefore $y = \frac{140}{2} = 70$, choice (D).

Remark: Two sides of the triangle are radii of the circle. Since all radii of a circle have equal length, these two sides are congruent. Recall that the angles opposite these sides share the same relationship and therefore are also congruent.

For more information on this technique, see **Strategy 29** in ***"The 32 Most Effective SAT Math Strategies."***

Definition: An **isosceles triangle** is a triangle with two congruent sides, or equivalently, a triangle with two congruent angles.

6. Number Theory

Solution by starting with choice (C): Let's start with choice (C) and begin listing some of the factors of 81: 1, 3, 9, 81… We can stop here since we already found 4 positive integer factors.

Let's try choice (D) next: 1, 2, 4, 8,…

Now choice (B): 1, 2, 5, 100,…

Now choice (E): 1, 3, 11, 33

Since choices (B), (C), (D), and (E) all have at least 4 factors, the answer must be choice (A). In fact, the only factors of 121 are 1, 11, and 121. So the answer is indeed choice (A).

For more information on this technique, see **Strategy 1** in ***"The 32 Most Effective SAT Math Strategies."***

*** Quick solution:** As it turns out, a "simple square" is just the square of a prime number. Since $121 = 11^2$ and 11 is prime, the answer is choice (A).

Further explanation: If p is prime, then the only factors of p^2 are 1, p, and p^2.

Remark: Note that choices (B), (C), and (D) have integers which are perfect squares, but they are not simple squares because they are not the square of a prime number. For example, $100 = 10^2$ but 10 is not prime (2 and 5 are factors).

For definitions of the **integers** and **positive integers** see the end of the solution to Problem 11 in Section 3 of Test 1 (pp. 14-15).

An integer d is a **factor** of an integer n if there is another integer k such that $n = dk$. For example, 5 is a factor of 100 because 100 = 5(20). In practice we can check if d is a factor of n simply by dividing n by d in our calculator. If the answer is an integer, then d is a factor of n. If the answer is not an integer (it contains digits after the decimal point), then d is not a factor of n.

A **prime number** is a positive integer that has **exactly** two factors (1 and itself). Here is a list of the first few primes:

2, 3, 5, 7, 11, 13, 17, 19, 23,...

Note that 1 is **not** prime. It only has one factor!

A **composite number** has **more** than two factors. Here is a list of the first few composites:

4, 6, 8, 9, 10, 12, 14, 15, 16,...

7. GEOMETRY

* **Algebraic solution:** The area of the triangle is $A = \frac{1}{2}bh = \frac{1}{2}(\frac{6}{7}h)h = \frac{6h^2}{14}$. The fraction $\frac{6}{14}$ can be reduced to $\frac{3}{7}$. So the answer is $\frac{3h^2}{7}$, choice (B).

Remarks: (1) The formula for the area of a triangle is $A = \frac{1}{2}bh$ where b is the length of the base of the triangle and h is the height of the triangle. This formula is given at the beginning of any math section of the SAT.

(2) The word "of" translates as multiplication. So $\frac{6}{7}$ of h is $\frac{6}{7}h$ or $\frac{6h}{7}$.

(3) To reduce the fraction $\frac{6}{14}$ in your calculator, simply divide 6 by 14, then type MATH ENTER ENTER.

Solution by picking numbers: Let's let $h = 7$. It then follows that $b = 6$, and the area of the triangle is $A = \frac{1}{2}bh = \frac{1}{2}(6)(7) = \mathbf{21}$. Now substituting 7 in for h into each answer choice yields

(A) $\frac{49}{3}$
(B) 21
(C) 3
(D) 42
(E) 84

Since (B) is the only choice that has become 21, we conclude that choice (B) is the answer.

Important note: (B) is **not** the correct answer simply because it is equal to 21. It is correct because all four of the other choices are **not** 21.

For more information on this technique, see **Strategy 4** in ***"The 32 Most Effective SAT Math Strategies."***

8. Number Theory

Solution by guessing: We can simply start guessing values for a and b, and use our calculator. Note that we can use the answer choices as a guide since a and b must be factors of the answer. For example, if we were to guess $a = 2$, $b = 3$, we would type the following into our TI-84 calculator:

(2^(1/2)*3^(1/3))^6.

The output would read 72 which is too small. So we know that at least one of a or b must be larger. This is the perfect time to use the "ENTRY" feature on your calculator. Press 2nd ENTER to pull up the previous computation. Now you can simply change the numbers 2 and 3 to your next guesses for a and b.

A little more guessing and checking should lead you to try $a = 3$, $b = 4$.

(3^(1/2)*4^(1/3))^6.

The output of this computation is 432. Thus, $a = 3$, $b = 4$, and so $ab = 12$, choice (B).

Remarks: (1) Students that are comfortable applying laws of exponents may first want to rewrite the given equation as $a^3b^2 = 432$. In this case, choosing $a = 3$, $b = 4$ leads to the calculator computation 3^3*4^2 with output 432.

(2) Switching the values for a and b will give different results. For example if we let $a = 4$ and $b = 3$, we get $a^3b^2 = 576$. Compare this with the choices $a = 3$ and $b = 4$ which give the desired result.

For more information on this technique, see **Strategy 3** in ***"The 32 Most Effective SAT Math Strategies."***

* **Quicker clever solution:** Using basic laws of exponents we have $\left(a^{\frac{1}{2}}b^{\frac{1}{3}}\right)^6 = a^3b^2 = aa^2b^2 = a(ab)^2$. So the given equation is equivalent to $a(ab)^2 = 432$.

We now begin taking guesses for the value of a and then divide 432 by these values. If we are left with a perfect square, then ab is the square root of this number.

Since 432 is not a perfect square, let's begin by guessing $a = 2$. We have $\frac{432}{2} = 216$ which is not a perfect square.

Let's try $a = 3$ next. We have $\frac{432}{3} = 144$ which is a perfect square. Therefore $ab = 12$, choice (B).

Remark: To determine if a positive integer is a perfect square, simply take the square root of the number in your calculator. If you get a positive integer, then the number was a perfect square. If you do not get an integer (there are digits after the decimal point), then the number was not a perfect square.

We have also used **Strategy 3** from ***"The 32 Most Effective SAT Math Strategies"*** in this solution.

For a review of the **Laws of Exponents** used here see the end of the solution to Problem 8 in Section 8 of Test 1 (p. 35).

9. Number Theory

* An integer has a factor of 10 precisely when it ends in a zero. The greatest three-digit integer that ends in a zero is **990**.

10. Number Theory

* We can solve this with a simple ratio. Begin by identifying 2 key words. In this case, such a pair of key words is "people" and "pounds."

people	20	150
pounds	4	x

Now draw in the division symbols and equal sign, cross multiply and divide the corresponding ratio to find the unknown quantity x.

$$\frac{20}{4} = \frac{150}{x}$$

$$20x = (4)(150)$$

$$20x = 600$$

$$x = \frac{600}{20} = \mathbf{30}.$$

For more information on this technique, see **Strategy 14** in ***"The 32 Most Effective SAT Math Strategies."***

11. Number Theory

*** Solution by guessing:** Let's take a guess for a positive even integer, say $n = 4$. Now, 50 percent of 4 is 2, and when 4 is increased by 2 we get 6. This is too small. So let's take a larger guess for n, say $n = 8$. Then we have that 50 percent of 8 is 4, and when we increase 8 by 4 we get 12. Since 12 is between 10 and 20, we see that a possible value for n is **8**.

For more information on this technique, see **Strategy 3** in ***"The 32 Most Effective SAT Math Strategies."***

Algebraic solution: First note that 50 percent of n is $.5n$. So n increased by 50 percent of itself is $n + .5n = 1.5n$. So we need to solve the inequality $10 < 1.5n < 20$. We divide through by 1.5 to get $\frac{10}{1.5} < n < \frac{20}{1.5}$. Now $\frac{10}{1.5}$ is approximately 6.67 and $\frac{20}{1.5}$ is approximately 13.33. So the possible values of n are **8**, **10**, and **12**.

12. Geometry

* Recall that to compute the perimeter of a rectangle we need to add up the lengths of all 4 sides. Since the length of one side of the rectangle is 40, and opposite sides of a rectangle are congruent we know that the lengths of two of the sides add up to $40 + 40 = 80$. So the sum of the lengths of the other two sides is $250 - 80 = 170$. Since these other two sides are also congruent, the width of the rectangle is $\frac{170}{2} = 85$. Finally, the area of the rectangle is $A = \ell w = (40)(85) = \mathbf{3400}$ square meters.

*** Quick computation:** $A = \ell w = (40)(\frac{250-2\cdot 40}{2})) = \mathbf{3400}$.

Remark: The formula for the area of a rectangle is given at the beginning of each math section on the SAT.

13. Algebra

Solution by guessing: Let's guess that the number of \$2 bulbs ordered was 200. Since twice as many \$1 bulbs were ordered, the number of \$1 bulbs was 400. The total cost was then 2(200) + 1(400) = 800 dollars. This is too much. So the number of \$2 bulbs ordered was less than 200.

Let's try 150 next for the number of \$2 bulbs ordered, so that the number of \$1 bulbs ordered was 300. In this case, the total cost was 2(150) + 1(300) = 600 dollars. This is correct. Thus, the number of bulbs ordered was 150 + 300 = **450**.

For more information on this technique, see **Strategy 3** in ***"The 32 Most Effective SAT Math Strategies."***

* **Algebraic solution (not recommended):** Let's let x be the number of \$2 bulbs ordered, so that the number of \$1 bulbs ordered is $2x$. Since the total cost for the bulbs ordered was \$600, we have $2x + 1(2x) = 600$. So $4x = 600$, and therefore $x = \frac{600}{4} = 150$. So the number of \$2 bulbs ordered was 150, and the number of \$1 bulbs ordered was 300. Therefore the total number of bulbs ordered was 150 + 300 = **450**.

14. Geometry

* **Solution using blocks:** We consider the expressions $x + y$ and $x - y$ as blocks . Let's let $a = x + y$ and $b = x - y$. So we are given $4ab = 40$, $b = 20$, and we want to find a. Substituting $b = 20$ into the first equation gives us $4a(20) = 40$, or equivalently $80a = 40$. So $a = \frac{40}{80}$ = **1/2** or **.5**.

For more information on this technique, see **Strategy 19** in ***"The 32 Most Effective SAT Math Strategies."***

Remark: Once you are comfortable with recognizing blocks there is no need to do a formal substitution. For example, in this problem you can simply replace $x - y$ by 20 in the first equation and solve for $x + y$. The algebra looks as follows.

$$4(x + y)(x - y) = 40$$
$$4(x + y)(20) = 40$$
$$80(x + y) = 40$$
$$x + y = \frac{40}{80} = \mathbf{1/2} \text{ or } \mathbf{.5}.$$

15. GEOMETRY

* Let's draw a picture.

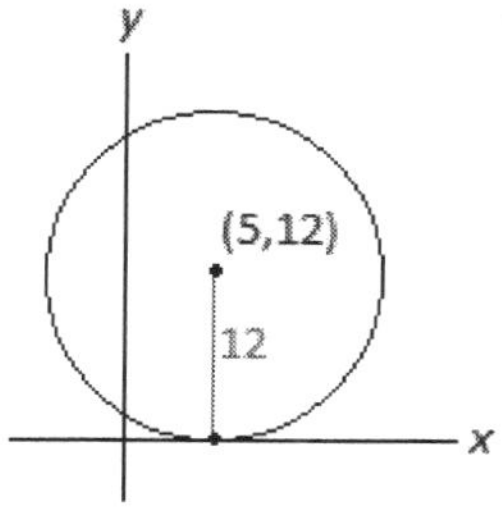

Just note that the radius of this circle is the distance from the center to the x-axis which is **12**.

For more information on this technique, see **Strategy 9** in ***"The 32 Most Effective SAT Math Strategies."***

16. NUMBER THEORY

* The total voting age population is 1200 + 1300 = 2500. The total that actually voted is then 40% of 2500 which is .4(2500) = 1000. The total number of registered voters is 1000 + 1200 = 2200. So the turnout for this election is $\frac{1000}{2200}$ = **5/11**, **.454**, or **.455**

17. GEOMETRY

* It is easier to see that there are 3 such segments that **do** lie on an edge of the figure. Therefore the number of segments that **do not** lie on an edge of the figure is 11 – 3 = **8**.

Clarification: Let's find the 3 edges that connect to vertex V. There are two on the top base, connecting from the left and right of V, and one in the back shown as a dotted vertical line connected to V.

18. FUNCTIONS

* First note that $AD = \frac{1}{2} - \frac{-1}{2} = \frac{1}{2} + \frac{1}{2} = 1$. Since the area of $ABCD$ is 4, we have that $CD = \frac{4}{1} = 4$. Thus, the length from the x-axis to C is 2. So $c = 2$. Now, observe that point C is on the graph of $y = px^3$. So $2 = p(\frac{1}{2})^3 = \frac{p}{8}$. Therefore $p = (2)(8) =$ **16**.

SECTION 8

1. ALGEBRA

Solution by starting with choice (C): Let's start with choice (C) and guess that $n = 6$. Substituting 6 for n into the left hand side of the equation yields $3(n - 4) = 3(6 - 4) = 3(2) = 6$. Since this is too small we can probably eliminate choices (A), (B), and (C) (but see the remark below).

Let's try choice (D) next and guess that $n = 10$. Substituting 10 for n into the left hand side of the equation yields $3(n - 4) = 3(10 - 4) = 3(6) = 18$. This is correct so that the answer is choice (D).

Remark: Usually on the SAT answer choices are given in increasing or decreasing order. Every now and then this principle gets violated. This sometimes happens when some of the answer choices have fractions and/or roots and others do not. In any case, this doesn't affect how you use the strategy. Just be aware that you may have to check answers that would have been eliminated under normal circumstances. For example in this problem, $\frac{22}{3}$ is actually larger than 6, and so is still a potential solution after eliminating choice (C).

For more information on this technique, see **Strategy 1** in ***"The 32 Most Effective SAT Math Strategies."***

*** Algebraic solution 1:**

$$3(n-4) = 18$$
$$n - 4 = 6$$
$$n = 6 + 4 = 10, \text{ choice (D).}$$

Algebraic solution 2:

$$3(n-4) = 18$$
$$3n - 12 = 18$$
$$3n = 18 + 12 = 30$$
$$n = \frac{30}{3} = 10, \text{ choice (D).}$$

2. Counting

Solution by writing a list: Let's label the stones by A, B, C, and D and let's label the metals by 1, 2, and 3. Now let's list all stone-metal combinations.

A1	A2	A3
B1	B2	B3
C1	C2	C3
D1	D2	D3

We see that there are 12 stone-metal combinations. This is choice (D).

For more information on this technique, see **Strategy 21** in ***"The 32 Most Effective SAT Math Strategies."***

* **Solution using the counting principle:** (4)(3) = 12, choice (D).

Remark: The **counting principle** says that if one event is followed by a second independent event, the number of possibilities is multiplied. The 2 events here are "choosing a stone," and "choosing a metal."

3. Algebra

* The word "sum" means addition, and "the square root of *b*" is $\sqrt{b}$. So "the sum of 3*a* and the square root of *b*" can be written $3a + \sqrt{b}$. "The sum of *a* and *b*" can be written $a + b$. So the square of the sum of *a* and *b* can be written $(a + b)^2$. Therefore an expression for the given statement is $3a + \sqrt{b}, = (a + b)^2$, choice (B).

4. Geometry

* Let's draw a picture.

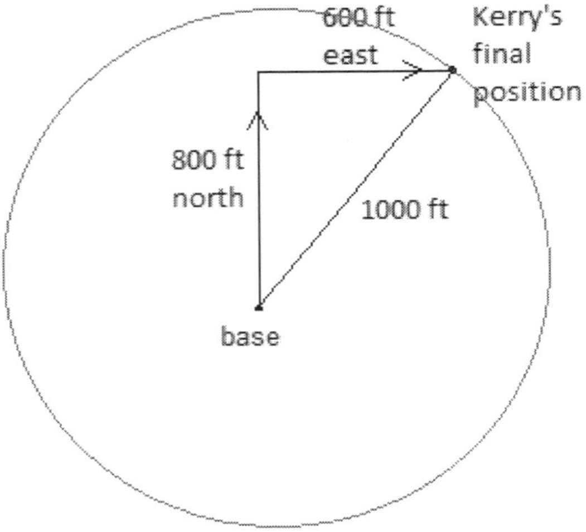

In the figure above, the receiver is at the center of a circle of radius 1000. The interior of the circle represents the range of the receiver. Therefore from Kerry's final position in the figure, she may walk south or west, but not north. This is choice (E).

For more information on this technique, see **Strategy 9** in ***"The 32 Most Effective SAT Math Strategies."***

5. Algebra

*** Solution by picking a number:** We can choose any value for x except 0. So let's let $x = 1$. The given equation then becomes $\frac{1}{4} = \frac{2}{a}$. So $a = 8$, choice (A).

Remark: We can see that $a = 8$ by simple observation or more formally by cross-multiplying.

Algebraic solution: We solve the equation for a.

$$\frac{x}{4} = \frac{2x}{a}$$

$$ax = 8x$$

$$a = 8$$

This is choice (A).

Remark: We can divide each side of the equation by x because we are given that $x \neq 0$.

6. Geometry

* This is a standard SAT problem involving two parallel lines cut by a transversal. Note that the transversal creates 8 angles, four of which have measure 50 degrees. The other four have measure 130 degrees as any two non-congruent angles are **supplementary**, i.e. they add up to 180 degrees.

So $u = s = r = 50$ and $t = 130$. Therefore $s + t + u = 50 + 130 + 50 = 230$, choice (A).

7. Geometry

* Let's draw a picture.

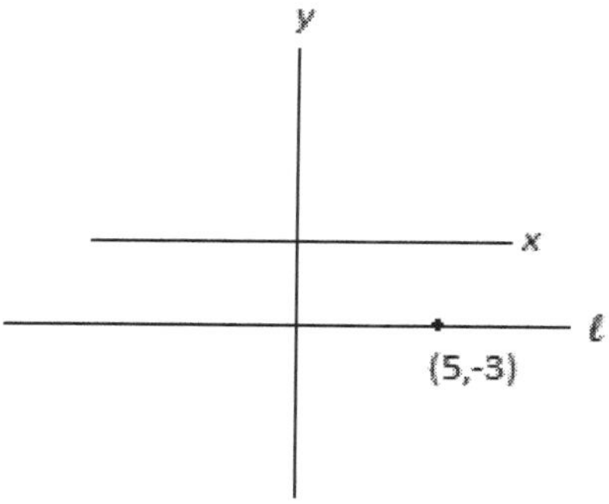

We see that the graph is a horizontal line. Thus, the equation is $y = -3$, choice (C).

Remarks: (1) A vertical line has an equation of the form $x = a$ where a is the x-coordinate of any point on the line. A horizontal line has an equation of the form $y = b$ where b is the y-coordinate of any point on the line.

(2) Answer choice (C) is the only choice that has the correct form, so we do not even have to worry about the y-coordinate of the point.

(3) Horizontal lines have a slope of zero. So in slope-intercept form the equation of the line is $y = 0x - 3$, or equivalently $y = -3$. The number -3 is there because the point (0,-3) is on the line.

For more information on this technique, see **Strategy 9** in ***"The 32 Most Effective SAT Math Strategies."***

8. FUNCTIONS

* We are given that $p(300) = 1900$. So we have

$$1900 = 17(300) - (10(300) + b)$$
$$1900 = 5100 - (3000 + b)$$
$$1900 = 5100 - 3000 - b$$
$$1900 = 2100 - b$$

So $b = 200$, choice (E).

9. ALGEBRA

* **Solution by processes of elimination:** Beginning with the integer 1, multiply each integer by itself to eliminate answer choices.

(1)(1) = 1 so we can eliminate choice (A).
(2)(2) = 4 so we can eliminate choice (B).
(3)(3) = 9.
(4)(4) = 16 so we can eliminate choice (D).
(5)(5) = 25 so we can eliminate choice (C).

Therefore the answer is choice (E).

10. PROBABILITY

* **Solution by process of elimination:** We can eliminate choices (A), (C) and (E) because 10, 18 and 30 are not divisible by 4. We can eliminate choice (D) because 20 is not divisible by 6. Therefore the answer is choice (B).

Verification that choice (B) works: Let's guess that there are a total of 12 marbles in the bag. Since the probability of selecting a red marble is $\frac{1}{4}$, there are $\frac{12}{4} = 3$ red marbles in the bag. Since the probability of selecting a blue marble is $\frac{1}{6}$, there are $\frac{12}{6} = 2$ blue marbles in the bag. This means that there must be $12 - 3 - 2 = 7$ yellow marbles in the bag. So $\frac{7}{12}$ of the marbles are yellow. Also, $\frac{1}{4} + \frac{1}{6} + \frac{7}{12} = 1$. Therefore the answer is choice (B).

Remark: To compute $\frac{1}{4}+\frac{1}{6}+\frac{7}{12}$ simply type the following into your calculator: 1/4 + 1/6 + 7/12 ENTER. The output will be 1.

11. STATISTICS

* We divide each side of the formula **Sum = Average · Number** by **Average** to rewrite the formula in the form $\frac{\textbf{Sum}}{\textbf{Average}}$ = **Number**. So k is the number of prices, choice (D).

For more information on this technique, see **Strategy 20** in ***"The 32 Most Effective SAT Math Strategies."***

Solution by picking numbers: Let's choose some prices, say 1 and 5 dollars. The sum of these prices is 6 dollars, the average of these prices is 3 dollars, and $k = \frac{6}{3} =$ **2. Put a nice big, dark circle around 2 so that you can find it easily later.** Now let's look at the value in each answer choice.

(A) 6
(B) 3
(C) 3
(D) 2
(E) 1

Since (A), (B), (C), and (E) each came out incorrect, the answer is choice (D).

Important note: (D) is **not** the correct answer simply because it is equal to 2. It is correct because all 4 of the other choices are **not** 2. **You absolutely must check all five choices!**

For more information on this technique, see **Strategy 4** in ***"The 32 Most Effective SAT Math Strategies."***

12. GEOMETRY

* Since the area of the square is 81, each side of the square has length 9. The perimeter of the figure outlined by the solid line is the sum of the perimeters of the 4 triangles minus the perimeter of the square (the dashed lines). This is 4(30) – 4(9) = 84, choice (D).

Remark: The area of a square is $A = s^2$ where s is the length of a side of the square. So if the area A is known, then $s = \sqrt{A}$. In this problem, the side length of the square is $\sqrt{81} = 9$.

13. Functions

* $g(2) = k$ is equivalent to "the point $(2, k)$ lies on the graph of g." So from the graph we see that $k = 5$. Now, $g(k) = g(5) = 2.5$ because the point (5,2.5) is on the graph of g. So the answer is choice (B).

14. Algebra

* **Solution by trying the extremes:** Let's compute xy for each pair (x,y) where x and y are the extreme values of the given intervals.

When $x = 0$ and $y = -1$, $xy = 0$.
When $x = 0$ and $y = 3$, $xy = 0$
When $x = 8$ and $y = -1$, $xy = -8$
When $x = 8$ and $y = 3$, $xy = 24$.

So the extreme values of xy are -8 and 24, and the answer must be choice (E).

Remark: Note that we get the least value of xy by letting $x = 8$ and $y = -1$. A common error would be to assume that we get the least value of xy by taking the least value of x and the least value of y (in this problem that gives $(0)(-1) = 0$ which is not the least value of xy).

15. Geometry

* Let's redraw the picture and name some of the angles.

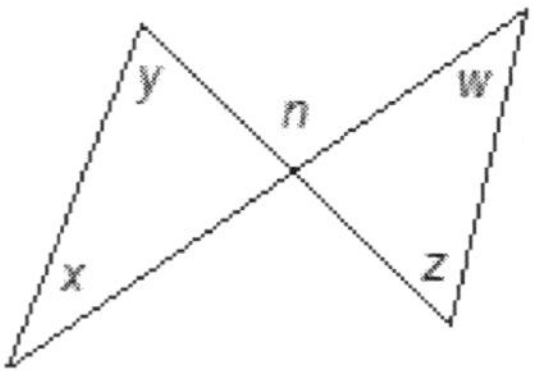

The measure of an exterior angle of a triangle is the sum of the measures of the two opposite interior angles of the triangle. So $n = x + y$, and $n = z + w$. Thus $x + y + z + w = 2n$, choice (B).

For more information on this technique, see **Strategy 30** in ***"The 32 Most Effective SAT Math Strategies."***

Remark: Note that the angle labeled n is an exterior angle of both triangles. We have used Strategy 30 twice here, once for each triangle.

16. NUMBER THEORY

Solution by picking numbers: Let's let the first term of the sequence be 3. It follows that the second term of the sequence is $(\frac{1}{3})(3) + 3 = 1 + 3 = 4$. So we have that $t = 3$ and the ratio of the second term to the first term is $\frac{4}{3}$. **Put a nice big, dark circle around $\frac{4}{3}$ so that you can find it easily later.** Now let's substitute 3 for t into each answer choice.

(A) 4

(B) 2

(C) $\frac{4}{3}$

(D) $\frac{2}{3}$

(E) 1

Since (A), (B), (D), and (E) each came out incorrect, the answer is (C).

Important note: (C) is **not** the correct answer simply because it is equal to $\frac{4}{3}$. It is correct because all 4 of the other choices are **not** $\frac{4}{3}$. **You absolutely must check all five choices!**

For more information on this technique, see **Strategy 4** in ***"The 32 Most Effective SAT Math Strategies."***

*** Algebraic solution (not recommended):** Since t is the first term of the sequence, it follows that the second term of the sequence is $\frac{1}{3}t + 3$. Thus, the ratio of the second term to the first term is $\frac{\frac{1}{3}t+3}{t} = \frac{t+9}{3t}$, choice (C).

Note: To get from the left hand side of the last equation to the right hand side we multiplied both the numerator and denominator of the fraction by 3. Note that in the numerator we must distribute the 3 to get $3(\frac{1}{3}t + 3) = t + 9$.

Blue Book Test 7 Fully Explained Solutions

Section 3

1. Number Theory

* We begin by identifying 2 key words. In this case, such a pair of key words is "pounds" and "rolls."

pounds	25	x
rolls	300	12

Choose the words that are most helpful to you. Now draw in the division symbols and equal sign, cross multiply and divide the corresponding ratio to find the unknown quantity x.

$$\frac{25}{300} = \frac{x}{12}$$

$$(25)(12) = 300x$$

$$300 = 300x$$

$$x = 1$$

So 1 pound of flour is needed to make 12 rolls, choice (A).

For more information on this technique, see **Strategy 14** in ***"The 32 Most Effective SAT Math Strategies."***

2. Algebra

Solution by picking numbers: Let's choose values for x and y, say $x = 2$ and $y = 5$. Note that with these choices $xy = 10$. We then have that

$$2 \cdot \frac{x}{y} \cdot y^2 = 2(\tfrac{2}{5}) \cdot 5^2 = 20.$$

This is choice (E).

For more information on this technique, see **Strategy 4** in ***"The 32 Most Effective SAT Math Strategies."***

*** Algebraic solution:** $2 \cdot \frac{x}{y} \cdot y^2 = 2xy = 2(10) = 20$, choice (E).

Note: To get from the first equation to the second equation we used one of the laws of exponents. We have $\frac{y^2}{y} = \frac{y^2}{y^1} = y^{2-1} = y^1 = y$.

3. ALGEBRA

Solution by picking numbers: Let's choose values for x and y, say $x = 31$ and $y = -1$. Note that with these choices $x + y = 30$ and $x > 8$. Now let's eliminate any answer choices that are false.

(A) False
(B) True
(C) False
(D) False
(E) False

Since (A), (C), (D), and (E) each came out false, the answer is choice (B).

Important note: (B) is **not** the correct answer simply because it is true. It is correct because all 4 of the other choices are false. **You absolutely must check all five choices!**

For more information on this technique, see **Strategy 4** in ***"The 32 Most Effective SAT Math Strategies."***

*** Algebraic solution:** We first solve the equation for y to get $y = 30 - x$. Since $x > 8$, we have $-x < -8$, and so $y = 30 - x < 30 - 8 = 22$, choice (B).

4. GEOMETRY

* Let's plot the points in xy-plane and draw the triangle.

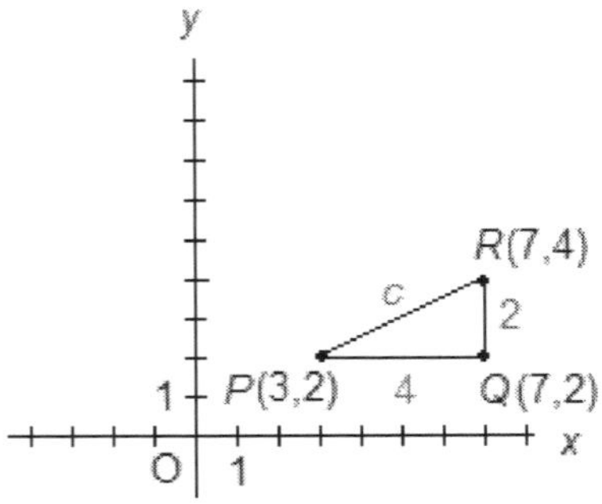

Note that $PQ = 4$ and $QR = 2$. By the Pythagorean Theorem we have that $c^2 = 4^2 + 2^2 = 20$. Thus, $PR = c = \sqrt{20}$.

Finally, the perimeter of ΔPQR is $PQ + QR + PR = 4 + 2 + \sqrt{20} = 6 + \sqrt{20}$, choice (C).

Note: If you cannot see that $PQ = 4$ by simple observation, you can also subtract the x-coordinates of the points to get $7 - 3 = 4$. Similarly, for QR you can subtract the y-coordinates of the points to get $4 - 2 = 2$.

For more information on this technique, see **Strategy 9** in ***"The 32 Most Effective SAT Math Strategies."***

5. Number Theory

Solution by searching for a pattern:

1st term: $8 = 8 + (0)9 = 8 + (1 - 1)9$
2nd term: $17 = 8 + (1)9 = 8 + (2 - 1)9$
3nd term: $26 = 8 + (2)9 = 8 + (3 - 1)9$
...

Following this pattern we see that $8 + (26 - 1)9$ is the 26th term in this sequence, choice (D).

*** Solution using the general term of an arithmetic sequence:**

Arithmetic sequence formula: $a_n = a_1 + (n - 1)d$

This question gives an arithmetic sequence with first term $a_1 = 8$ and common difference $d = 9$. Therefore the general term is given by the formula $a_n = 8 + (n - 1)9$. The question is asking us to substitute 26 in for n. Therefore the answer is choice (D).

6. Geometry

*** Quick solution:** To get all six angle measures we need to know at least two measures of angles that lie along the same line. In other words we can just pick the answer choice where the angles are vertical (vertical angles **do not** lie along the same line). This is choice (A).

Solution by starting with choice (C): Let's start with choice (C) and assume we know s and x. Since s, t, and x add up to 180 degrees we can find t. The other three angles are vertical to these three so we can find them as well. Therefore we can eliminate choice (C).

Continuing in this fashion we see that for choices (B), (D), and (E), the two given measures are for angles that form a straight line. Thus we can find all six angles just as we did for choice (C).

For the measures in choice (A) this cannot be done because the measures given are for angles that are vertical. So the answer is (A).

7. Number Theory

Solution by picking numbers: Let's choose 2 numbers that differ by 1, say 5 and 6. Then $t = 5 + 6 = 11$. Note that the greater of the two numbers is **6. Put a nice big, dark circle around 6 so that you can find it easily later.** Now let's substitute 11 in for t in each answer choice.

(A) 5
(B) 5.5
(C) 6
(D) 6.5
(E) 10.5

Since (A), (B), (D), and (E) each came out incorrect, the answer is (C).

Important note: (C) is **not** the correct answer simply because it is equal to 6. It is correct because all four of the other choices are **not** 6. **You absolutely must check all five choices!**

For more information on this technique, see **Strategy 4** in ***"The 32 Most Effective SAT Math Strategies."***

* **Algebraic solution (not recommended):** Let x be the greater of the two numbers. Since the two numbers differ by 1, it follows that the smaller number is $x - 1$. We are given that the sum of the two numbers is t. So we have $(x - 1) + x = t$, or equivalently $2x - 1 = t$. We now solve this equation for x. We have $2x - 1 = t$. So $2x = t + 1$, and thus, $x = \frac{t+1}{2}$. This is choice (C).

8. Statistics

* First note that there are 13 students total (including the new one), and the median number of siblings per student is 1. So we want the average number of siblings for the 13 students to be 1. Equivalently, we want the sum of the number of siblings for the 13 students to be (1)(13) = 13. The old sum was 0(3) + (1)(6) + (2)(2) + (3)(1) = 13. So the new student must have 0 siblings, choice (A).

Notes: (1) If you are having trouble seeing that the median is 1, you can simply list all the numbers of siblings in increasing order.

0 0 0 1 1 1 1 1 1 2 2 3

Now note that there are several 1's right in the middle. So if we throw in a new student the median will still be 1.

(2) To change the average to a sum we used the formula

Sum = Average · Number

For more information on this technique, see **Strategy 20** in ***"The 32 Most Effective SAT Math Strategies."***

9. Algebra

Solution by taking a guess: Let's begin guessing values for x. Let's start with a guess of 5. If $x = 5$, then $2(x - 3) = 2(5 - 3) = 2(2) = 4$. This is too small. So let's choose a larger guess, say $x = 7$. In ths case we have that $2(x - 3) = 2(7 - 3) = 2(4) = 8$. This is correct, so $x = 7$.

Now, $\frac{x-3}{x+3} = \frac{7-3}{7+3} = \frac{4}{10}$ = **2/5** or **.4**.

For more information on this technique, see **Strategy 3** in ***"The 32 Most Effective SAT Math Strategies."***

Algebraic solution 1: We solve for x.

$$2(x-3)=8$$
$$x-3=4$$
$$x=7$$

Now, $\frac{x-3}{x+3}=\frac{7-3}{7+3}=\frac{4}{10}=$ **2/5** or **.4**.

Note: To get from the first equality to the second equality we divided each side of the equation by 2. To get from the second equality to the third equality we added 3 to each side of the equation.

Algebraic solution 2:

$$2(x-3)=8$$
$$2x-6=8$$
$$2x=14$$
$$x=7$$

Now, $\frac{x-3}{x+3}=\frac{7-3}{7+3}=\frac{4}{10}=$ **2/5** or **.4**.

*** Mental math:** 2 times 4 is 8, so $x-3=4$. Since $7-3$ is 4, $x=7$. Now, $\frac{x-3}{x+3}=\frac{7-3}{7+3}=\frac{4}{10}=$ **2/5** or **.4**.

10. Algebra

Solution by guessing: Let's take a guess for the number, say 150. Then twice the number is 300, and when we decrease this by 3 we get 297. This is too big.

So let's try 130 for the number next. Twice this number is 260, and when we decrease this by 3 we get 257. This is still just a bit too big.

Let's try 128 for the number next. Twice this number is 256, and when we decrease this by 3 we get 253. This is correct. Therefore the number is **128**.

For more information on this technique, see **Strategy 3** in ***"The 32 Most Effective SAT Math Strategies."***

*** Algebraic solution:** Let x be the number. Then twice the number is $2x$, and so twice the number decreased by 3 is $2x-3$. So we are given that $2x-3=253$. Adding 3 to each side of this equation gives $2x=256$. Dividing each side of this equation by 2 gives $x=$ **128**.

11. Data Analysis

* Let's begin to fill in the table.

	High-tops	Low-tops	Total
White	3600		
Black	900	1500	2400
Total	4500	5500	10,000

We got the total number of high tops by 10,000 – 5500 = 4500. We then got the number of black high-tops by 4500 – 3600 = 900. Finally, we got the total number of black sneakers by 900 + 1500 = **2400**.

12. Functions

* Let's focus on point *R*. First note that the *x*-coordinate of point *R* is equal to the *x*-coordinate of point *S*, and so it is 1. Next note that *PS* = 2. Since *PQRS* is a rectangle, *QR* = 2 also. Since the perimeter of *PQRS* is 10, it follows that *RS* = 3 (because 2 + 2 + 3 + 3 = 10). Therefore the *y*-coordinate of point *R* is 3.

Now note that point *R* lies on the graph of $y = ax^2$. Since the coordinates of point *R* are (1,3), we have $3 = a(1)^2$. So *a* = **3**.

13. Algebra

* When *a* = 2 and *c* = 3 we get 2*b* + *b* = 2 + 2(3) = 8. So 3*b* = 8, and therefore *b* = **8/3**.

Note: We can also grid in one of the decimals **2.66** or **2.67**.

14. Geometry

* **Solution by picking a number:** Let's begin by choosing a value for *y* between 45 and 55, say *y* = 50.

This is a standard SAT problem involving two parallel lines cut by a transversal. In this example there are actually two transversals. It's useful to isolate just one of them. We do this below.

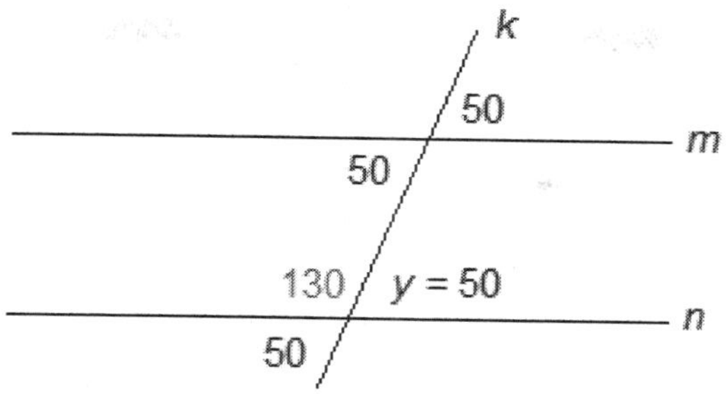

Note that the transversal k creates 8 angles, four of which have measure 50 degrees. The other four are 130 degrees (only one is labeled in the picture). Any two non-congruent angles are **supplementary**, ie. they add up to 180 degrees. Now let's draw in the second transversal.

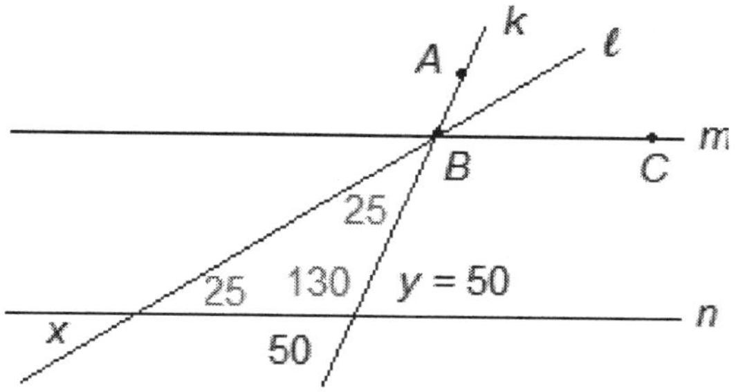

Note that since line ℓ bisects $\angle ABC$, the 50 degree angle right below line m is split into two 25 degree angles. We then use the fact that angles sum to 180 degrees in a triangle to get the other 25 degree angle. Finally, since vertical angles are congruent, x = **25**.

Note: Other choices for y lead to values of x between 22.5 and 27.5.

For more information on this technique, see **Strategy 4** in ***"The 32 Most Effective SAT Math Strategies."*** **Strategy 9** is also relevant here.

Complete geometric solution (not recommended): Let's label the angles in the triangle in the given figure so we can refer to them easily.

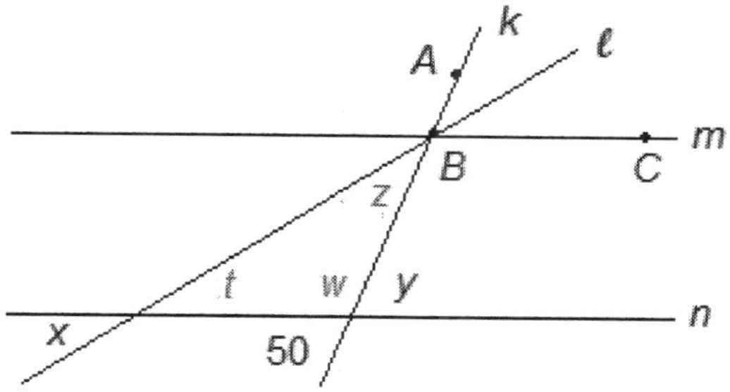

Using basic geometry we have $w = 180 - y$ and $z = \frac{y}{2}$. It therefore follows that $t = 180 - (180 - y + \frac{y}{2}) = 180 - 180 + y - \frac{y}{2} = \frac{y}{2}$. Since vertical angles are congruent, $x = \frac{y}{2}$. Now since $45 < y < 55$, we have $22.5 < \frac{y}{2} < 27.5$. So $22.5 < x < 27.5$.

15. Counting

Solution by listing: Let's let Aaron, Bill, Carl and David be the experienced plumbers and let's let Ethan, Fred, Gary, and Hank be the trainees. We now list all the combinations of 1 experienced plumber and 2 trainees. To save time we will just use the first letter of each name.

AEF	AEG	AEH	AFG	AFH	AGH
BEF	BEG	BEH	BFG	BFH	BGH
CEF	CEG	CEH	CFG	CFH	CGH
DEF	DEG	DEH	DFG	DFH	DGH

We see that the number of possible teams is (6)(4) = **24**.

For more information on this technique, see **Strategy 21** in ***"The 32 Most Effective SAT Math Strategies."***

*** Solution using combinations and the counting principle:** The number of ways to choose 1 experienced plumber from 4 is ${}_4C_1 = 4$. The number of ways to choose 2 trainees from 4 is ${}_4C_2 = 6$. By the counting principle, the number of ways to choose 1 experienced plumber and 2 trainees is then (4)(6) = **24**.

Remarks: (1) To compute ${}_4C_1$ on your graphing calculator, type 4 into your calculator, then in the **MATH** menu scroll over to **PRB** and select **nCr** (or press **3**). Then type 1 and press **ENTER**. You will get 4.

(2) The **counting principle** says that if one event is followed by a second independent event, the number of possibilities is multiplied. The 2 events here are "choosing 1 experienced plumber," and "choosing 2 trainees."

16. Geometry

* The area of the smaller circle is $A = \pi r^2 = \pi(6)^2 = 36\pi$ square inches. Therefore the area of the larger circle is $36\pi + 64\pi = 100\pi$ square inches. So the radius of the larger circle in inches is **10**.

17. Number Theory

* **Direct solution:** The positive factors of n are 1, p, q, r, pq, pr, qr, and n. There are no other positive factors because p, q, and r are prime. So the number of positive factors of n is **8**.

Solution by picking numbers: Lets choose prime number values for p, q, and r, say $p = 3$, $q = 5$, and $r = 7$. Then $pqr = 105$. Let's now write all factor pairs for 105.

$$105 = (1)(105) = (3)(35) = (5)(21) = (7)(15)$$

So the positive factors of 105 are 1, 3, 5, 7, 15, 21, 35, and 105. We see that the number of positive factors of 105 is **8**.

18. Functions

* We are given a quadratic function. Let's put it into standard form.

$$h(t) = c - (d - 4t)^2$$
$$h(t) = c - (4t - d)^2$$
$$h(t) = c - [4(t - \tfrac{d}{4})]^2$$
$$h(t) = c - 16(t - \tfrac{d}{4})^2$$
$$h(t) = -16(t - \tfrac{d}{4})^2 + c$$

The graph of this equation is a parabola that opens downward with vertex $(\frac{d}{4}, c)$. So $\frac{d}{4} = 2.5$ and $c = 106$. Thus, $d = 10$. So we now have

$$h(t) = 106 - (10 - 4t)^2$$

Finally, $h(1) = 106 - (10 - 4)^2 = 106 - 6^2 = 106 - 36 =$ **70**.

Remark: The **standard form for a quadratic function** is

$$\boldsymbol{y - k = a(x - h)^2}.$$

The graph is a parabola with **vertex** at (h, k). The parabola opens upwards if $a > 0$ and downwards if $a < 0$.

SECTION 7

1. NUMBER THEORY

*** Solution by starting with choice (E):** Since the word "greatest" is in the problem we start with the largest answer choice which is choice (E). We divide 59 by 3 in our calculator and get about 19.6667. Since the quotient is not an integer we can eliminate choice (E).

We try choice (D) next and divide 58 by 3 in our calculator to get about 19.3333. This is also not an integer and so we eliminate choice (D).

We try choice (C) next and divide 57 by 3 in our calculator to get 19. Since 19 is an integer, 57 is divisible by 3, and the answer is choice (C).

Remarks: (1) If we had started with choice (C) here we would see immediately that 57 is divisible by 3. However we cannot be guaranteed that this is the answer since it is still possible that there is a greater value divisible by 3.

(2) It is actually quicker to check for divisibility by 3 without using a calculator. If the sum of the digits of the number is divisible by 3, then so is the number itself. For example, $5 + 9 = 14$. Since 14 is not divisible by 3, 59 is not divisible by 3. Similarly, 58 is not divisible by 3, but 57 is because $5 + 7 = 12$, and 12 is divisible by 3.

For more information on this technique, see **Strategy 2** in ***"The 32 Most Effective SAT Math Strategies."***

2. GEOMETRY

Solution by starting with choice (C): The letter M shown has only one line of symmetry – a vertical line. So choice (C) is not the answer. The letter X shown has at least two lines of symmetry – a vertical and horizontal line. So the answer is choice (D).

Note: If the X is drawn to scale, then there are two more lines of symmetry – in this case each of the two lines drawn as part of the X is a line of symmetry as well.

For more information on this technique, see **Strategy 1** in ***"The 32 Most Effective SAT Math Strategies.***

3. Algebra

* **Solution by picking a number:** Let's choose a value for n, say $n = 3$. Then Bobby has done 3 chores for the week, and so he receives a total of 6 + 10 = **16** dollars. **Put a nice big, dark circle around 16 so that you can find it easily later.** Now let's substitute 3 in for n in each answer choice.

(A) 10 + 3 = 13
(B) (10 + 2)(3) = (12)(3) = 36
(C) 10(3) + 2 = 30 + 2 = 32
(D) 10 + 2(3) = 10 + 6 = 16
(E) (10 + 3) (2) = 13(2) = 26

Since (A), (B), (C), and (E) each came out incorrect, the answer is (D).

Important note: (D) is **not** the correct answer simply because it is equal to 16. It is correct because all four of the other choices are **not 16**. **You absolutely must check all five choices!**

For more information on this technique, see **Strategy 4** in ***"The 32 Most Effective SAT Math Strategies."***

* **Algebraic solution:** Bobby receives \$2 for each chore he does during the week. Therefore he receives \$2n for n chores. He also receives an additional \$10 for the week. So the total dollar amount that Bobby receives for the week is $10 + 2n$, choice (D).

4. Geometry

* Figure A has 13 squares. Since the total area of Figure A is 26 sq cm, the area of each square is $\frac{26}{13} = 2$ sq cm.

Now, Figure B has 8 squares. Therefore the area of Figure B is 8(2) = 16 sq cm, choice (C).

5. Data Analysis

* We can immediately eliminate choice (A) and (D) because Albert and Smith had a decrease in units sold. Now, by observation we can see that Goldberg had the greatest increase, choice (B).

Notes: (1) We are looking for the greatest difference between the heights of the two rectangles.

(2) If you are having trouble seeing that Goldberg's rectangles have the greatest difference, you can simply compute the three differences.

Goldberg: 250 – 150 = 100
Patel: 250 – 225 = 25
Wang: 300 – 250 = 50

Now note that Goldberg has the greatest difference.

6. Statistics

Solution by starting with choice (C): Let's start with choice (C) and guess that $x = 9$. We then have that the average of 6, 6, 12, 16, and 9 is $\frac{6+6+12+16+9}{5} = \frac{49}{5} = 9.8$. Since $9.8 \neq 9$ we can eliminate choice (C).

Let's try choice (D) next and guess that $x = 10$. We then have that the average of 6, 6, 12, 16, and 10 is $\frac{6+6+12+16+10}{5} = \frac{50}{5} = 10$. This is correct so that the answer is choice (D).

For more information on this technique, see **Strategy 1** in ***"The 32 Most Effective SAT Math Strategies."***

*** Solution by changing an average to a sum:** We use the formula

Sum = Average · Number

to see that $6 + 6 + 12 + 16 + x = 5x$. So $40 + x = 5x$. Subtracting x from each side of this equation gives $40 = 4x$. Thus, $x = \frac{40}{4} = 10$, choice (D).

For more information on this technique, see **Strategy 20** in ***"The 32 Most Effective SAT Math Strategies."***

7. Geometry

* Since the angle measures of a triangle sum to 180 degrees, we have that $2y = 90 - 40 = 50$. Thus, $y = \frac{50}{2} = 25$.

Again using the fact that the angle measures of a triangle sum to 180 degrees, we have $z + y + 2y + 40 = 180$. So $z + 25 + 50 + 40 = 180$. Therefore $z = 180 - 25 - 50 - 40 = 65$, choice (C).

8. Number Theory

* If 13 is selected, then the integer printed is 2(13) = 26 because 13 is odd. If 26 is selected, then the integer printed is 26 because 26 is even. If 52 is printed, then the integer printed is 52 because 52 is even. So the answer is choice (C).

9. Algebra

Solution by picking numbers: Let's choose values for m and s, say $m = 2$, and $s = 5$. In 2 minutes and 5 seconds there are 2(60) + 5 = **125** seconds. **Put a nice big, dark circle around 125 so that you can find it easily later.** Now let's substitute 2 in for m and 5 in for s in each answer choice.

(A) $60(2) + 5 = 125$

(B) $2 + 60(5) = 302$

(C) $60(2 + 5) = 420$

(D) $\frac{2+5}{60} \sim .1167$

(E) $\frac{2}{60} + 5 \sim 5.033$

Since (B), (C), (D), and (E) each came out incorrect, the answer is (A).

Important note: (A) is **not** the correct answer simply because it is equal to 125. It is correct because all four of the other choices are **not** 125. **You absolutely must check all five choices!**

For more information on this technique, see **Strategy 4** in ***"The 32 Most Effective SAT Math Strategies."***

* **Algebraic solution:** Since there are 60 seconds in a minute, m minutes is equal to $60m$ seconds. So the total number of seconds in m minutes and s seconds is $60m + s$, choice (A).

10. Algebra

Solution by plugging in numbers: Since the answer choices only have 0, 1, and 2 in them, let's just plug these numbers into the left hand side of the equation.

$x = 0$: $(2(0) - 2)(2 - 0) = (-2)(2) = -4$. Since $-4 \neq 0$, we can eliminate choices (A) and (E).

$x = 1$: $(2(1) - 2)(2 - 1) = (0)(1) = 0$. So 1 is a possible value of x, and we can eliminate choice (C).

$x = 2$: : $(2(2) - 2)(2 - 2) = (2)(0) = 0$. So 2 is a possible value of x, and we see that the answer is choice (D).

* **Algebraic solution:** We set each factor equal to zero to get $2x - 2 = 0$ and $2 - x = 0$.

For the first equation, we add 2 to each side to get $2x = 2$. We then divide each side by 2 to get $x = 1$.

For the second equation, we add x to each side to get $2 = x$.

So 1 and 2 are the two solutions, choice (D).

11. ALGEBRA

Solution by picking a number: Let's choose a value for y, say $y = 2$. Then $y^9 = 2^9 = 512$. So $x^3 = 512$ and $x = \sqrt[3]{512} = \mathbf{8}$. **Put a nice big, dark circle around 8 so that you can find it easily later.** Now let's substitute 2 in for y in each answer choice.

(A) $\sqrt{2}$
(B) 4
(C) 8
(D) 64
(E) 4096

Since (A), (B), (D), and (E) each came out incorrect, the answer is (C).

Important note: (C) is **not** the correct answer simply because it is equal to 8. It is correct because all four of the other choices are **not** 8. **You absolutely must check all five choices!**

For more information on this technique, see **Strategy 4** in ***"The 32 Most Effective SAT Math Strategies."***

* **Algebraic solution:** We raise each side of the given equation to the $\frac{1}{3}$ power to get $x = (y^9)^{1/3} = y^{9(1/3)} = y^3$, choice (C).

For a review of the **Laws of Exponents** used here see the end of the solution to Problem 8 in Section 8 of Test 1 (p. 35).

12. GEOMETRY

* We can eliminate choices (C) and (D) because $\overline{OC}$ and $\overline{OD}$ have positive slope.

To get from point O to point A, we travel down 3 and right 1. Therefore the slope of $\overline{OA}$ is $\frac{-3}{1}$ = -3. So we can eliminate choice (A).

To get from point O to point B, we travel down 1 and right 3. Therefore the slope of $\overline{OB}$ is $\frac{-1}{3}$. So we can eliminate choice (B).

The answer is therefore choice (E).

Notes: To get from point D to point C, we travel down 2 and right 2. Therefore the slope of $\overline{DC}$ is $\frac{-2}{2}$ = -1.

For a review of **slope** see the end of the solution to Problem 12 in Section 3 of Test 1 (pp. 15-17).

13. NUMBER THEORY

* **Solution by starting with choice (C):** Let's start with choice (C). The number 15 is both odd and a multiple of 5. So we can eliminate choice (C). We can eliminate choices (B) and (D) for the same reason (use 25 for choice (B) and 15 for choice (D)).

Let's try choice (E) next. The odd number would be 21 and the multiple of 5 would be 30. This leaves 34 for the birthday which is of course impossible. So we can eliminate choice (E).

Therefore the answer must be choice (A).

Remark: In choice (A), the odd number is 13, the multiple of 5 is 20. This leaves 14 for the birthday which is possible.

14. ALGEBRA

* We square each side of the equation to get

$$x + 9 = (x - 3)^2$$
$$x + 9 = (x - 3)(x - 3)$$

$$x + 9 = x^2 - 3x - 3x + 9$$
$$x + 9 = x^2 - 6x + 9$$
$$x = x^2 - 6x$$

This is choice (C).

15. Number Theory

* It's easier to first count the integers from 1 to 100 that **are** the square of an integer. Let's list them.

1, 4, 9, 16, 25, 36, 49, 64, 81, 100

We see that there are 10 integers from 1 to 100 that are the square of an integer. Therefore the number of integers from 1 to 100 that are **not** the square of an integer is 100 – 10 = 90, choice (E).

Note: $1^2 = 1$ and $10^2 = 100$. So the set of all integers from 1 to 100 that are the square of an integer consist of the squares of the integers 1 through 10. This is a faster way to see that there are 10 of them without listing each integer.

16. Geometry

* First note that the total distance for the trip is 16 + 15 + 4 = 35 miles. Now, the problem becomes much simpler if we draw *AD*, and "move" *BC* and *CD* as shown below.

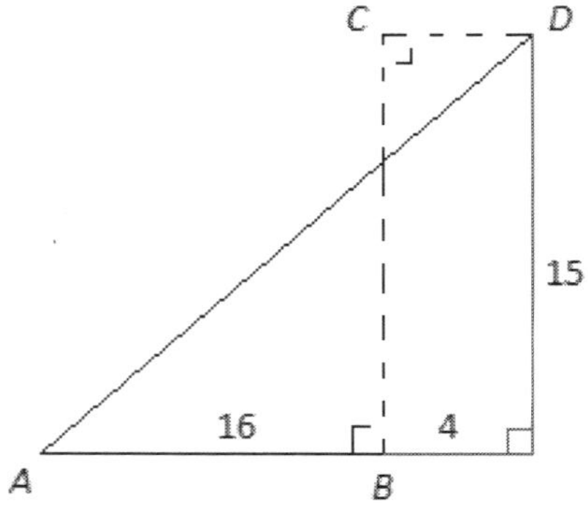

We now have a single right triangle and we can either use the Pythagorean Theorem, or better yet just notice that 15 = (5)(3) and 20 = (5)(4). Thus the hypotenuse of the triangle is (5)(5) = 25.

So the trip from *A* to *D* directly is 25 miles. Since 35 – 25 = 10, the trip would be 10 miles shorter, choice (C).

Remarks: (1) The 20 comes from adding 16 and 4.

(2) If we didn't notice that the triangle was a multiple of a 3-4-5 triangle, then we would use the Pythagorean Theorem as follows.

$$AD^2 = 15^2 + 20^2 = 225 + 400 = 625. \text{ So } AD = 25.$$

17. GEOMETRY

The smaller circle has area $A = \pi r^2 = \pi(\frac{1}{2})^2 = \frac{\pi}{4}$. The larger circle has area $A = \pi r^2 = \pi(1)^2 = \pi$. Therefore the requested ratio is $\pi \div \frac{\pi}{4} = \frac{\pi}{1} \cdot \frac{4}{\pi} = \frac{4}{1}$. So the answer is 4 : 1, choice (D).

* **Quick solution:** When the radius of a circle is doubled, the area of the circle is multiplied by $2^2 = 4$. So the answer is 4 : 1, choice (D).

18. NUMBER THEORY

* If we add up the consecutive integers from -22 to 22 we get 0. So let's start adding consecutive integers beginning with 23.

$$23 + 24 = 47$$
$$23 + 24 + 25 = 72$$

Therefore $-22 + (-21) + ... + (-1) + 0 + 1 + ... + 21 + 22 + 23 + 24 + 25 = 72$.

So $x = 25$, choice (B).

19. ALGEBRA

* We first raise each side of the first equation to the $\frac{-3}{4}$ power to get

$$x = (k^{-2})^{-3/4} = k^{-2(-3/4)} = k^{3/2}.$$

We next raise each side of the second equation to the $\frac{3}{4}$ power to get

$$y = (n^2)^{3/4} = n^{2\,(3/4)} = n^{3/2}.$$

So $xy = k^{3/2}\, n^{3/2} = (kn)^{3/2}$, and therefore

$$(xy)^{-2/3} = [(kn)^{3/2}]^{-2/3} = (kn)^{(3/2)(-2/3)} = (kn)^{-1} = \frac{1}{kn} = \frac{1}{nk}.$$

This is choice (A).

20. FUNCTIONS

* To get from the point (-1,3) to the point (2,1) we need to move right 3 and down 2. Therefore $g(x) = f(x - 3) - 2$. So $h = -3$ and $k = -2$. Finally, we have $hk = (-3)(-2) = 6$, choice (E).

Remarks: The graph of g is a **translation** of the graph of f. The easiest way to see how the whole graph is translated is to track a single point. In this case we tracked the point (-1,3). More formally 2 – -1 = 2 + 1 = 3, and 1 – 3 = -2. This shows that to get the graph of g we need to move the graph of f right 3 and down 2. We could have tracked the point (1,-3) instead. In this case we are moving (1,-3) to (4,-5). The horizontal shift is 4 – 1 = 3, and the vertical shift is -5 – -3 = -5 + 3 = -2.

For a lesson on **transformations** see the end of the solution to Problem 7 in Section 5 of Test 2 (p. 62).

SECTION 9

1. PROBABILITY

* The total number of cars is 10. The number of red cars is 6. Therefore the desired probability is $\frac{6}{10} = \frac{3}{5}$, choice (B).

Remarks: (1) To reduce the fraction $\frac{6}{10}$ in your calculator, type

6 / 10 ENTER MATH ENTER ENTER

(2) Here we have used the **Simple Probability Principle** which says the following. To compute a simple probability where all outcomes are equally likely, divide the number of "successes" by the total number of outcomes.

2. GEOMETRY

*** Solution by using a representation of the picture satisfying the given information:** Note that although the figure is not necessarily drawn to scale here, the figure given is a representation that satisfies the given information. It is easy to see in this picture that $w \neq x$. Therefore $w = x$ CANNOT be concluded, and the answer is choice (A).

Solution by starting with choice (C): First note that the triangle is isosceles because $AB = BC$.

Let's start with choice (C) and note that $x = y$ because $\overline{BD}$ is an angle bisector of angle ABC. So we can eliminate choice (C).

Let's look at choice (D) next and note that $AD = DC$ because we are given that $\overline{BD}$ bisects $\overline{AC}$. So we can eliminate choice (D).

Let's look at choice (B) and note that $w = z$ because these angles are opposite two congruent sides. So we can eliminate choice (B).

We can eliminate choice (E) because $\overline{BD}$ bisects $\overline{AC}$ and the triangle is isosceles (see Remark (1) below).

By process of elimination, the answer is choice (A).

Remarks: (1) In general, for an **isosceles** triangle, the **median, altitude**, and **angle bisector** from the vertex opposite the two congruent angles are all equal.

(2) It is consistent with what is given that $x = y = 30$ and $w = z = 60$. In this case, $w \neq x$ showing that choice (A) is the answer.

For the definitions of an isosceles triangle, median, altitude, and angle bisector see the notes at the end of Problem 19 in Section 2 of Test 5 (pp. 145-146).

3. PERCENTS

* **Quick solution:** Since 15 percent is half of 30 percent, 15 percent of m is $\frac{1}{2}(40) = 20$, choice (B).

Algebraic solution 1: 30 percent of m can be written as $.3m$. So we are given that $.3m = 40$. Dividing each side by 2 gives $.15m = 20$, choice (B).

Algebraic solution 2: As in the last solution we are given $.3m = 40$. We divide each side of this equation by .3 to get $m = \frac{40}{.3}$. So we have that $.15m = .15(\frac{40}{.3}) = 20$, choice (B).

Note: All of the calculations above can be done easily in your calculator.

For more information on converting between decimals and percents see the notes at the end of Problem 15 in Section 3 of Test 1 (p. 12).

4. Number Theory

* **Solution by picking a number:** Let's choose a value for *n*, say $n = -3$. Let's plug in -3 for *n* into each answer choice.

(A) -1.5
(B) -6
(C) -1
(D) -5
(E) 5

Since (A), (B), (C), and (D) each came out incorrect, the answer is (E).

For more information on this technique, see **Strategy 4** in ***"The 32 Most Effective SAT Math Strategies."***

5. Number Theory

* We simply divide 1.2 by 1 in our calculator and then convert back to a fraction to get $\frac{6}{5}$. So the answer is 6 to 5, choice (D).

Remarks: (1) We do not actually need to divide by 1 since anything divided by 1 is itself. In particular 1.2 divided by 1 is 1.2

(2) To convert 1.2 to a fraction in your calculator type

1.2 MATH ENTER ENTER

6. Data Analysis

* Each house represents 5 million homes and there are 3.5 houses. So the number of homes represents 3.5(5) = 17.5 million homes, choice (D).

Note: There is no need to change 5 million into the number 5,000,000 because the answers in the answer choices are given in millions.

7. Number Theory

* If we add b^2 to each side of the given equation we get $a^2 = 7 + b^2$. Now let's take guesses for *b* until $7 + b^2$ is a perfect square.

If $b = 1$, then $7 + b^2 = 7 + 1^2 = 8$
If $b = 2$, then $7 + b^2 = 7 + 2^2 = 11$
If $b = 3$, then $7 + b^2 = 7 + 3^2 = 16$

Since 16 is a perfect square, $a^2 = 16$, and therefore $a = 4$, choice (B).

Remark: The equation $a^2 = 16$ actually has two solutions $a = 4$ and $a = -4$. But we are given that a is positive so we use $a = 4$.

For more information on this technique, see **Strategy 3** in ***"The 32 Most Effective SAT Math Strategies."***

8. NUMBER THEORY

*** Solution by picking numbers:** Let's choose values for u and w consistent with the picture, say $u = -.8$ and $w = -.5$. Then we have that $u - w = -.8 - -.5 = -.8 + .5 = -.3$, and so $|u - w| = \mathbf{.3}$. This is where x is, choice (C).

For more information on this technique, see **Strategy 4** in ***"The 32 Most Effective SAT Math Strategies.***

9. ALGEBRA

Solution by picking a number: Let's choose a value for n, say $n = 3$. We first increase 3 by 5 to get 8. We then multiply 8 by 5 to get 40. We then decrease 40 by 5 to get 35. We then divide 35 by 5 to get **7. Put a nice big, dark circle around 7 so that you can find it easily later.** Now let's substitute 3 in for n in each answer choice.

(A) -2
(B) 2
(C) 3
(D) 7
(E) 40

Since (A), (B), (C), and (E) each came out incorrect, the answer is (D).

For more information on this technique, see **Strategy 4** in ***"The 32 Most Effective SAT Math Strategies."***

*** Algebraic solution (not recommended):** n increased by 5 is $n + 5$. When we multiply this result by 5 we get $5(n + 5) = 5n + 25$. When we decrease this result by 5 we get $5n + 20$. When we divide this result by 5 we get $\frac{5n+20}{5} = \frac{5n}{5} + \frac{20}{5} = n + 4$, choice (D).

10. Algebra

Solution by picking numbers: Let's choose a value for n, say $n = 3$. So Philip put up 3 posters. Each poster requires 4(6) = 24 inches, or 2 feet of tape. So he used 3(2) = 6 feet of tape. The number of feet of tape left on the roll is 300 – 6 = **294**. **Put a nice big, dark circle around 294 so that you can find it easily later.** Now let's substitute 3 in for n in each answer choice.

(A) $300 - 6(3) = 282$
(B) $300 - 2(3) = 294$
(C) $300 - 3 = 297$
(D) $300 - \frac{1}{2}(3) = 298.5$
(E) $300 - \frac{1}{4}(3) = 299.25$

Since (A), (C), (D), and (E) each came out incorrect, the answer is (B).

For more information on this technique, see **Strategy 4** in ***"The 32 Most Effective SAT Math Strategies."***

* **Algebraic solution (not recommended):** Each poster requires 4(6) = 24 inches, or 2 feet of tape. So Phillip used $2n$ feet of tape. Therefore the number of feet of tape left on the roll is $300 - 2n$, choice (B).

11. Geometry

* Let's draw a picture.

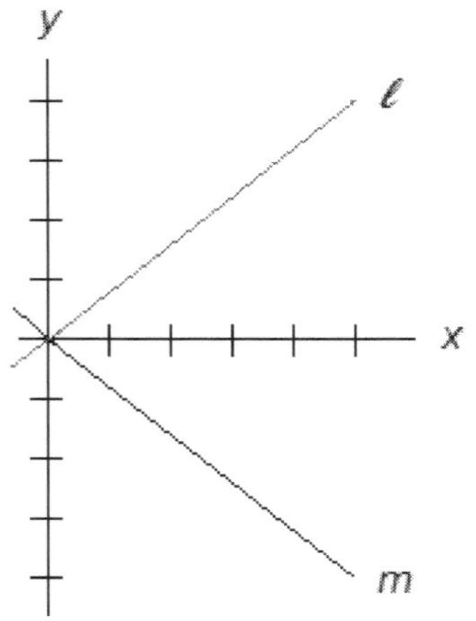

Note that line m was drawn first. To make the picture as simple as possible we start at the origin (the point (0,0)), and then move down 4, right 5 to get to the next point on the line.

Now, for line ℓ to be the reflection of line m in the x-axis, we must move up 4, right 5 from the origin. So the slope of line ℓ is $\frac{4}{5}$, choice (B).

Remark: A common mistake is to assume that these two lines will be perpendicular. Reflecting a line in the x-axis almost never results in a perpendicular line. The only time this will happen is if the slope of the original line is 1 or -1.

For more information on this technique, see **Strategy 9** in ***"The 32 Most Effective SAT Math Strategies."***

12. ALGEBRA

Solution by starting with choice (C): Let's start with choice (C) and guess that $p = 1$. Then $n = 3p = 3(1) = 3$. So $n \neq p$, and we can eliminate (C).

Let's try choice (A) next and guess that $p = 0$ (because it is easier to plug in than the other choices). Then $n = 3p = 3(0) = 0$. So $n = p$, and the answer is choice (A).

For more information on this technique, see **Strategy 1** in ***"The 32 Most Effective SAT Math Strategies."***

*** Algebraic solution:** Since we want n to equal p, we substitute n for p in the first equation to get $p = 3p$. We subtract p from each side of this equation to get $0 = 2p$. Finally we divide each side of this equation by 2 to get $p = \frac{0}{2} = 0$, choice (A).

13. GEOMETRY

*** Solution by picking numbers:** Let's choose values for the degree measures of the triangle so that $z = 30$ and the sum of the angle measures is 180 degrees. For example, we can choose 30, 70, and 80. The picture looks like this.

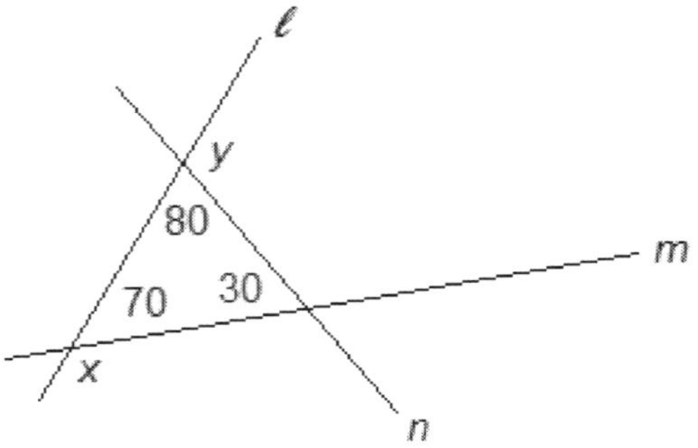

From this picture we see that $x = 180 - 70 = 110$ and $y = 180 - 80 = 100$. Therefore $x + y = 110 + 100 = 210$, choice (D).

Note: Any choice for the degree measures of the triangle such that the sum of the angle measures is 180 degrees and $z = 30$ will give the same answer for $x + y$.

For more information on this technique, see **Strategy 4** in ***"The 32 Most Effective SAT Math Strategies."*** **Strategy 9** is also relevant.

14. Functions

*** Solution by plugging in numbers and graphing:** Let's choose positive values for b and c, say $b = 2$ and $c = 3$. So the function is $f(x) = x^2 + 2x + 3$. We put this in our graphing calculator by first pressing the Y= button and then typing X^2 + 2X + 3. Press ZOOM 6 to graph this function in a standard window. Now simply note that the graph looks like choice (E).

*** Quick solution:** Since c is positive, the graph intersects the y-axis above the x-axis. The only answer choice that satisfies this requirement is choice (E).

Note: The general form for a quadratic function is

$$y = ax^2 + bx + c.$$

The graph of this function is a parabola whose vertex has x-coordinate

$$-\frac{b}{2a}$$

The parabola opens upwards if $a > 0$ and downwards if $a < 0$.

The y-intercept of this parabola is the point $(0,c)$.

15. GEOMETRY

* We use the **Generalized Pythagorean Theorem.**

The distance from A to the lower front right vertex is 1. The distance from the lower front right vertex to the lower rear right vertex is 2. The distance from the lower rear right vertex to B is 1. By the Generalized Pythagorean Theorem $AB^2 = 1^2 + 2^2 + 1^2 = 1 + 4 + 1 = 6$. So $AB = \sqrt{6}$, choice (D).

Notes: (1) The **Generalized Pythagorean Theorem** says that the length d of the long diagonal of a rectangular solid is given by $d^2 = a^2 + b^2 + c^2$ where a, b and c are the length, width and height of the rectangular solid.

(2) In this problem we are not looking for the long diagonal of the given cube. We are looking for the long diagonal of one quarter of this rectangular solid. We get this solid by slicing the original cube in half two ways. We first take the right half of the cube, and then we take the bottom half of the resulting solid.

16. ALGEBRA

* **Solution by starting with choice (C):** Let's start with choice (C) and guess that $a = \frac{3}{2}$. Then $a - 2 = \frac{-1}{2}$. Now, $(\frac{3}{2})^2 - \frac{3}{2} = .75$, and $(\frac{-1}{2})^2 - \frac{-1}{2} = .75$. Since both came out the same, the answer is choice (C).

For more information on this technique, see **Strategy 1** in ***"The 32 Most Effective SAT Math Strategies."***

Algebraic solution: We are given that $a^2 - a = (a - 2)^2 - (a - 2)$. So we have $a^2 - a = a^2 - 5a + 6$ (see below for details on this computation). We subtract a^2 and add a to each side of this equation to get $0 = -4a + 6$. We now add $4a$ to each side of this equation to get $4a = 6$. Finally, we divide each side of this last equation by 4 to get $a = \frac{6}{4} = \frac{3}{2}$, choice (C).

Computation: $(a - 2)^2 = (a - 2)(a - 2) = a^2 - 2a - 2a + 4 = a^2 - 4a + 4$. So $(a - 2)^2 - (a - 2) = a^2 - 4a + 4 - a + 2 = a^2 - 5a + 6$.

Alternatively we can perform this computation as follows.

$$(a-2)^2 - (a-2) = (a-2)(a-2) - (a-2) = (a-2)(a-2-1) =$$
$$(a-2)(a-3) = a^2 - 3a - 2a + 6 = a^2 - 5a + 6.$$

Blue Book Test 8
Fully Explained Solutions

Section 3

1. Number Theory

* Change the two fractions to decimals by dividing in your calculator. Dividing 1 by 5 gives 0.2. Dividing 1 by 4 gives .25. Since 0.21 is between these two the answer is choice (D).

Remark: We can compare two decimals by looking at the first position where they disagree. For example, 0.24 is less than 0.25 because 4 is less than 5. If a digit is missing, there is a hidden 0 there. Thus 0.2 is also less than 0.25 because 0.2 is the same as 0.20 and 0 is less than 5 (remember that we look at the **first** position where the decimals disagree).

For more information on this technique, see **Strategy 15** in ***"The 32 Most Effective SAT Math Strategies."***

2. Geometry

* **Solution by drawing a picture:** Let's plot the five points.

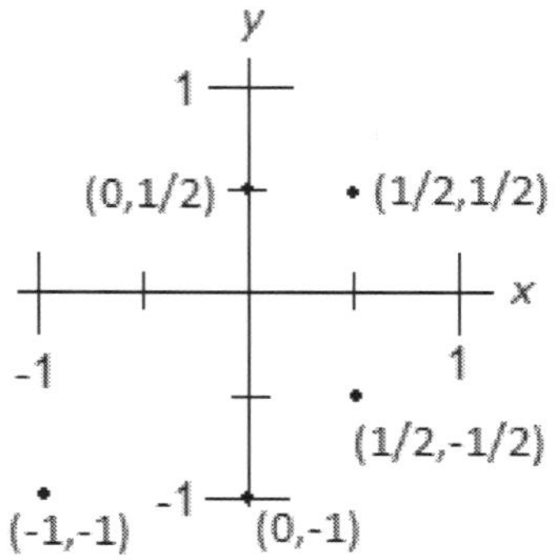

Now just observe that $(0,\frac{1}{2})$ is closest to the origin, choice (B).

Remark: If you are having trouble seeing that $(0,\frac{1}{2})$ is closer to the origin than $(\frac{1}{2},\frac{1}{2})$, just note that the legs of a right triangle are always shorter than the hypotenuse. See the figure below.

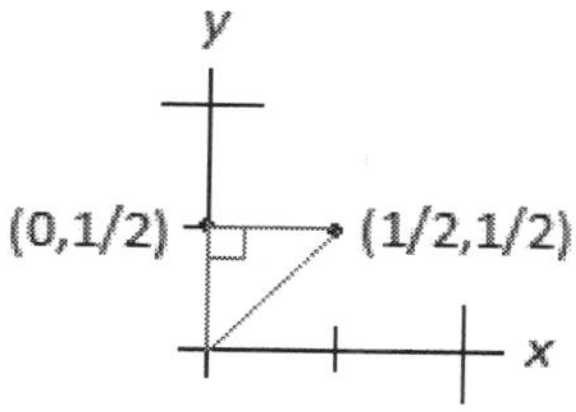

Another way to see this it to draw a circle centered at the origin with radius $\frac{1}{2}$. Note that the point $(0, \frac{1}{2})$ is on this circle and all other points are outside this circle. See the figure below.

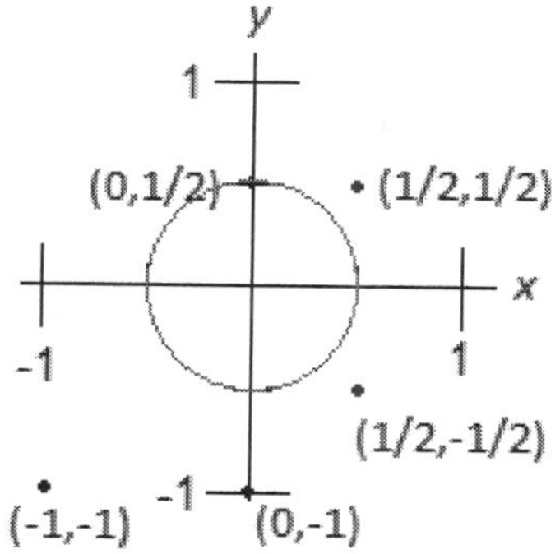

For more information on this technique, see **Strategy 9** in ***"The 32 Most Effective SAT Math Strategies."***

3. Geometry

* **Algebraic solution:** Since *AB* is a line, $5x = 180$. So $x = \frac{180}{5} = 36$. Now, we have $7x + y = 360$. So $y = 360 - 7x = 360 - 7(36) = 108$, choice (A).

4. Algebra

Solution by starting with choice (C): Let's start with choice (C) and guess that $x = 100$. Then $65(x + 1) = 65(100 + 1) = 65(101) = 6{,}565$. Since this is correct, the answer is choice (C).

For more information on this technique, see **Strategy 1** in ***"The 32 Most Effective SAT Math Strategies."***

* **Algebraic solution 1:** Divide each side of the equation by 65 to get

$$\frac{6,565}{65} = x + 1$$

$$101 = x + 1$$

So $x = 100$, choice (C).

Algebraic solution 2: Distribute the 65 on the right hand side of the equation to get

$$6,565 = 65x + 65.$$

Now subtract 65 from each side of this equation to get

$$6,500 = 65x.$$

Finally, divide each side of this equation by 65 to get $x = \frac{6,500}{65} = 100$, choice (C).

5. Number Theory

* Using basic laws of exponents we have $m^x \cdot m^7 = m^{x+7}$ and $(m^5)^y = m^{5y}$. So $m^{x+7} = m^{28}$ and $m^{5y} = m^{15}$. Thus, $x + 7 = 28$ and $5y = 15$. Therefore $x = 21$ and $y = 3$. So $x + y = 21 + 3 = 24$, choice (D).

For a review of the **Laws of Exponents** used here see the end of the solution to Problem 8 in Section 8 of Test 1 (p. 35).

6. Data Analysis

* The total decrease from 1987 to 1990 was approximately

$$156,000 - 114,000 = 42,000.$$

Thus, the approximate decrease per year was $\frac{42,000}{3} = 14,000$, choice (C).

7. Geometry

* Since $x = y$, both triangle are isosceles right triangles. An isosceles right triangle is the same as a 45, 45, 90 triangle. So we can simply use the formula given for this triangle at the beginning of each math section of the SAT. We have that $AB = s\sqrt{2} = 4$. So $BE = s = \frac{4}{\sqrt{2}}$. Similarly, we have that $BD = s\sqrt{2} = 8$. So $CB = s = \frac{8}{\sqrt{2}}$. Finally, $CE = CB + BE = \frac{8}{\sqrt{2}} + \frac{4}{\sqrt{2}} \sim 8.49$, choice (B).

Notes: (1) That last computation is easiest to do in our graphing calculator.

(2) Instead of using the formula for a 45, 45, 90 triangle, the Pythagorean Theorem can be used instead. For example, to find AE, we can solve the equation $s^2 + s^2 = 4^2$. So $2s^2 = 16$, and thus, $s^2 = 8$. Therefore $s = \sqrt{8}$.

For more information on this technique, see **Strategy 27** in ***"The 32 Most Effective SAT Math Strategies."***

8. Algebra

* **Solution by picking numbers:** Let's choose values for d and c. Let's say $d = 8$ and $c = 4$. So it costs 8 dollars for 8 ounces, or equivalently, 1 dollar per ounce. Also each ounce makes 4 cups of coffee so that it costs **.25** dollars per cup. **Put a nice big, dark circle around .25 so that you can find it easily later.** Now let's substitute 8 for d and 4 for c into each answer choice.

(A) $\frac{8}{32} = .25$
(B) $\frac{32}{8} = 4$
(C) $\frac{32}{8} = 4$
(D) $\frac{64}{4} = 16$
(E) 256

Since (B), (C), (D), and (E) each came out incorrect, the answer is choice (A).

Important note: (A) is **not** the correct answer simply because it is equal to .25. It is correct because all 4 of the other choices are **not .25**. **You absolutely must check all five choices!**

Remark: 8 was actually a "risky" choice for *d* since the number 8 appears in the answer choices. In this case it worked out okay and only one of the answer choices came out correct.

For more information on this technique, see **Strategy 4** in ***"The 32 Most Effective SAT Math Strategies."***

9. Algebra

* We simply cross multiply to get $ab = (10)(12) = \mathbf{120}$.

10. Number Theory

* We divide each term by 5 to get the next term. So we simply divide 6 by 5 twice in our calculator. We can type 6 / 5 ENTER / 5 ENTER. The output is **.24**

Note: We can also grid in the fraction **6/25**.

11. Geometry

* Let's draw a picture.

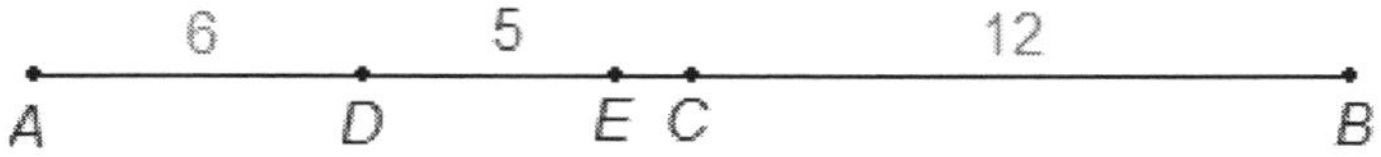

Since C is the midpoint of $\overline{AB}$, we have $AC = CB = 12$. Since D is the midpoint of $\overline{AC}$, we have $AD = DC = 6$. So if we place E to the right of D, we have $AE = 6 + 5 = \mathbf{11}$.

Remark: We could also have placed E to the left of D in which case we have $AE = 6 - 5 = \mathbf{1}$.

12. Number Theory

Solution by guessing: Let us try some guesses for the 5th integer.

5th	4th	3rd	2rd	1st	Sum
50	49	48	47	46	240
30	29	28	27	26	140
35	34	33	32	32	165
38	37	36	35	34	180
39	38	37	36	35	185

Thus, the answer is **39**.

Remark: You should use your calculator to compute these sums. This will be quicker and you are less likely to make a careless error.

For more information on this technique, see **Strategy 3** in ***"The 32 Most Effective SAT Math Strategies."***

Algebraic solution: If we name the least integer x, then the second, third, fourth and fifth integers are $x + 1$, $x + 2$, $x + 3$, and $x + 4$, respectively. So we have

$$x + (x + 1) + (x + 2) + (x + 3) + (x + 4) = 185$$
$$5x + 10 = 185$$
$$5x = 175$$
$$x = \frac{175}{5} = 35$$

The fifth integer is $x + 4 =$ **39**.

*** Quick computation:** Divide 185 by 5 to get the third integer: $\frac{185}{5} = 37$. It follows that the greatest integer is 37 + 2 = **39**.

Remark: The following algebraic steps show why the last method gives the correct solution.

$$x + (x + 1) + (x + 2) + (x + 3) + (x + 4) = 185$$
$$5x + 10 = 185$$
$$5(x + 2)= 185$$
$$x + 2 = \frac{185}{5} = 37$$

So $x + 4 = 37 + 2 =$ **39**.

13. Percents

* **Quick solution:** 20 percent of the dollar amount of salesman's sales, in dollars, was 2500 – 1200 = 1300. Therefore the dollar amount of his sales for that month was (1300)(5) = **6500**.

Algebraic solution: We solve the equation $1200 + .2x = 2500$. Subtracting 1200 from each side of this equation yields $.2x = 1300$. Finally, we divide each side of this last equation by .2 to get $\frac{1300}{.2}$ = **6500**.

Remark: We change 20% to a decimal by moving the decimal point to the left 2 places. Note that there is a hidden decimal point to the right of the zero.

14. Geometry

* First note that a there are 360 degrees in one full revolution of a circle. We now set up a simple ratio. Begin by identifying 2 key words. In this case, such a pair of key words is "degrees" and "grams."

degrees	40	360
grams	x	2.5

Now draw in the division symbols and equal sign, cross multiply and divide the corresponding ratio to find the unknown quantity x.

$$\frac{40}{x} = \frac{360}{2.5}$$

$$(40)(2.5) = 360x$$

$$100 = 360x$$

$$x = \frac{100}{360} = \mathbf{5/18}$$

Note: We can also grid in either of the decimals **.277** or **.278**.

For more information on this technique, see **Strategy 14** in ***"The 32 Most Effective SAT Math Strategies."***

15. ALGEBRA

*We use the special factoring formula $x^2 - y^2 = (x + y)(x - y)$. So we have

$$x^2 - y^2 = 10$$
$$(x + y)(x - y) = 10$$
$$5(x - y) = 10$$
$$x - y = \frac{10}{5} = \mathbf{2}.$$

16. GEOMETRY

* We let c be the length of a side of the shaded square and use the Pythagorean Theorem to get $A = c^2 = 2^2 + 1^2 = \mathbf{5}$.

Notes: (1) Since the figure does not say "Figure not drawn to scale," we may assume it is. It follows that the four triangles are congruent. Now simply choose any of the right triangles and note that the legs have lengths 2 and 1.

(2) If c is the length of a side of the shaded square, then the area of the shaded square is $A = c^2$. Since the question is asking for the **area** of the shaded square, there is no need to find c.

For more information on this technique, see **Strategy 6** in ***"The 32 Most Effective SAT Math Strategies."***

* **Alternative solution:** The area of the large square is $A = 3^2 = 9$, and the area of each triangle is $A = \frac{1}{2}bh = \frac{1}{2}(1)(2) = 1$. So the area of the shaded square is $9 - 4(1) = \mathbf{5}$.

For more information on this technique, see **Strategy 23** in ***"The 32 Most Effective SAT Math Strategies."***

17. NUMBER THEORY

* The question can be rephrased as "The remainder is 2 when 13 is divided by what number?" Well, when 13 is divided by **11** the remainder is 2. Indeed, 13 = 11(1) + 2. So the answer is **11**.

Remark: If you do not see that the answer is 11 right away, just start dividing 13 by various positive integers and keeping track of the remainders.

13 = 2(1) + 11. So when 13 is divided by 2 the remainder is 11.
13 = 3(1) + 10. So when 13 is divided by 3 the remainder is 10.
13= 4(1) + 9. So when 13 is divided by 4 the remainder is 9.
...

and so on

Visual solution: Draw 13 circles on your paper. We want 2 to be left over. So we need to take 11 of them. In other words, divide 13 by 11 to get a remainder of 2.

18. STATISTICS

* The sum of the test scores of the class of p students is $70p$.

The sum of the test scores of the class of n students is $92n$.

Adding these we get the sum of the test scores of both classes combined: $70p + 92n$.

We can also get this sum directly from the problem.

$$86(p + n) = 86p + 86n.$$

So we have that $70p + 92n = 86p + 86n$.

We get p to one side of the equation by subtracting $70p$ from each side, and we get n to the other side by subtracting $86n$ from each side.

$$6n = 16p$$

We can get $\frac{p}{n}$ to one side by performing **cross division.** We do this just like cross multiplication, but we divide instead. Dividing each side of the equation by $16n$ will do the trick (this way we get rid of n on the left, and 16 on the right).

$$\frac{p}{n} = \frac{6}{16} = \frac{3}{8}.$$

So we can grid in **3/8** or **.375**.

For more information on this technique, see **Strategy 20** in ***"The 32 Most Effective SAT Math Strategies."***

SECTION 7

1. NUMBER THEORY

* $1 + 5 + 5 + 1 + 1 + 1 + 1 + 1 + 1 = 17$, choice (B).

Notes: (1) There are 9 letters in the word, 2 of which are worth 5 points each, and the other 7 worth 1 point each.

(2) The computation can be done a bit quicker as $2(5) + 7(1) = 17$.

2. ALGEBRA

* We divide each side of the equation by 2 to get $x - 5 = 10$, choice (B).

Note: When we divide the left hand side by 2, we have to divide **each** term by 2: $\frac{2x}{2} = x$ and $\frac{10}{2} = 5$

Alternative: We can factor out 2 on the left hand side: $2x - 10 = 2(x - 5)$

So we have

$$2x - 10 = 20$$
$$2(x - 5) = 20$$
$$x - 5 = \frac{20}{2} = 10$$

This is choice (B).

For more information on this technique, see **Strategy 16** in ***"The 32 Most Effective SAT Math Strategies."***

3. NUMBER THEORY

Solution by picking a number: Let's choose a value for t, say $t = 3$. We substitute 3 in for t in each answer choice.

(A) $3 + 2 = 5$	odd
(B) $2(3) - 1 = 5$	odd
(C) $3(3) - 2 = 7$	odd
(D) $3(3) + 2 = 11$	odd
(E) $5(3) + 1 = 16$	even

Since (A), (B), (C), and (D) each came out odd, the answer is choice (E).

For more information on this technique, see **Strategy 4** in ***"The 32 Most Effective SAT Math Strategies."***

* **Direct solution:** The following describes what happens when you add and multiply various combinations of even and odd integers.

$$\begin{array}{ll} e+e=e & ee=e \\ e+o=o & eo=e \\ o+e=o & oe=e \\ o+o=e & oo=o \end{array}$$

For example, the sum of an even and an odd integer is odd ($e+o=o$).

Note that in choice (E) we have (odd)(odd) + odd = odd + odd = even (or more compactly, $oo + o = o + o = e$).

4. Geometry

* The perimeter of triangle *DEF* is 4 + 8 + 9 = 21. Therefore the perimeter of triangle *ABC* is also 21. So $AB = \frac{21}{3} = 7$, choice (C).

5. Data Analysis

* We are given that the store sold 900 Other Brands. So 900 is 20% of the sales. The total sales is therefore 900(5) = 4500, choice (E).

Formal algebraic solution: If we let x be the total number of sales, then we are given $.2x = 900$. So $x = \frac{900}{.2} = 4500$, choice (E).

For more information on converting between decimals and percents see the notes at the end of Problem 5 in Section 3 of Test 1 (p. 12).

6. Geometry

* Let's convert the given measurements to yards. We have that 12 feet is $\frac{12}{3} = 4$ yards, and 18 feet is $\frac{18}{3} = 6$ yards. So the amount of carpeting needed is (4)(6) = 24 square yards, choice (C).

Notes: (1) Here we used the formula for the area of a rectangle: $A = \ell w$.

(2) We can also first multiply (12)(18) = 216 square feet, and then convert to square yards by dividing by $3^2 = 9$. So $\frac{216}{9} = 24$. Note that it would be incorrect to divide by 3 here.

7. Geometry

Solution by starting with choice (C): Let's start with choice (C) and guess that the puppy weighs 4 pounds. Then from the third piece of information, the bunny weighs 9 – 4 = 5 pounds. From the second piece of information, the kitten weighs 8 – 4 = 4 pounds. So the kitten and the bunny together weigh 4 + 5 = 9 pounds, contradicting the first piece of information. So we can eliminate choice (C). A moment's thought allows us to eliminate choices (A) and (B) as well.

Let's try choice (D) next. If the puppy weighs 5 pounds, then the bunny weighs 9 – 5 = 4 pounds, and the kitten weighs 8 – 5 = 3 pounds. So the kitten and bunny together weigh 3 + 4 = 7 pounds. This agrees with the first piece of information. So the answer is choice (D).

For more information on this technique, see **Strategy 1** in ***"The 32 Most Effective SAT Math Strategies."***

*** Algebraic solution:** Let k, b, and p represent the kitten's, bunny's, and puppy's weights, respectively. Then we have the following system of equations.

$$\begin{aligned} k + b &= 7 \\ k + p &= 8 \\ b + p &= 9 \end{aligned}$$

We subtract the first equation from the second equation.

$$\begin{array}{c} k + p = 8 \\ \underline{k + b = 7} \\ p - b = 1 \end{array}$$

We now add this equation to the third equation from above.

$$\begin{array}{c} b + p = 9 \\ \underline{p - b = 1} \\ 2p = 10 \end{array}$$

Finally, divide each side of this equation by 2 to get $p = \frac{10}{2} = 5$, choice (D).

8. Number Theory

* This is a simple ratio. We begin by identifying 2 key words. In this case, such a pair of key words is "inches" and "feet."

inches	.25	x
feet	16	40

Now simply cross multiply and divide the corresponding ratio to find the unknown quantity x.

$$\frac{.25}{16} = \frac{x}{40}$$

$$(.25)(40) = 16x$$

$$x = \frac{10}{16} = \frac{5}{8}$$

This is choice (B).

For more information on this technique, see **Strategy 14** in **"The 32 Most Effective SAT Math Strategies."**

9. Geometry

* We are given that $(p,0)$ is a point of intersection of the two graphs. This means that this point satisfies both equations. So using the first equation we have $0 = -p^2 + 9$. Thus, $p^2 = 9$ and therefore $p = 3$, choice (A).

Remarks: (1) The equation $p^2 = 9$ actually has two solutions $p = 3$ and $p = -3$. But we are given that p is positive so we use $p = 3$.

(2) We could have also used the second equation to get $0 = p^2 - 9$. Solving this for p^2 gives $9 = p^2$ and so $3 = p$.

10. Number Theory

* Together the two machines make 300 + 450 = 750 bolts per hour. Let's now set up a ratio. We identify 2 key words. Let's choose "bolts" and "minutes."

bolts	750	900
minutes	60	x

At first glance it might seem to make more sense to choose "hours" as our second key word, but choosing the word "minutes" is more efficient because

(a) The answer that we're looking for must be in minutes.
(b) It's extremely simple to convert 1 hour into 60 minutes.

We now find x by cross multiplying and dividing.

$$\frac{750}{60} = \frac{900}{x}$$

$$750x = 54{,}000$$

$$x = \frac{54{,}000}{750} = 72$$

So, the answer is choice (B).

For more information on this technique, see **Strategy 14** in ***"The 32 Most Effective SAT Math Strategies."***

11. Number Theory

*** Solution by plugging in points:** Note that when $t = 0$, $g(t) = 2$. So let's substitute $t = 0$ into each answer choice and eliminate any choices that do not come out to 2.

(A) 1
(B) 1
(C) 1
(D) 2
(E) 2

Since (A), (B), and (C) each came out incorrect we can eliminate them.

We still have to choose between choices (D) and (E). So let's use another of the given points. Note that when $t = 1$, $g(t) = 0$. So let's substitute $t = 1$ into choices (D) and (E) and eliminate any choice that does not come out to 0.

(D) $-1 + 2 = 1$
(E) $-2(1) + 2 = 0$

Since (D) came out incorrect we can eliminate it, and the answer is therefore choice (E).

For more information on this technique, see **Strategy 5** in ***"The 32 Most Effective SAT Math Strategies."***

12. Data Analysis

* **Solution by starting with choice (C):** Let's start with choice (C) and check if more 12th graders than 11th graders travel 6 or more miles to school. Well 3 twelfth graders travel 6 or more miles to school, and 2 eleventh graders travel 6 or more miles to school. So the statement is true, and the answer is choice (C).

For more information on this technique, see **Strategy 1** in ***"The 32 Most Effective SAT Math Strategies."***

13. Counting

Solution by writing a list: Let's try to list the numbers in **increasing order**.

304	314	324	334	344
354	364	374	384	394

And that's it. We see that the answer is 10, choice (A).

For more information on this technique, see **Strategy 19** in ***"The 32 Most Effective SAT Math Strategies."***

* **Solution using the counting principle:** There is 1 possibility for the hundreds digit (3), 10 possibilities for the tens digit (0, 1, 2, 3, 4, 5, 6, 7, 8, or 9), and 1 possibility for the units digit (4). The counting principle says that we multiply the possibilities to get (1)(10)(1) = 10, choice (A).

14. Geometry

* The equation $y = mx + b$ is in slope-intercept form. The number b is where the graph hits the y-axis. From the given graph, we see $b = -1$. The graph of the equation $y = -3mx + b$ also hits the y-axis at $b = -1$. Only choice (D) satisfies this condition. So the answer is choice (D).

More details: Note that these details are unnecessary for solving this problem, but may help in getting a general understanding of the slope-intercept form of an equation of a line.

The slope of the line in the given graph is $\frac{-1}{3}$. To see this simply note that to get from the x-intercept (-3,0) to the y-intercept (0,-1) we need to move down 1, then right 3. So we have $m = \frac{-1}{3}$, and as per the solution above, $b = -1$. So $-3m = -3(\frac{-1}{3}) = 1 = \frac{1}{1}$. So to graph the new line we start on the y-axis at -1, then move up 1, right 1 to get a second point. This agrees with the graph in choice (D).

For more information on this technique, see **Strategy 28** in ***"The 32 Most Effective SAT Math Strategies."***

For more information on slope see the notes at the end of Problem 12 in Section 3 of Test 1 (pp. 15-17).

15. GEOMETRY

* Since the volume of the cube is 8, the length of a side of the cube is 2. The distance from the center of the cube to the base of the cube is half the length of a side of the cube. So the answer is 1, choice (A).

Remarks: (1) To see that the length of a side of the cube is 2, note that $2^3 = 8$, or more formally take the cube root of 8 to get $\sqrt[3]{8} = 2$.

(2) If you are having trouble seeing that the distance from the center of the cube to the base of the cube is half the length of a side of the cube, look at the following cross section of the cube.

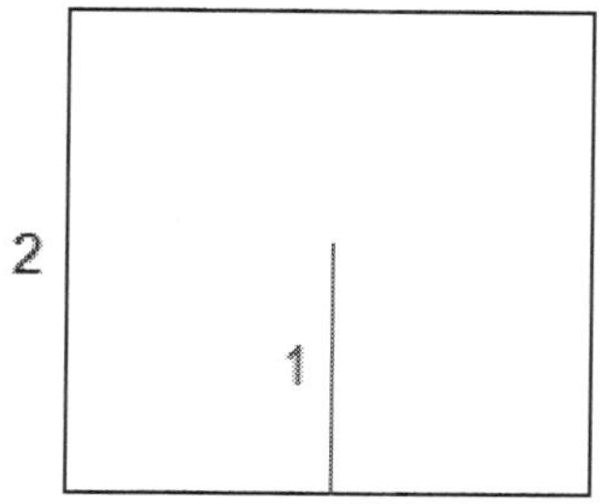

16. NUMBER THEORY

Solution by picking numbers: Let's choose values for x and z, say $x = 2$ and $z = 4$. Then $y = \frac{5 \cdot 2^3}{4} = 10$. Now let's double the values we chose for x and z so that $x = 4$ and $z = 8$. Then $y = \frac{5 \cdot 4^3}{8} = 40$. So we see that the value of y is multiplied by 4, choice (E).

Algebraic solution: If we replace x by $2x$ and y by $2y$ in the given expression we get $y = \frac{5(2x)^3}{2z} = \frac{5 \cdot 8x^3}{2z} = \frac{20x^3}{z} = 4(\frac{5x^3}{z})$. So we see that the value of y is multiplied by 4, choice (E).

* **Quick solution:** If x is doubled, then x^3 is multiplied by 8. So if x and z are doubled, then $\frac{x^3}{z}$ is multiplied by $\frac{8}{2} = 4$. So the answer is choice (E).

Note: The constant 5 in the given formula does not affect what happens to y when x and z are doubled.

17. FUNCTIONS

Solution by starting with choice (C): We start with choice (C) and guess that $n = 3$. We compute $V(3)$ in our calculator by typing 5000*(4/5)^3 and we get an output of 2560. This is too small so we need to **decrease** the value of n (if you do not see this it's okay – just keep plugging in answer choices for n until you get 3,200 for $V(n)$).

Let's try $n = 2$ next. We compute $V(2)$ in our calculator by typing 5000*(4/5)^2 and we get an output of 3200. This is correct. So the answer is choice (B).

Remark: Decreasing the value of n increases the value of $V(n)$ because $\frac{4}{5}$ is a number between 0 and 1.

For more information on this technique, see **Strategy 1** in ***"The 32 Most Effective SAT Math Strategies."***

* **Algebraic solution:** We are being asked to find n when $V(n) = 3{,}200$. So we need to solve the following equation.

$$3200 = 5000(\tfrac{4}{5})^n$$

$$\frac{3200}{5000} = (\tfrac{4}{5})^n$$

$$\frac{16}{25} = (\tfrac{4}{5})^n$$

$$(\tfrac{4}{5})^2 = (\tfrac{4}{5})^n$$

So $n = 2$, choice (B).

18. NUMBER THEORY

* The pattern is to swap the leftmost two letters, then swap the rightmost two letters, then repeat. We continue until we get back ABC.

Start	ABC
Step 1	BAC
Step 2	BCA
Step 3	CBA
Step 4	CAB
Step 5	ACB
Step 6	ABC

The answer is 6, choice (D).

19. STATISTICS

*** Solution by process of elimination:** Let's consider a list of eleven different numbers.

1 2 3 4 5 6 7 8 9 10 11

Note that the median is 6.

Now let's consider each answer choice.

(A) 2 4 6 8 10 12 14 16 18 20 22

The median of this list is 12. So we can eliminate choice (A).

(B) 11 12 13 14 15 16 17 18 19 20 21

The median of this list is 16. So we can eliminate choice (B).

(C) Let's increase the smallest number 1 to 12. So now the list is

2 3 4 5 6 7 8 9 10 11 12

The median of this list is 7. So we can eliminate choice (C).

(D) Let's decrease the largest number 11 to 0. So now the list is

0 1 2 3 4 5 6 7 8 9 10

The median of this list is 5. So we can eliminate choice (D).

Therefore the answer is choice (E).

Note: Increasing the largest number in a list of 11 numbers does not affect which number is in the middle. This is why the answer is (E).

20. GEOMETRY

* It does not say "Figure not drawn to scale." So let's assume it is. Then $CT = 3$ because it looks like half the radius. Similarly $RC = 3$, and thus $AR = 8 - 3 = 5$ (because the length plus the width of the rectangle is 8). Now SR is a radius, so $SA = 6 - 5 = 1$. BR (not drawn) is also a radius. So $BR = 6$. Since both diagonals of a rectangle are congruent, $AC = 6$. The circumference of a circle of radius 6 is $C = 2\pi r = 2\pi(6) = 12\pi$. Arc SBT is a quarter circle, and thus has length $SBT = \frac{12\pi}{4} = 3\pi$. Finally, we just add: $SA + AC + CT + SBT = 1 + 6 + 3 + 3\pi = 10 + 3\pi$, choice (B).

For more information on this technique, see **Strategy 6** in ***"The 32 Most Effective SAT Math Strategies."***

Remark: Although the above method gives us the correct answer, the method of solution is actually **not** correct. Note that triangle RAC is a right triangle, and therefore should satisfy the Pythagorean Theorem. But $AR^2 + RC^2 = 5^2 + 3^2 = 34$. So AC should be approximately 5.83, and **not** 6. The error that we made was in assuming that $RC = CT$. Note that this error does not matter as far as getting the solution is concerned, but the more advanced student should try to solve this problem the correct way (not on the SAT, but at home for practice).

A correct solution for the advanced student: This is quite difficult, and is only included for completeness. Since the length plus the width of the rectangle is 8, if we let $RC = x$, then $AR = 8 - x$. Recall that AC is congruent to BR, and so $AC = 6$, the radius of the circle. By the Pythagorean Theorem, $x^2 + (8 - x)^2 = 6^2$. So $x^2 + 64 - 16x + x^2 = 36$. Simplifying this gives us $2x^2 - 16x + 28 = 0$. We divide through by 2 to get $x^2 - 8x + 14 = 0$. We can use the quadratic formula to solve for x.

$$x = \frac{8 \pm \sqrt{(-8)^2 - 4(1)(14)}}{2} = \frac{8 \pm \sqrt{8}}{2} = \frac{8 \pm 2\sqrt{2}}{2} = 4 \pm \sqrt{2}$$

We let $RC = x = 4 - \sqrt{2}$ so that $AR = 8 - x = 8 - (4 - \sqrt{2}) = 4 + \sqrt{2}$. We also have $CT = 6 - (4 - \sqrt{2}) = 2 + \sqrt{2}$ and $SA = 6 - (4 + \sqrt{2}) = 2 - \sqrt{2}$. Finally $SA + AC + CT + SBT = (2 - \sqrt{2}) + 6 + (2 + \sqrt{2}) + 3\pi = 10 + 3\pi$, choice (B).(See the original solution above to see where 3π comes from.)

Remark: We could have chosen x to be $4 + \sqrt{2}$. The solution would come out the same. The value of x that we chose matches the picture a little better.

SECTION 9

1. ALGEBRA

Solution by starting with choice (A): Let's start with choice (A) and guess that $m = 4$. We now substitute 4 in for m into the given expression to get $3m - 1 = 3(4) - 1 = 12 - 1 = 11$. Since 11 is greater than 10, the answer is choice (A).

Remark: We started with choice (A) here because the word "greater" is in the problem. Otherwise we would have started with choice (C).

For more information on this technique, see **Strategy 2** in ***"The 32 Most Effective SAT Math Strategies."***

*** Algebraic solution:**

$$3m - 1 > 10$$
$$3m > 11$$
$$m > \frac{11}{3} \sim 3.667$$

So we need to choose a number greater than 3.667. The only number in the answer choices satisfying this requirement is 4, choice (A).

2. ALGEBRA

Solution by picking a number: Let's choose a value for a, say $a = 2$. The given equation then becomes $2 \times k = 2$. So $k = \mathbf{1}$. **Put a nice big, dark circle around 1 so that you can find it easily later.** Now let's substitute 2 in for a into each answer choice.

(A) -2
(B) -1
(C) 0
(D) 1
(E) 2

Since (A), (B), (C), and (E) each came out incorrect, the answer is (D).

Important note: (D) is **not** the correct answer simply because it is equal to 1. It is correct because all 4 of the other choices are **not 1**. **You absolutely must check all five choices!**

For more information on this technique, see **Strategy 4** in ***"The 32 Most Effective SAT Math Strategies."***

* **Algebraic solution:** We divide each side of the given equation by a to get $k = \frac{a}{a} = 1$, choice (D).

3. ALGEBRA

* Since vertical angles are congruent, the angle inside the triangle across from x has measure 80 degrees. Similarly, the angle inside the triangle across from y has measure 70 degrees. So $z = 180 - 80 - 70 = 30$, choice (A).

4. GEOMETRY

Solution by starting with choice (C): Let's start with choice (C) and guess that the direct route is 15 kilometers. Since the scenic route is 5 kilometers longer than the direct route, it follows that the scenic route is 20 kilometers. The round trip is therefore 15 + 20 = 35 kilometers. This is correct. So the answer is choice (C).

For more information on this technique, see **Strategy 1** in ***"The 32 Most Effective SAT Math Strategies."***

* **Algebraic solution:** Let x be the direct route, in kilometers. It follows that the scenic route, in kilometers, is $x + 5$. We are given $x + (x + 5) = 35$. So $2x + 5 = 35$. Subtract 5 from each side of this equation to get $2x = 30$. Finally, divide each side of this last equation by 2 to get $x = 15$, choice (C).

5. PROBABILITY

* The light is <u>not</u> red for 50 seconds out of 80 seconds. Therefore the probability the light will not be red is $\frac{50}{80} = \frac{5}{8}$, choice (B).

6. ALGEBRA

Let y be the increase in heating expenses, and let x be the increase in water-temperature setting.

Solution 1: Since y is proportional to x, $y = kx$ for some constant k. We are given that $y = 24$ when $x = 20$, so that $24 = k(20)$, or $k = \frac{24}{20} = \frac{6}{5}$. So $y = \frac{6x}{5}$. When $x = 15$, we have $y = \frac{6(15)}{5} = 18$, choice (B).

* **Solution 2:** Since y is proportional to x, $\frac{y}{x}$ is a constant. So we get the following ratio: $\frac{24}{20} = \frac{y}{15}$. Cross multiplying gives $360 = 20y$, so that $y = 18$, choice (B).

Solution 3: The graph *of* $y = f(x)$ is a line passing through the points (0,0) and (20,24). The slope of this line is $\frac{24-0}{20-0} = \frac{6}{5}$. Writing the equation of the line in slope-intercept form we have $y = \frac{6}{5}x$. As in solution 1, when $x = 15$, we have $y = \frac{6(15)}{5} = 18$, choice (B).

For a quick lesson on **Direct Variation** see the end of the solution to Problem 5 in Section 2 of Test 5 (pp. 136-137).

7. GEOMETRY AND STATISTICS

* Since the angles of a triangle have measures that sum to 180 degrees, $u + v + w = 180$ and $x + y = 90$. So $u + v + w + x + y = 90 + 180 = 270$. So the average of u, v, w, x, and y is $\frac{u+v+w+x+y}{5} = \frac{270}{5} = 54$, choice (E).

8. ALGEBRA

Solution by starting with choice (C): Let's start with choice (C) and guess that $x = \frac{3}{4} = .75$. Then $x^2 = .5625$ and $x^3 = .421875$. Now simply note that $x^3 < x^2 < x$. So the answer is choice (C).

Remark: The calculations above should be done in your calculator.

For more information on this technique, see **Strategy 1** in ***"The 32 Most Effective SAT Math Strategies."***

* **Direct solution:** We are looking for a number x such that $x^3 < x^2 < x$. The values of x that satisfy this are all x such that $0 < x < 1$. That is we are looking for a positive proper fraction, choice (C).

9. Geometry

* The slope of a line passing through (0,0) and (x,y) is $\frac{y}{x}$. So $\frac{k}{h} = \frac{3}{1} = 3$, choice (A).

10. Algebra

* **Solution by guessing:** Trial and error will lead to $m = -2$ and $k = -22$. So $m - k = -2 - (-22) = -2 + 22 = 20$, choice (E).

For more information on this technique, see **Strategy 3** in ***"The 32 Most Effective SAT Math Strategies."***

Complete algebraic solution: The equation $|m - 3| = 5$ is equivalent to $m - 3 = 5$ or $m - 3 = -5$. So $m = 8$ or $m = -2$. Since we are given $m < 0$, we have $m = -2$.

Similarly, we have the equation $|k + 7| = 15$ is equivalent to $k + 7 = 15$ or $k + 7 = -15$. So $k = 8$ or $k = -22$. Since we are given $k < 0$, we have $k = -22$.

Finally, $m - k = -2 - (-22) = -2 + 22 = 20$, choice (E).

11. Algebra

* 5W flows twice as fast as 10W, thus 4 times as fast as 15W, and so 8 times as fast as 20W, choice (C).

12. Geometry

* Since $PB = 4$, we have $PA = AB = 2$. Since $PR = 6$, $PQ = QR = 3$. Since triangle PAQ is **similar** to triangle PBR, $BR = 2AQ = 2(4) = 8$. So the perimeter of $QABR$ is $QA + AB + BR + RQ = 4 + 2 + 8 + 3 = 17$.

This is answer choice (E).

For more information on **Similar Triangles** see the end of the solution to Problem 10 in Section 2 of Test 2 (p. 47).

13. Functions

* $g(5) = 5^2 + 5 = 25 + 5 = 30$ and $h(4) = 4^2 - 4 = 16 - 4 = 12$. Therefore we have $g(5) - h(4) = 30 - 12 = 18$, choice (D).

14. Functions

Solution by picking a number: Let's choose a value for m, say $m = 5$. Then $h(m + 1) = h(6) = 6^2 - 6 = 36 - 6 =$ **30**. **Put a nice big, dark circle around 30 so that you can find it easily later.** Now let's substitute 5 in for m into each answer choice.

(A) $g(5) = 5^2 + 5 = 25 + 5 = 30$
(B) $g(5) + 1 = 30 + 1 = 31$
(C) $g(5) - 1 = 30 - 1 = 29$
(D) $h(5) + 1 = 5^2 - 5 + 1 = 25 - 5 + 1 = 21$
(E) $h(5) - 1 = 5^2 - 5 - 1 = 25 - 5 - 1 = 19$

Since (B), (C), (D), and (E) each came out incorrect, the answer is choice (A).

Important note: (A) is **not** the correct answer simply because it is equal to 30. It is correct because all 4 of the other choices are **not 30**. **You absolutely must check all five choices!**

For more information on this technique, see **Strategy 4** in ***"The 32 Most Effective SAT Math Strategies."***

* **Direct solution:** We compute $h(m + 1)$ directly.

$$h(m + 1) = (m + 1)^2 - (m + 1) = m^2 + 2m + 1 - m - 1 = m^2 + m = g(m)$$

This is choice (A).

Some computational details:

(1) $(m + 1)^2 = (m + 1)(m + 1) = m^2 + m + m + 1 = m^2 + 2m + 1$.

(2) $-(m + 1) = -m - 1$. Don't forget to distribute the minus sign here!

15. Percents

* Let x be the amount it costs the store to buy a sweater. We are given that 28 is 40 percent more than x. As an equation this is $28 = 1.4x$. So we have that the store's cost is $x = \frac{28}{1.4} = 20$. We must now take 30 percent off of 20. Taking 30 percent **off of** 20 is the same as taking 70 percent **of** 20. So the answer is $.7(20) = 14$, choice (B).

Remark: (1) We change a percent to a decimal by moving the decimal point to the left two places. The number 70 has a "hidden" decimal point after the 0. So 70 percent as a decimal is .70 = .7.

(2) We can also take 30 percent off of 20 by taking 30 percent of 20 and then subtracting this from 20.

So 30 percent of 20 is .3(20) = 6. Thus, 30 percent off of 20 is 20 – 6 = 14.

16. Geometry

* Let's begin by drawing a picture.

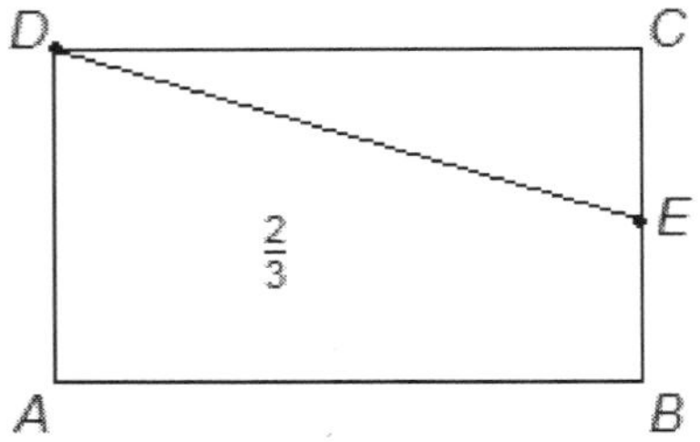

This picture alone really sheds some light on the situation. Let's now chop up our picture into 4 equal parts.

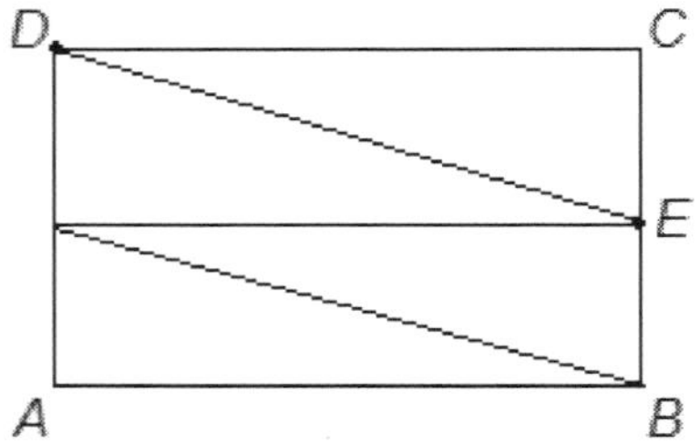

To get the area of one of those pieces simply divide $\frac{2}{3}$ by 3. In our calculator we get

$$.22222222222 \text{ or } \frac{2}{9} \text{ if we change back to a fraction.}$$

This is $\frac{1}{4}$ of the area of the rectangle, so we simply multiply this result by 4 to get the answer. We get $\frac{8}{9}$, choice (C).

For more information on this technique, see **Strategy 9** in ***"The 32 Most Effective SAT Math Strategies."***

Blue Book Test 9 Fully Explained Solutions

Section 2

1. Number Theory

* Let's simply look at each number in set X and see if it is also in set Y.

30 is **not** in set Y 31 is **not** in set Y 32 **is** in set Y 33 **is** in set Y

So there are **Two** numbers in set X that are also in set Y, choice (A).

Remark: The question is asking us to find the **intersection** of X and Y. The **intersection** of sets X and Y is the set $X \cap Y$ consisting of the elements common to both sets.

2. Number Theory

* Linda traveled 20 miles in 1 hour. So Linda's average speed was 20 miles per hour, choice (C).

Notes: Linda travelled twice as far as Peg. So Linda traveled 2(10) = 20 miles. It took Linda half the time, and $\frac{1}{2}$ of 2 is 1.

3. Algebra

Solution by picking a number: Let's choose a value for k, say $k = 4$. It follows that $x = 4(4 - 2) = 4(2) = 8$. So $x + 1 = 9$. **Put a nice big, dark circle around 9 so that you can find it easily later.** Now let's substitute 4 in for k into each answer choice.

(A) 4^2 – 4 = 12
(B) 4^2 – 3*4 = 4
(C) 4^2 – 2*4 + 1 = 9
(D) 4^2 + 2*4 + 1 = 25
(E) 4^2 – 1 = 15.

Since (A), (B), (D), and (E) each came out incorrect, the answer is (C).

Important note: (C) is **not** the correct answer simply because it is equal to 9. It is correct because all 4 of the other choices are **not 9**. **You absolutely must check all five choices!**

For more information on this technique, see **Strategy 4** in ***"The 32 Most Effective SAT Math Strategies."***

* **Algebraic solution:** $x + 1 = k(k - 2) + 1 = k^2 - 2k + 1$, choice (C).

4. GEOMETRY

* The equation $y = ax + b$ is in slope-intercept form. The number b is where the graph hits the y-axis. From the given graph, we see $b = 1$. The graph of the equation $y = 2ax + b$ also hits the y-axis at $b = 1$. Only choices (B) and (C) satisfy this condition. So we can eliminate choices (A), (D), and (E).

Now, the line with equation $y = 2ax + b$ has a slope of $2a$ which is twice the slope of the line with equation $y = ax + b$. This means it rises twice as fast as we move from left to right . So the answer is choice (B).

For more information on this technique, see **Strategy 28** in ***"The 32 Most Effective SAT Math Strategies."***

For more information on **slope** see the notes at the end of Problem 12 in Section 3 of Test 1 (pp. 15-17).

5. GEOMETRY

Solution by plugging in answer choices: This is one of those rare instances where the answer choices are not listed in increasing or decreasing order. So let's just start with one of the easier numbers, say choice (A). So we are guessing that $x = 2$. We need to find the length of the hypotenuse of the triangle. The quickest way to do this is to note that the given triangle is an isosceles right triangle. This is the same as a 45, 45, 90 triangle. By looking at the formula for this special triangle given at the beginning of the SAT math section we see that the hypotenuse has length $2\sqrt{2}$. So the perimeter is $2 + 2 + 2\sqrt{2} = 4 + 2\sqrt{2}$. So choice (A) is the answer.

Note: (1) We could also use the Pythagorean Theorem to find the length of the hypotenuse of the triangle. If we are assuming that $x = 2$, then we have $c^2 = 2^2 + 2^2 = 4 + 4 = 8$. So $c = \sqrt{8}$. This makes the perimeter $4 + \sqrt{8}$. To see that this is equal to $4 + 2\sqrt{2}$, we can just put each of these expressions into our calculator and note that they are both approximately equal to 6.828.

(2) Since we can use a calculator it is not necessary to simplify $\sqrt{8}$. But for those who would like to see it anyway $\sqrt{8} = \sqrt{4 \cdot 2} = \sqrt{4}\sqrt{2} = 2\sqrt{2}$.

Here we have used a slight modification of **Strategy 1** in ***"The 32 Most Effective SAT Math Strategies."***

* **Algebraic solution:** As in the previous solution observe that the given triangle is a 45, 45, 90 triangle. Using the formula for this special triangle given at the beginning of the section, the length of the hypotenuse is $x\sqrt{2}$. Thus, the perimeter of the triangle is $x + x + x\sqrt{2} = 2x + x\sqrt{2}$. So we have $2x + x\sqrt{2} = 4 + 2\sqrt{2}$. So $x = 2$, choice (A).

6. Statistics

* After Sam takes the test there will be 3 students that received a 95 on the test. Let's list the scores of the students in increasing order.

60, 70, 70, 75, 75, 80, 80, 80, 85, 90, 90, 90, 90, 95, 95, 95, 100

Note that 95 appears three times in the list (as opposed to only two times) because that is the score that Sam received. If we strike off numbers in pairs – one from the left and one from the right until we are down to only one number, we will see that only the number 85 is left. So the median is 85, choice (C).

7. Geometry

Solution by picking a number: Let's choose a value for x, say $x = 16$. Then the total capacity of 16 containers of one size is 16 gallons. So each of these containers has a capacity of 1 gallon.

The total capacity of 8 containers of the other size is also 16 gallons. So each of these containers has a capacity of 2 gallons.

So the second container is the larger one and it has a capacity of **2** gallons. **Put a nice big, dark circle around 2 so that you can find it easily later.** Now let's substitute 16 in for *x* into each answer choice.

(A) 64
(B) 32
(C) 8
(D) 2
(E) 1

Since (A), (B), (C), and (E) each came out incorrect, the answer is (D).

For more information on this technique, see **Strategy 4** in ***"The 32 Most Effective SAT Math Strategies."***

*** Algebraic solution (not recommended):** The total capacities of each of the two different containers are $\frac{x}{16}$ and $\frac{x}{8}$. Both of these expressions have the same numerator. Since the second expression has a **smaller** denominator it is a **larger** number. So the answer is choice (D).

8. Geometry

*** Solution by picking a number:** Let's choose a value for the slope of one side of the rectangle, say $m = 1$. The side parallel to this side also has slope 1. The other sides are perpendicular to these sides, and therefore have slopes that are the negative reciprocal of 1. That is the other two sides each have a slope of -1. So the product of the slopes of all four sides of the rectangle is (1)(1)(-1)(-1) = 1, choice (D).

Notes: (1) We can choose any side of the rectangle, and choose any value for the slope of that side except zero. If one of the sides had a slope of zero, then the sides would be parallel to the axes.

(2) Perpendicular lines have slopes that are negative reciprocals of each other. The negative reciprocal of $1 = \frac{1}{1}$ is $\frac{-1}{1} = -1$.

(3) It might be helpful to draw a picture here.

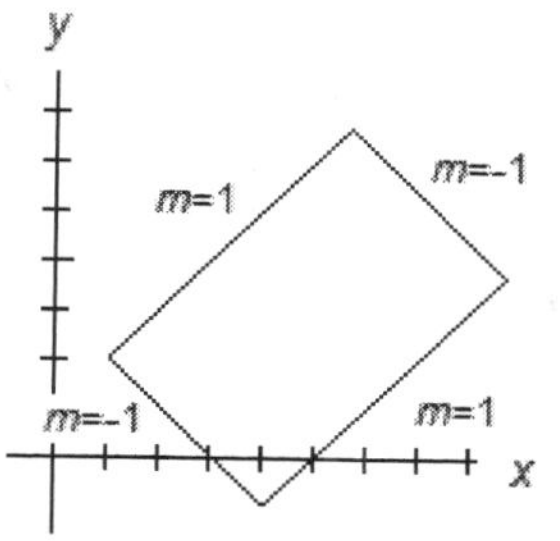

Geometric solution: If the slope of one side of the rectangle is m (where m is any nonzero number), then the slopes of the other three sides are m, $\frac{-1}{m}$, and $\frac{-1}{m}$. So the product of the slopes of all four sides of the rectangle is $(m)(m)(\frac{-1}{m})(\frac{-1}{m}) = 1$, choice (D).

9. Number Theory

* There are 60 minutes in an hour. So 60 – 20 = 40 of the minutes were not commercials. Therefore the fraction of the hour-long program that was not commercials is $\frac{40}{60}$ = **2/3**.

Note: We can also grid in one of the decimals **.666** or **.667**.

10. Number Theory

* If we let x be the number, then the product of 0.3 and the number is $.3x$. So we want to solve the equation $.3x = 1$. We divide each side of this equation by .3 to get $x = \frac{1}{.3} = 3.333333...$

So we can grid in the decimal **3.33** or the fraction **10/3**.

Remarks: (1) The word **product** means to multiply. So the product of 0.3 and x is $.3x$.

(2) We can get the answer in our TI-84 calculator by typing

1/.3 MATH ENTER ENTER.

(3) We could also write .3 as the fraction $\frac{3}{10}$. The equation then becomes $\frac{3}{10}x = 1$. We then multiply each side of this equation by the reciprocal of $\frac{3}{10}$ which is $\frac{10}{3}$ to get $x = (1)(\frac{10}{3})$ = **10/3**.

11. ALGEBRA

* We are given that $x = 10$, $y = 3$, and $z = 5$. Therefore we have

$$x^y - z^y = 10^3 - 5^3 = 1000 - 125 = \mathbf{875}.$$

12. GEOMETRY

* **Solution by guessing:** Let's take a guess for *UT*, say $UT = 3$. Since *URST* is a square, $ST = UT = 3$. Also, $PT = PU + UT = 5 + 3 = 8$. So the area of *PQST* is $A = 8 \cdot 3 = 24$. Since 24 is more than 10 but less than 30 we can grid in **3**.

Below is a picture of what has just been described.

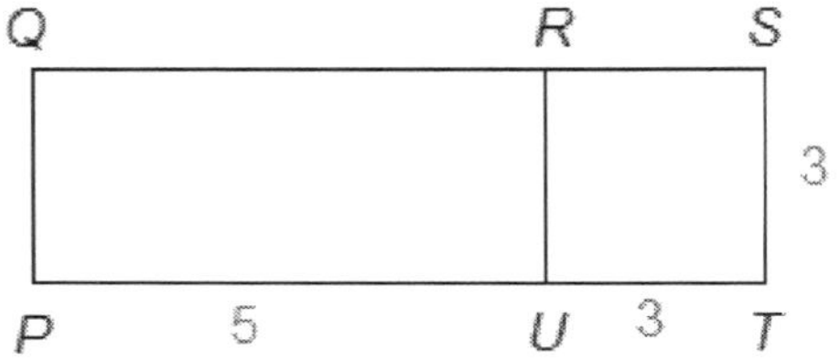

For more information on this technique, see **Strategy 3** in ***"The 32 Most Effective SAT Math Strategies."***

Algebraic solution: Let $x = UT$. Then $ST = x$, and $PT = PU + PT = 5 + x$. The area of *PQST* is then $A = x(5 + x) = 5x + x^2 = x^2 + 5x$. We are told that

$$10 < x^2 + 5x < 30.$$

At this point it is probably best to go back to the guessing strategy. For example, if we let $x = 3$, we have $x^2 + 5x = 3^2 + 5(3) = 9 + 15 = 24$. Since 24 is more than 10 but less than 30 we can grid in **3**.

Remark: Solving the inequality $10 < x^2 + 5x < 30$ would require solving two separate quadratic inequalities followed by some further analysis. This would be time consuming and more difficult than anything actually required on the SAT. Students taking precalculus or a higher level math class may want to solve this inequality for practice, but there is no benefit in doing so for SAT preparation.

13. Number Theory

Solution by guessing: Let's take a guess for the number of balloons that were in the box. Note that the number of balloons must be divisible by 3 and substantially greater than 18. Let's guess that the number of balloons in the box was 60. Since $\frac{1}{3}$ of the balloons were red, there were 20 red balloons. Since there were half as many green balloons as red ones, there were 10 green balloons. So the total number of balloons was $20 + 10 + 18 = 48$, too small.

So let's try less balloons, say 48. Then $\frac{1}{3}(48) = 16$ of the balloons were red and so $\frac{1}{2}(16) = 8$ of the balloons were green. This gives us that there are a total of $16 + 8 + 18 = 42$ balloons. This is still too small but we're heading in the right direction.

Let's try 36 balloons. Then $\frac{1}{3}(36) = 12$ of the balloons were red and so $\frac{1}{2}(12) = 6$ of the balloons were green. This gives a total of $12 + 6 + 18 = 36$ balloons. This is correct. So the answer is **36**.

For more information on this technique, see **Strategy 3** in ***"The 32 Most Effective SAT Math Strategies."***

* **Algebraic solution:** Let x be the total number of balloons in the box. Then $\frac{1}{3}x + \frac{1}{2}(\frac{1}{3}x) + 18 = x$. Let's multiply each side of this equation by 6 to eliminate the denominators. So $2x + x + 108 = 6x$, or $3x + 108 = 6x$. Subtracting $3x$ from each side of this equation gives us $108 = 3x$. Now divide each side by 3 to get $36 = x$. So we can grid in **36**.

14. Counting and Geometry

Let's draw a picture

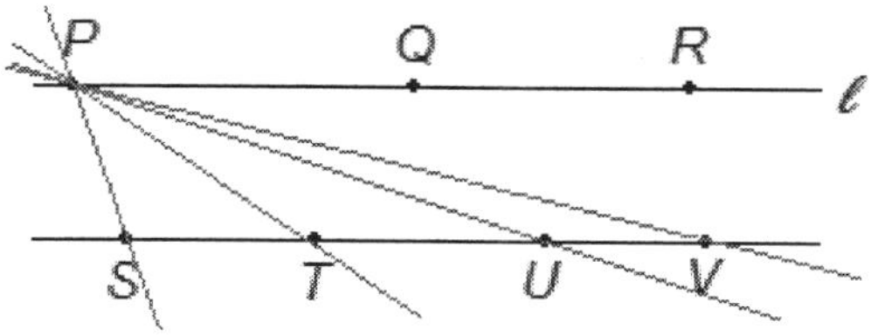

In the figure above we drew the three distinct points on line ℓ, the four distinct points on the line parallel to line ℓ, and all the different lines that contain P and exactly one of the other points. Note that there are 4 such lines. Similarly, there are 4 such lines containing Q and exactly one of the other points. And there are 4 such lines containing R and exactly one of the other points. This gives $4 + 4 + 4 =$ **12** such lines.

For more information on this technique, see **Strategy 9** in ***"The 32 Most Effective SAT Math Strategies."***

* **Quick solution:** There are 3 ways to choose one point from line ℓ and 4 ways to choose one point from the line parallel to line ℓ. By the counting principle we get $(3)(4) =$ **12**.

Remark: The **counting principle** says that if one event is followed by a second independent event, the number of possibilities is multiplied.

15. Algebra

***Solution by guessing:** First note that $2^7 = 128$. Now, let's take a guess for x, say $x = 3$. Then we have

$$2^x + 2^x + 2^x + 2^x = 2^3 + 2^3 + 2^3 + 2^3 = 8 + 8 + 8 + 8 = 32.$$

This is too small. So let's take a larger guess, say $x = 5$. Then we have

$$2^x + 2^x + 2^x + 2^x = 2^5 + 2^5 + 2^5 + 2^5 = 32 + 32 + 32 + 32 = 128.$$

This is correct. So the answer is **5**.

Algebraic solution: $2^x + 2^x + 2^x + 2^x = 4(2^x) = 2^2 \cdot 2^x = 2^{2+x}$. So $2 + x = 7$, and therefore $x = 7 - 2 =$ **5**.

Notes: (1) For the first equality note that adding the same expression to itself 4 times is the same as multiplying that expression by 4.

(2) For the second equality we rewrote 4 as 2^2 to get a common base.

(3) For the third equality we used a basic law of exponents.

(4) From the first three notes we see that the given equation is equivalent to the equation $2^{2+x} = 2^7$. Since the bases here are equal we can set the exponents equal to each other.

For a review of the **Laws of Exponents** used here see the end of the solution to Problem 8 in Section 8 of Test 1 (p. 35).

16. Statistics

*** Solution by changing averages to sums:** We use the formula

Sum = Average · Number.

Since the **Average** of the integers is 15, and the **Number** of things we are averaging is 5, the **Sum** of the integers is (15)(5) = 75.

Now, to make one of the integers as large as possible we will make the other 4 as small as possible. The smallest positive integer is 1, so we make 4 of the integers 1. Thus the 5th integer is 75 – 1 – 1 – 1 – 1 = **71**.

For more information on this technique, see **Strategy 20** in ***"The 32 Most Effective SAT Math Strategies."***

17. Number Theory

* Alice first retraces her 10 steps to get back to where she started. It then takes her 7 more steps to get to Alice. So Alice requires 7 steps for 10 of Corinne's steps. Therefore each of Alice's steps is $\frac{10}{7}$ of each of Corinne's steps. So we can grid in **10/7**, **1.42**, or **1.43**.

Remark: Many students get confused as to whether the answer should be $\frac{10}{7}$ or $\frac{7}{10}$. To help you decide, just think about if Alice's steps should be bigger or smaller than Corinne's. Well it takes Alice less steps to get to the same position as Corinne. So Alice's steps are bigger. The answer should therefore be greater than 1. In other words, the numerator should be larger than the denominator.

18. Functions

* $f(2m) = (2m)^2 + 18 = 4m^2 + 18$ and $2f(m) = 2(m^2 + 18) = 2m^2 + 36$. So $4m^2 + 18 = 2m^2 + 36$. We now subtract $2m^2$ from each side of this equation to get $2m^2 + 18 = 36$. Subtract 18 from each side of this new equation to get $2m^2 = 18$. Now divide by 2 to get $m^2 = 9$. Finally $m =$ **3**.

Remark: The equation $m^2 = 9$ actually has two solutions: $m = 3$, $m = -3$. But we take $m = 3$ because the question says m is a positive number. Also, you can't grid in a negative number so the answer to a grid in question always has to be positive.

SECTION 5

1. NUMBER THEORY

* Since we already have 4 terms of the sequence, we just need to apply the given rule twice. We add 1 to 30 to get 31. We then double 31 to get 62. So the fifth term of the sequence is 62.

We now add 1 to 62 to get 63. We then double 63 to get 126. So the sixth term of the sequence is 126, choice (E).

Note:

$2(2 + 1) = 2(3) = 6$
$2(6 + 1) = 2(7) = 14$
$2(14 + 1) = 2(15) = 30$
$2(30 + 1) = 2(31) = 62$
$2(62 + 1) = 2(63) = 126$

2. ALGEBRA

Solution by picking numbers: We choose values for a, x, and y that satisfy the two given equations. Since $ax = 15$, we can let $a = 5$ and $x = 3$. Now since $a(x + y) = 45$, we have $5(3 + y) = 45$. So y must be 6 (see the Remark below if you require more explanation). Thus, $ay = 5\cdot 6 = 30$, choice (E).

Remarks: (1) To see that y must be 6, we need to solve the equation $5(3 + y) = 45$. We can solve this *informally* by noting that since $5\cdot 9 = 45$, we must have $3 + y = 9$. Now note that since $3 + 6 = 9$, y must be 6.

(2) We can also solve the equation $5(3 + y) = 45$ formally by first dividing each side of the equation by 5 to get $3 + y = 9$, and then subtracting 3 from each side of this equation to get $y = 6$.

(3) For one other formal solution to $5(3 + y) = 45$, we can first distribute the 5 to get $15 + 5y = 45$. We then subtract 15 from each side of this equation to get $5y = 30$. Finally, we divide each side of this equation by 5 to get $y = 6$.

(4) Once we choose values for two of the variables, the third is determined. It is easiest to choose values for a and x first, and then figure out what y must be.

(5) Many other choices for a and x will work. For example, if we choose the values $a = 15$, $x = 1$, then it follows that $y = 2$, and we have $ay = 30$ as before.

For more information on this technique, see **Strategy 4** in ***"The 32 Most Effective SAT Math Strategies."***

* **Algebraic solution:** $a(x + y) = ax + ay = 15 + ay$. Since $a(x + y) = 45$, we have $15 + ay = 45$. Subtracting 15 from each side of this equation gives $ay = 45 - 15 = 30$, choice (E).

3. NUMBER THEORY

* The middle graph is in miles per hour. We therefore focus our attention on the middle graph and ignore the other two. The length of the interval from 30 to 60 is $60 - 30 = 30$. Since there are 4 subintervals between 30 and 60, the length of each subinterval is $\frac{30}{4} = 7.5$. Therefore the given needle position indicates that the speed is $30 + 7.5 = 37.5$ miles per hour, choice (B).

Note about intervals and subintervals: If $a < b$, the length of the interval from a to b is $b - a$. If there are n subintervals between a and b, the length of each subinterval is $\frac{b-a}{n}$.

4. COUNTING

* **Solution by listing:** We list all the possibilities.

456 465 546 564 645 654

We can easily see that there are 6 integers, choice (C).

For more information on this technique, see **Strategy 21** in ***"The 32 Most Effective SAT Math Strategies."***

Solution using the counting principle: There are 3 possible integers for the ones place. After placing one of these integers in the ones place, there are 2 integers left for the tens place. Finally, there is 1 integer left for the hundreds place. By the counting principle we get $(3)(2)(1) = \mathbf{6}$ arrangements, choice (C).

Remark: The **counting principle** says that if one event is followed by a second independent event, the number of possibilities is multiplied.

* **Solution using permutations:** There are 3 integers, and we are arranging all 3 of them. So there are ${}_3P_3 = 3! = 1 \cdot 2 \cdot 3 = 6$ arrangements, choice (C).

For more information on **permutations** see Problem 14 from Section 8 of Test 1 (p. 38)

5. GEOMETRY

* There are 3 rectangular faces and 2 triangular faces. Therefore the total surface area of the figure is $3r + 2t$, choice (B).

Note: To compute the surface area of a three-dimensional figure we simply add up the areas of the faces that make up the figure. In this case we have $r + r + r + t + t = 3r + 2t$.

6. NUMBER THEORY

* **Solution by starting with choice (C):** Let's start with choice (C) and guess that $n = 3$. We then have $\frac{n+1}{2^n} = \frac{3+1}{2^3} = \frac{4}{8} = \frac{1}{2}$. So the answer is (C).

For more information on this technique, see **Strategy 1** in ***"The 32 Most Effective SAT Math Strategies."***

7. STATISTICS

* **Solution by converting averages to sums:** We change the average to a sum using the formula

Sum = Average · Number

The **Average** is given to be p, and the **Number** is given to be 14. Therefore the **Sum** is $(p)(14) = 14p$, choice (E).

For more information on this technique, see **Strategy 20** in ***"The 32 Most Effective SAT Math Strategies."***

8. Geometry

* t is the average of the y-coordinates of A and C. So $t = \frac{-1+5}{2} = \frac{4}{2} = 2$, choice ©.

The **midpoint** of a line segment is the point on the segment midway between the two endpoints of the segment.

9. Algebra

* When a product is equal to zero, one of the factors **must** be zero. So we must have $k = 0$, $2x + 3 = 0$, or $x - 1 = 0$.

If $x - 1 = 0$, then $x = 1$. But we are given that $x > 1$. So $x - 1 \neq 0$.

If $2x + 3 = 0$, then $2x = -3$, and so $x = \frac{-3}{2}$. Again, $x > 1$, so $2x + 3 \neq 0$.

So we must have $k = 0$, choice (B).

10. Logic

* The statement "All men in the Williams family are over six feet tall" is equivalent to the **conditional** statement "If you are a man in the Williams family, then you are over six feet tall." The **contrapositive** of this statement is "If you are under six feet tall, then you are not a man in the William's family." This last statement is equivalent to "No man under six feet tall is a member of the William's family," choice (A).

The Contrapositive

A statement of the form "if p, then q" is known as a **conditional** statement. An example of such a statement is "If you are a man in the Williams family, then you are over six feet tall." Another common way to say this is "All men in the Williams family are over six feet tall." There are 3 other statements that often come up in association with a conditional statement. Let's use the example above to illustrate.

Conditional: If you are a man in the Williams family, then you are over six feet tall.

Converse: If you are over six feet tall, then you are a man in the William's family.

Inverse: If you are not a man in the William's family, then you are not over six feet tall.

Contrapositive: If you are not over six feet tall, then you are not a man in the William's family.

The most important thing to know for the SAT is that the contrapositive is logically equivalent to the original conditional statement! The converse and inverse are not.

11. GEOMETRY

Solution by starting with choice (C): The circumference of a circle is $C = 2\pi r$. Let's start with choice (C) as our first guess. If $r = 1$, then we have $C = 2\pi(1) = 2\pi$. Since this is too big we can eliminate choices (C), (D), and (E). Let's try choice (B) next. If $r = \frac{1}{2}$, then $C = 2\pi(\frac{1}{2}) = \pi$. So the answer is choice (B).

For more information on this technique, see **Strategy 1** in ***"The 32 Most Effective SAT Math Strategies."***

* **Algebraic solution:** We use the circumference formula $C = 2\pi r$, and substitute π in for C.

$$C = 2\pi r$$

$$\pi = 2\pi r$$

$$\frac{\pi}{2\pi} = r$$

So we have $\frac{1}{2} = r$, and the answer is choice (B).

12. ALGEBRA

Solution 1: Since y is directly proportional to x^2, $y = kx^2$ for some constant k. We are given that $y = \frac{1}{8}$ when $x = \frac{1}{2}$, so that $\frac{1}{8} = k(\frac{1}{2})^2$. Therefore $\frac{1}{8} = k(\frac{1}{4})$. Multiplying each side of this equation by 8 gives us that $1 = 2k$, so that $k = \frac{1}{2}$. So $y = \frac{1}{2}x^2$. When $y = \frac{9}{2}$, we have $\frac{9}{2} = \frac{1}{2}x^2$ so that $9 = x^2$, and $x = 3$, choice (D).

* **Solution 2:** Since y is directly proportional to x^2, $\frac{y}{x^2}$ is a constant. So we get the following ratio: $\frac{\frac{1}{8}}{\left(\frac{1}{2}\right)^2} = \frac{\frac{9}{2}}{x^2}$. Cross multiplying gives $\frac{1}{8}x^2 = \frac{9}{2}(\frac{1}{2})^2$. So $\frac{1}{8}x^2 = \frac{9}{8}$. Multiply each side of this equation by 8 to get $x^2 = 9$. So $x = 3$, choice (D).

Note: The equation $x^2 = 9$ actually has two solutions. The **square root property** says that $x = 3$ or $x = -3$. But we are being asked for the positive value of x in the question.

For a quick lesson on **Direct Variation** see the end of the solution to Problem 5 in Section 2 of Test 5 (pp. 136-137).

13. Algebra

Solution by picking numbers: Let's choose a value for x, say $x = 1$. Then

$6u = 4(1) = 4$, so that $u = \frac{4}{6} \sim .66667$.

$5v = 4(1) = 4$, so that $v = \frac{4}{5} = .8$.

$7w = 4(1) = 4$, so that $w = \frac{4}{7} \sim .5714$.

We see that $w < u < v < x$, choice (D).

For more information on this technique, see **Strategy 4** in ***"The 32 Most Effective SAT Math Strategies."***

* **Quick solution:** Since $4 < 5 < 6 < 7$, we have $w < u < v < x$, choice (D).

Remark: This is tricky to see. If you don't see why the inequalities seem to be going the wrong way, look at the solution by picking numbers. This should help you to understand what is happening.

14. Algebra and Functions

* We begin by setting $h(t)$ equal to -60 and solving for t.

$$h(t) = -60$$
$$2(t^3 - 3) = -60$$
$$t^3 - 3 = -30$$
$$t^3 = -27$$
$$t = -3$$

Finally, we have $2 - 3t = 2 - 3(-3) = 2 + 9 = 11$, choice (B).

15. Number Theory

Solution by picking numbers: Let's choose values for x and y, say $x = 6$ and $y = 10$. Then $xy = 60$ which is divisible by 15. So we **cannot** eliminate I. We have $3x + 5y = 3(6) + 5(10) = 18 + 50 = 68$ which is **not** divisible by 15. So we can eliminate II. Finally, $5x + 3y = 5(6) + 3(10) = 30 + 30 = 60$. So we **cannot** eliminate III.

Since we eliminated II, we can eliminate choices (C) and (E). A good guess at this point would be choice (D).

The answer is in fact choice (D).

For more information on this technique, see **Strategy 4** in ***"The 32 Most Effective SAT Math Strategies."***

Notes: (1) At this point you may want to choose new values for x and y to see if I and III still work. This will give more evidence to support that the answer is choice (D).

(2) Any choice that you make for x and y will work for I and III. Unfortunately, this only provides evidence that choice (D) is the correct answer. There is still a small chance we could be wrong.

(3) This particular method of solution does not guarantee the correct answer for this problem (but it gives a very good guess which turns out to be correct).

*** Direct solution:** Since x is divisible by 3 and y is divisible by 5, xy is divisible by both 3 and 5. Therefore xy is divisible by 15. So I works.

Since x is divisible by 3, $5x$ is divisible by 15. Since y is divisible by 5, $3y$ is divisible by 15. Since both $5x$ and $3y$ are divisible by 15, $5x + 3y$ is divisible by 15. So III works.

There is no reason to believe that $3x + 5y$ should always be divisible by 15. In fact (as we've seen in the first solution), if we let $x = 6$ and $y = 10$ we see that $3x + 5y$ is **not** divisible by 15.

So the answer is choice (D).

16. Geometry

Solution by picking a number: Let's choose a value for y, say $y = 120$. We get the following picture.

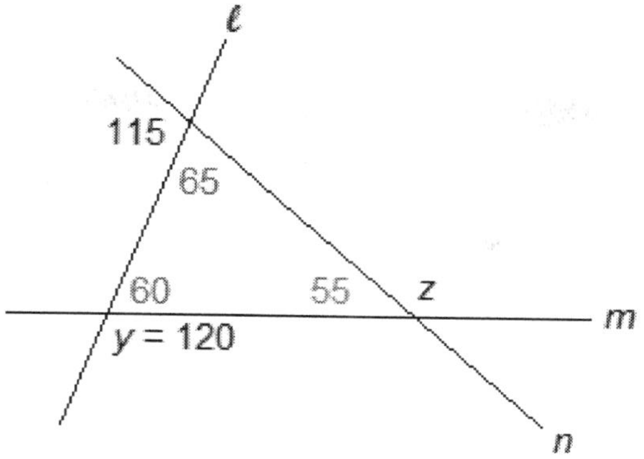

Note that we get the angles inside the triangle from 180 – 120 = 60, 180 – 115 = 65, and then 180 – 60 – 65 = 55. So $z = 180 - 55 = 125$.

Finally, $y + z = 120 + 125 = 245$, choice (E).

For more information on this technique, see **Strategy 4** in ***"The 32 Most Effective SAT Math Strategies."***

*** Geometric solution:** Let's label the angles inside the triangle.

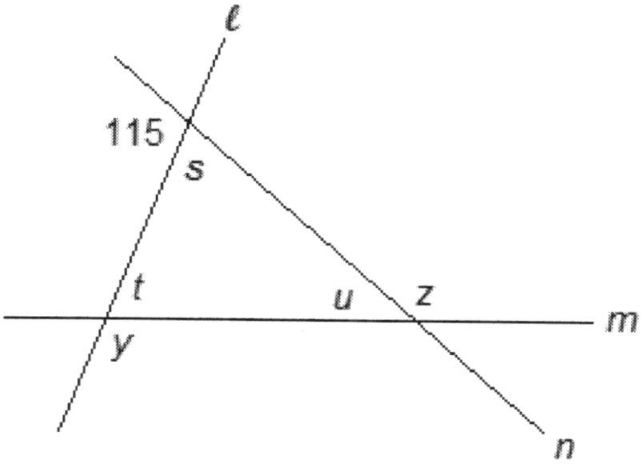

We now use the fact that the measure of an exterior angle to a triangle is the sum of the measures of the opposite interior angles of the triangle. So

$$y = s + u \text{ and } z = s + t. \text{ So } y + z = s + (s + t + u) = 65 + 180 = 245.$$

Therefore the answer is choice (E).

Notes: (1) $s = 180 - 115 = 65$.

(2) Since s, t, and u are the three measures of the angles of a triangle, we have $s + t + u = 180$.

For more information on this technique, see **Strategy 30** in ***"The 32 Most Effective SAT Math Strategies."***

17. Number Theory

* If n is the least of the three integers, then the integers are n, $n + 2$, and $n + 4$. The sum of these integers is $n + (n + 2) + (n + 4) = 3n + 6$. So we have $3n + 6 = 111$, choice (D).

For the definition of **consecutive odd integers** see the end of the solution to Problem 16 in Section 2 of Test 5 (p. 143).

18. Geometry

* We are given that $18(2) + 18(b) = 45$. So $36 + 18b = 45$. Subtracting 36 from each side of this equation yields $18b = 45 - 36 = 9$. So $b = \frac{9}{18} = \frac{1}{2}$.

Now, to get the <u>degree</u> measure of each of the arcs of length b note that b is $\frac{1}{90}$th of the circle (see Remarks below for further explanation). Since there are 360 degrees in a circle, this degree measure is $\frac{360}{90} = 4$, choice (A).

Remarks: (1) To see that an arc of length b is $\frac{1}{90}$th of the circle, note that $45 \div \frac{1}{2} = 45 \cdot 2 = 90$.

(2) Once we have that $b = \frac{1}{2}$, we can also find the degree measure of an arc of length b by setting up the following ratio:

$$\frac{x}{360} = \frac{\frac{1}{2}}{45}$$

$$45x = 180$$

$$x = \frac{180}{45} = 4$$

19. Statistics

Solution by picking a number: Let's let $n = 1$. Note that 10 percent of 300 is $.1(300) = 30$. Since Andrew paid \$300 this year, 1 year from now he will pay \$330. So we have $330 = 300x^1$. Dividing eah side of this equation by 300 gives us $x = x^1 = \frac{330}{300} = 1.1$, choice (C).

For more information on this technique, see **Strategy 4** in ***"The 32 Most Effective SAT Math Strategies."***

*** Direct solution (not recommended):** 10 percent as a decimal is .1. So to increase a number by 10% we multiply by 1 + .1 = 1.1. If we multiply 300 by 1.1 *n* times, we get $300(1.1)^n$. So $x = 1.1$, choice (C).

20. Geometry

* Note that the quadrilateral is a rhombus. Let's add more information to the picture. Let's choose a value for *AB*, say *AB* = 2.

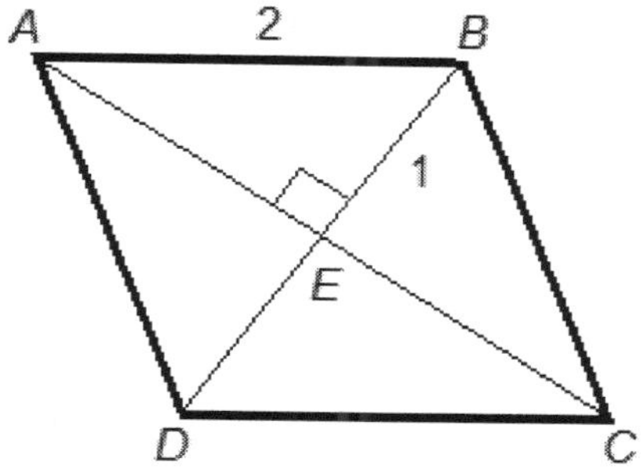

Since *BD* = *AB*, *BD* = 2 as well. In a rhombus, the diagonals bisect each other, and are perpendicular to each other. It follows that *BE* = 1 and angle *AEB* is a right angle. So triangle *AEB* is a 30, 60, 90 triangle, and $AE = \sqrt{3}$. Thus, $AC = 2\sqrt{3}$, and it follows that $\frac{AC}{BD} = \frac{2\sqrt{3}}{2} = \frac{\sqrt{3}}{1}$. So the answer is choice (B).

Note: If we let *BE* = *x*, then *BD* = 2*x*, and by a similar argument to the solution above *AB*= 2*x* and $AC = 2x\sqrt{3}$. So $\frac{AC}{BD} = \frac{2x\sqrt{3}}{2x} = \frac{\sqrt{3}}{1}$, as before.

SECTION 8

1. ALGEBRA

Solution by starting with choice (C): Let's start with choice (C) and guess that $k = 10$. We now substitute 10 in for k into the right hand side of the given equation to get $100(6k + 7) = 100(6 \cdot 10 + 7) = 100(67) = 6700$. Since this is equal to the left hand side of the equation, the answer is (C).

For more information on this technique, see **Strategy 1** in ***"The 32 Most Effective SAT Math Strategies."***

* **Algebraic solution 1:** We divide each side of the given equation by 100 to get $67 = 6k + 7$. Now subtract 7 from each side of this equation to get $60 = 6k$. Finally, divide each side of this equation by 6 to get $k = \frac{60}{6} = 10$, choice (C)

Algebraic solution 2: Distribute on the right hand side of the given equation to get $6700 = 600k + 700$. Now subtract 700 from each side of this equation to get $6000 = 600k$. Finally, divide each side of this equation by 600 to get $k = \frac{6000}{600} = 10$, choice (C).

2. NUMBER THEORY

Solution by starting with choice (C): Let's start with choice (C) and guess that $n = -3$. Then 3 more than n is 0 which is **not** a negative number. So we can eliminate choices (C), (D), and (E).

Let's try choice (B) next and guess that $n = -4$. Then 3 more than n is -1 which is a negative number, and 5 more than n is 1 which is a positive number. So the answer is choice (B).

For more information on this technique, see **Strategy 1** in ***"The 32 Most Effective SAT Math Strategies."***

* **Algebraic solution:** We are given $n + 3 < 0$ and $n + 5 > 0$. Subtracting 3 from each side of the first inequality gives $n < -3$. Subtracting 5 from each side of the second inequality gives $n > -5$. So we are looking for a value of n such that $-5 < n < -3$. Since $n = -4$ satisfies this inequality, the answer is choice (B).

3. Geometry

* Simply note that $z = \frac{1}{2}x + \frac{1}{2}y = \frac{1}{2}(70) + \frac{1}{2}(40) = 35 + 20 = 55$, choice (E).

4. Probability

* **Solution by starting with choice (C):** Let's start with choice (C) and guess that there are 52 pieces of fruit in the basket. Then the number of apples in the basket is $\frac{2}{5}(52) = 20.8$. Since 20.8 is not an integer, there cannot be 52 pieces of fruit in the basket and the answer is choice (C).

* **Quick solution:** The total number of pieces of fruit must be a multiple of 5. So the answer is 52, choice (C).

Remark: Here we have used the **Simple Probability Principle** which says the following. To compute a simple probability where all outcomes are equally likely, divide the number of "successes" by the total number of outcomes.

5. Geometry

* Since the square has sides of length 3, the **perimeter** of the square is $4(3) = 12$. Since the triangle is equilateral and has perimeter equal to the perimeter of the square, one side of the triangle has length $\frac{12}{3} = 4$, choice (C).

6. Number Theory

* **Solution by picking a number:** Let's choose a value for k, say $k = 3$, and let's substitute $x = -1$ and $k = 3$ into each answer choice.

(A) $2(3)(-1) = -6$
(B) $4(3)(-1)^2 = 12$
(C) $6(3)(-1)^3 = -18$
(D) $8(3)(-1)^4 = 24$
(E) $10(3)(-1)^5 = -30$.

We see that the greatest value is choice (D).

7. Data Interpretation

* Let's let s, c, and r represent the speeds at which Josephine swims, cycles, and runs, respectively. Since she runs faster than she swims, we have $r > s$. Since she cycles faster than she runs, we have $c > r$. So we have $s < r < c$. Note that s, r, and c are the slopes of the line segments corresponding to swimming, cycling and running. Since swimming is first, the graph should start with the line segment with the smallest slope. Since cycling is second, the second line segment should have the largest slope. This only happens in choice (E).

8. Algebra

* $(\sqrt{6},k)$ satisfies both equations. From the first equation we see that $k = (\sqrt{6})^2 - 7 = 6 - 7 = -1$. From the second equation $k = -(\sqrt{6})^2 + j = -6 + j$. So $-1 = -6 + j$. Therefore $j = -1 + 6 = 5$, choice (A).

9. Algebra

Solution by starting with choice (C): Let's start with choice (C) and guess that a possible value for x is $x = 6$. Then $|2 - x| = |2 - 6| = |-4| = 4$. This is too big, so we can eliminate choice (C).

Let's try choice (A) next. Then $|2 - x| = |2 - 4| = |-2| = 2$. Since $2 < 3$, the answer is choice (A).

For more information on this technique, see **Strategy 1** in ***"The 32 Most Effective SAT Math Strategies."***

* **Algebraic solution:** The absolute value inequality is equivalent to

$$-3 < 2 - x < 3$$
$$-5 < -x < 1$$
$$5 > x > -1$$

So $-1 < x < 5$. The only number in the answer choices satisfying this inequality is choice (A).

10. Algebra

* A **regular** polygon is a polygon with all sides equal in length, and all angles equal in measure.

The total number of degrees in the interior of an n-sided polygon is $(n-2) \cdot 180$. For example, a five-sided polygon (or pentagon) has

$$(5-2) \cdot 180 = 3 \cdot 180 = 540 \text{ degrees}$$

in its interior. Therefore each angle of a regular pentagon has

$$\frac{540}{5} = 108 \text{ degrees.}$$

Finally, $x = 180 - 108 = 72$, choice (C).

Remark: For those of us that do not like to memorize formulas, there is a quick visual way to determine the total number of degrees in the interior of an n-sided polygon. Simply split the polygon up into triangles and quadrilaterals by drawing nonintersecting line segments between vertices. Then add 180 degrees for each triangle and 360 degrees for each quadrilateral. For example, here is one way to do it for a pentagon.

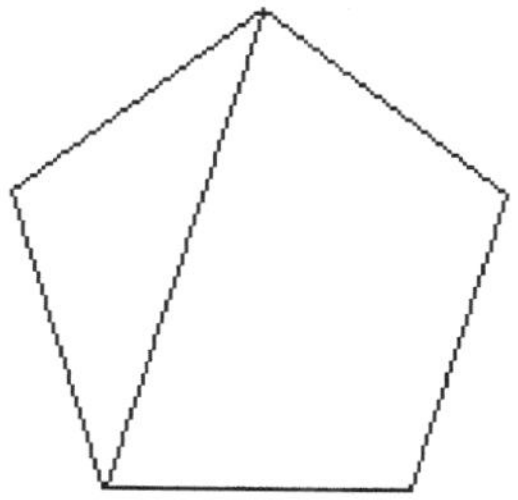

Since the pentagon has been split up into 1 triangle and 1 quadrilateral, the pentagon has 180 + 360 = **540** degrees. This is the same number we got from the formula.

11. Number Theory

Solution by starting with choice (C): Let's start with choice (C) and guess that the length of the tool is 16 inches. It follows that the length of the drawing of the tool is $\frac{3}{8}(16) = 6$. This is correct. So the answer is (C).

For more information on this technique, see **Strategy 1** in ***"The 32 Most Effective SAT Math Strategies."***

*** Algebraic solution:** Let x be the length of the tool and let d be the length of the drawing of the tool. We are given that $d = \frac{3}{8}x$, and $d = 6$. So $6 = \frac{3}{8}x$. We can now solve this equation by multiplying each side of the equation by $\frac{8}{3}$. So $x = \frac{8}{3}(6) = 16$, choice (C).

12. Number Theory

Solution by picking a number: Let's choose a value for x, say $x = 1$. Then $\frac{x+3}{2} = \frac{1+3}{2} = \frac{4}{2} = 2$, so that x satisfies the given condition. Now let's check whether each answer choice is true or false.

(A) False
(B) True
(C) False
(D) False
(E) True

So we can eliminate choices (A), (C), and (D).

Now, note that we can also use $x = -1$. Indeed, $\frac{-1+3}{2} = \frac{-2}{2} = -1$. So we can eliminate choice (B), and the answer is choice (E).

*** Direct solution:** In order for $\frac{x+3}{2}$ to be an integer, $x + 3$ must be even. So x must be odd, choice (E).

Remark: The following describes what happens when you add and multiply various combinations of even and odd integers.

$$\begin{array}{ll} e+e=e & ee=e \\ e+o=o & eo=e \\ o+e=o & oe=e \\ o+o=e & oo=o \end{array}$$

For example, the sum of an even and an odd integer is odd ($e + o = o$).

13. Geometry

* The coordinates of point Q are (3,3) and the coordinates of point S are (11,5). Therefore the slope of line QS is $\frac{5-3}{11-3} = \frac{2}{8} = \frac{1}{4}$, choice (B).

For more information on this technique, see **Strategy 28** in ***"The 32 Most Effective SAT Math Strategies."***

Note: Slope = $m = \frac{\text{rise}}{\text{run}} = \frac{y_2 - y_1}{x_2 - x_1}$

14. Number Theory

Solution by guessing: Let's guess values for n and then check what $n + 3$ and $n + 10$ are beginning with $n = 2$.

$n = 2$	$n + 3 = 5$	$n + 10 = 12$
$n = 3$	$n + 3 = 6$	$n + 10 = 13$
$n = 4$	$n + 3 = 7$	$n + 10 = 14$

We see that when $n = 4$, we have $n + 3$ and $n + 10$ both divisible by 7. So $p = 7$, choice (B).

For more information on this technique, see **Strategy 1** in ***"The 32 Most Effective SAT Math Strategies."***

15. Geometry

* Point D is furthest from point Y because $\overline{YD}$ is the diagonal of the bottom square. Point D is also furthest from point X because $\overline{XD}$ is the long diagonal of the cube. Therefore $\angle XDY$ has the least measure, choice (D).

16. Algebra

* $x^2y - xy^2 = xy(x - y) = (7)(5) = 35$, choice (D).

BLUE BOOK TEST 10 FULLY EXPLAINED SOLUTIONS

SECTION 2

1. ALGEBRA

* The original price of each pencil was $\frac{4.50}{3}$ = \$1.50. When we increase the cost per pencil by \$0.50 we have that the new cost per pencil is \$2. So 5 of these pencils will cost 5(2) = \$10, choice (E).

2. ALGEBRA

Solution by plugging in points: From the table we see that when $x = 1$, we have $y = 3$. Let's substitute 1 in for x into each answer choice.

(A) 2
(B) 5
(C) 3
(D) 4
(E) 3

We can eliminate choices (A), (B), and (D) because they did not come out to 3.

Let's use the next column from the table. When $x = 2$, we have $y = 7$. Let's substitute 2 in for x into the remaining answer choices.

(C) 6
(E) 7

We can now eliminate choice (C) because it did not come out to 7. Therefore the answer is choice (E).

For more information on this technique, see **Strategy 5** in ***"The 32 Most Effective SAT Math Strategies."***

Solution using the point-slope equation of a line: We can choose any two points on the line to find the slope of the line. Let's use (1,3) and (2,7). Then the slope of the line is $m = \frac{7-3}{2-1} = 4$. Let's write the equation of the line in point-slope form using the point (1,3) and the slope $m = 4$. We have $y - 3 = 4(x - 1) = 4x - 4$. So $y = 4x - 1$, choice (E).

For more information on slope see the notes at the end of Problem 12 in Section 3 of Test 1 (pp. 15-17).

The **point-slope form of an equation of a line** is $y - y_0 = m(x - x_0)$ where m is the slope of the line and (x_0, y_0) is any point on the line.

* **Quick solution:** Note that each increase in x by 1 unit yields an increase in y by 4 units. Thus, the slope is $m = 4$. We can find b by subtracting 4 from 3. So $b = 3 - 4 = -1$. So an equation of the line in slope-intercept form is $y = 4x - 1$.

3. Algebra

Solution by starting with choice (C): Let's start with choice (C) and guess that $BC = 3$. Then $AB = 2BC = 2(3) = 6$ (see Remark below). So $AC = 9$. This is too large so we can eliminate choices (C), (D), and (E).

Let's try choice (B) next and guess that $BC = 2$. Then $AB = 4$, and $AC = 6$. This is correct so that the answer is choice (B).

Remark: We are given that the **circumference** of the circle with center A is twice the circumference of the circle with center C. Recall that the formula for the circumference of a circle is $C = 2\pi r$. Since this is a linear equation, it follows that the **radius** of the circle with center A is twice the radius of the circle with center C. That is, $AB = 2BC$.

For more information on this technique, see **Strategy 1** in ***"The 32 Most Effective SAT Math Strategies."***

* **Algebraic solution:** Let $BC = x$. It follows that $AB = 2x$. So $x + 2x = 6$. That is $3x = 6$, and so $x = \frac{6}{3} = 2$, choice (B).

Definition: The **radius** of a circle is a line segment that joins the center of the circle with any point on its circumference.

4. Geometry

* **Solution by starting with choice (C):** The coordinates of point C are (-2,5). In this case $|x| - |y| = |-2| - |5| = 2 - 5 = -3$. So we can eliminate choice (C).

Let's try choice (D) next. The coordinates of point D are (4,3). In this case $|x| - |y| = |4| - |3| = 4 - 3 = 1$. So we can eliminate choice (C).

Let's try choice (B) next. The coordinates of point B are (-4,-1). In this case $|x| - |y| = |-4| - |-1| = 4 - 1 = 3$. So the answer is choice (B).

For more information on this technique, see **Strategy 1** in ***"The 32 Most Effective SAT Math Strategies."***

5. Data Analysis

* According to the chart, 30% of the people said their age was less than 20 and 20% said their age was at least 20 but less than 40. All together this is 50%. So .5(1000) = 500 people said that their age was less than 40, choice (D).

6. Number Theory

* When a positive integer is divided by 3, the remainder can only be 0, 1, or 2. This eliminates choices (A), (B), (C), and (E). Therefore the answer is choice (D).

Further remarks: Remainders are cyclical. This means that if we start with an integer divisible by 3 (remainder 0), then the next integer will have a remainder of 1 when divided by 3, the next integer a remainder of 2, and the next a remainder of 0 again, etc. The pattern looks like this.

$$0, 1, 2, 0, 1, 2, 0, 1, 2, 0, \ldots$$

For example, when we divide 3 by 3 we get a quotient of 1 and a remainder of 0. In other words, $3 = 3(1) + 0$.

When we divide 4 by 3 we get a quotient of 1 and a remainder of 1. In other words, $4 = 3(1) + 1$.

When we divide 5 by 3 we get a quotient of 1 and a remainder of 2. In other words, 5 = 3(1) + 2.

Now we have to be careful. When we divide 6 by 3, the quotient is now 2 and the remainder is 0. That is, 6 = 3(2) + 0.

So the remainders start over.

7. GEOMETRY

Solution 1: Since y varies inversely as x, $y = \frac{k}{x}$ for some constant k. We are given that $y = 15$ when $x = 5$, so that $15 = \frac{k}{5}$, or $k = 75$. So $y = \frac{75}{x}$. When $x = 25$, we have $y = \frac{75}{25} = 3$, choice (C).

Solution 2: Since y varies inversely as x, xy is a constant. So we get the following equation: $(5)(15) = 25y$ So $75 = 25y$, and $y = \frac{75}{25} = 3$, choice (C).

*** Solution 3:** $\frac{(5)(15)}{25} = 3$, choice (C).

Here is a quick lesson in **inverse variation:**

The following are all equivalent ways of saying the same thing:

(1) y varies inversely as x
(2) y is inversely proportional to x
(3) $y = \frac{k}{x}$ for some constant k
(4) xy is constant

The following is a consequence of (1), (2) (3) or (4).

(5) The graph of $y = f(x)$ is a hyperbola.

Note: (5) is not equivalent to (1), (2), (3) or (4).

For example, in the equation $y = \frac{12}{x}$, y varies inversely as x. Here is a partial table of values for this equation.

x	1	2	3	4
y	12	6	4	3

Note that we can tell that this table represents an inverse relationship between x and y because (1)(12) = (2)(6) = (3)(4) = (4)(3) = 12. Here the **constant of variation** is 12.

Here is a graph of the equation. On the left you can see the full graph. On the right we have a close-up in the first quadrant.

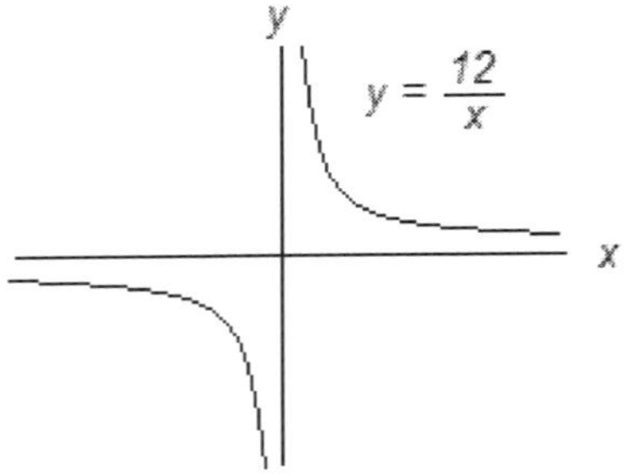

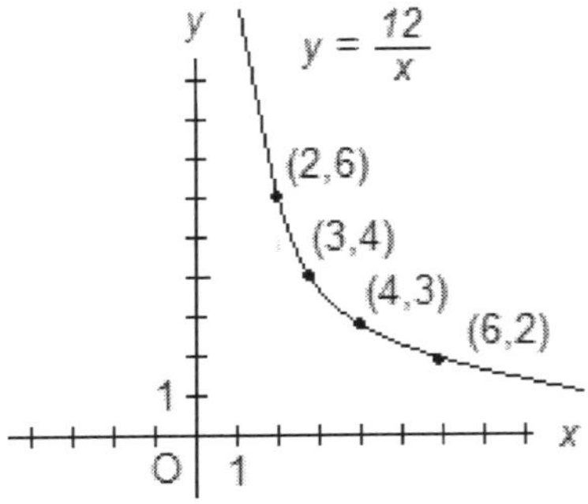

8. GEOMETRY

Solution by picking a number: Let's choose a value for z, say $z = 0$. Then from the first equation $2x = 2y$, or equivalently $x = y$. From the second equation $2x + 2y = 20$, or $x + y = 10$. Since $x = y$, We have $2x = 10$, or $x = 5$. So $y = 5$. So the answer is choice (A) or choice (E). Since this is the last multiple choice question we can quasi-eliminate choice (E). So the answer is most likely choice (A).

For more information on this technique, see **Strategy 4** in ***"The 32 Most Effective SAT Math Strategies."*** Also see **Strategy 10** for the method of Quasi-Elimination.

*** Solution by performing a simple operation:** Let's line up the equations and subtract.

$$\begin{array}{r} 2x + 2y + z = 20 \\ \underline{2x - 2y + z = 0} \\ 4y = 20 \end{array}$$

So $y = \frac{20}{4} = 5$, choice (A).

Remarks: (1) In order to line up the equations nicely we had to subtract $2y$ from each side of the first equation.

(2) $2y - (-2y) = 2y + 2y = 4y$.

For more information on this technique, see **Strategy 16** in ***"The 32 Most Effective SAT Math Strategies."***

9. Algebra

Solution by guessing: Let's take a guess for x, say $x = 6$. Then we have $2(x - 3) = 2(6 - 3) = 2(3) = 6$. This is too small so we will take a larger guess.

Let's try $x = 7$. Then $2(x - 3) = 2(7 - 3) = 2(4) = 8$. This is too big so we will take a smaller guess.

Let's try $x = 6.5$. Then $2(x - 3) = 2(6.5 - 3) = 2(3.5) = 7$. This is correct. So the answer is **6.5**.

For more information on this technique, see **Strategy 3** in ***"The 32 Most Effective SAT Math Strategies."***

* **Algebraic solution:** Distributing the left hand side of the equation gives $2x - 6 = 7$. Adding 6 to each side of the equation gives $2x = 7 + 6 = 13$. Finally, we divide each side of this equation by 2 to get $x =$ **13/2** or **6.5**.

10. Geometry

* We substitute 4 for x and solve for y.

$$y - 4 = 3(x - 2)$$
$$y - 4 = 3(4 - 2)$$
$$y - 4 = 3(2)$$
$$y - 4 = 6$$
$$y = \mathbf{10}.$$

11. Number Theory

* Car A used $\frac{60}{20} = 3$ gallons of gasoline. So the number of miles car B travelled when it had used the same amount of gasoline as car A was $3(15) =$ **45**.

12. Geometry

* Since the angles of a quadrilateral sum to 360 degrees, the missing angle in the quadrilateral measures $360 - 65 - 100 - 120 = 75$ degrees. Therefore $x = 180 - 75 =$ **105**.

13. Number Theory

* Let's write out the sequence.

20, 8, 14, 11, 12.5

So the first term of the sequence that is not an integer is **12.5** or **25/2**.

Notes: The average of 20 and 8 is $\frac{20+8}{2} = \frac{28}{2} = 14$. The average of 8 and 14 is $\frac{8+14}{2} = \frac{22}{2} = 11$. The average of 14 and 11 is $\frac{14+11}{2} = \frac{25}{2} = 12.5$.

14. Number Theory

* **Solution by picking a number:** Let's choose a value for z, say $z = 50$ (this seems like a good choice since it is the product of the two denominators). Then

$y = \frac{3}{10} \cdot 50 = 15$ (the word "of" indicates multiplication),

and $x = \frac{1}{5} \cdot 15 = 3$. Therefore $x = \frac{3}{50} \cdot z$. So we can grid in **3/50** or **.06**.

Algebraic solution: $x = \frac{y}{5}$ and $y = \frac{3z}{10}$. Then

$$x = \frac{3z}{10} \div 5 = \left(\frac{3z}{10}\right) \cdot \left(\frac{1}{5}\right) = \frac{3z}{50}.$$

Thus, the answer is **3/50** or **.06**.

15. Geometry

*Triangle ABE is a 30, 60, 90 right triangle. Using the formula given for this triangle at the beginning of any math section of the SAT we see that $BE = 8\sqrt{3}$. So the area of the square is $(BE)^2 = (8\sqrt{3})^2 =$ **192**.

For more information on this technique, see **Strategy 27** in ***"The 32 Most Effective SAT Math Strategies."***

16. Number Theory

* We can represent the weight of the peanuts by $5x$ and the weight of the cashews by $2x$ for some number x. Then the total weight is $7x$ which must be equal to 4. $7x = 4$ implies that $x = \frac{4}{7}$. Since we want the number of pounds of cashews, we need to find $2x$. This is $2\left(\frac{4}{7}\right) =$ **8/7** or **1.14**.

Important note: After you find x make sure you look at what the question is asking for. A common error is to give an answer of $\frac{4}{7}$. But the number of pounds of cashews is **not** equal to x. It is equal to $2x$.

Alternate solution: We set up a ratio of the number of pounds of cashews to the total number of pounds in the mixture.

cashews	2	x
total	7	4

$$\frac{2}{7} = \frac{x}{4}$$

$$8 = 7x$$

x = **8/7** or **1.14**

For more information on this technique, see **Strategy 14** in **"The 32 Most Effective SAT Math Strategies."**

17. Geometry

* **Solution by choosing a line:** Let's choose a specific line m. An easy choice is the line passing through (0, 0) and (8, 1). Now plug these two points into the slope formula to get $\frac{1-0}{8-0}$ = **1/8**.

Remarks: (1) Here we have used the slope formula $m = \frac{y_2 - y_1}{x_2 - x_1}$.

(2) If the line j passes through the origin (the point (0, 0)) and the point (a,b) with $a \neq 0$, then the slope of line j is simply $\frac{b}{a}$.

Complete geometric solution: The slope of line OA is $\frac{3}{8}$ = .375 (see Remark (2) above) and the slope of line OB is 0. Therefore we can choose any number strictly between 0 and .375 that fits in the answer grid.

18. Statistics

* Let's list the numbers in the second column from least to greatest.

1238 1351 1459 1552

1351 will me the median if x is less than or equal to 1351. Since no two years had the same enrollment, the greatest possible value for x is **1350**.

SECTION 5

1. ALGEBRA

Solution by starting with choice (C): Let's start with choice (C) and guess that $x = 41$. Then $\frac{x}{x-2} = \frac{41}{39} \sim 1.05128$. But $\frac{39}{37} \sim 1.05405$. So choice (C) is not the answer. (Note that we got the decimal approximations by dividing in our calculator.)

Let's try choice (B) next and guess that $x = 39$. Then $\frac{x}{x-2} = \frac{39}{37}$. So the answer is choice (B).

For more information on this technique, see **Strategy 4** in ***"The 32 Most Effective SAT Math Strategies."***

* **Solution by direct observation:** Just observe that 37 is 2 less than 39. So $x = 39$, choice (C).

Algebraic solution (not recommended): We begin by cross multiplying to get $37x = 39(x - 2)$. Distributing on the right gives $37x = 39x - 78$. Now subtract $37x$ from each side of this equation to get $0 = 2x - 78$. Add 78 to each side of this equation to get $78 = 2x$. Dividing each side by 2 gives us $x = \frac{78}{2} = 39$, choice (B).

2. DATA ANALYSIS

* z is the total number of students in the advanced biology class. There are three ways to get this total.

(1) add the total number of juniors and seniors: $w + x = z$.

(2) add the total number of boys and girls: $m + t = z$.

(3) Add the junior boys, senior boys, junior girls, and senior girls:

$$k + n + r + s = z$$

Method (3) happens to be answer choice (E).

3. Number Theory

* The measure of an exterior angle of a triangle is the sum of the measures of the two opposite interior angles of the triangle. So we have $x + 25 = 60$. So $x = 60 - 25 = 35$, choice (C).

For more information on this technique, see **Strategy 30** in ***"The 32 Most Effective SAT Math Strategies."***

Alternative solution: The unlabeled angle in the triangle is supplementary with the angle measuring 60 degrees, and therefore has a measure of $180 - 60 = 120$ degrees. Since the angle measures in a triangle sum to 180 degrees, we have $x + 25 + 120 = 180$, or equivalently $x = 180 - 25 - 120 = 35$, choice (C).

4. Algebra

* **Solution by starting with choice (C):** First note that the difference between the cost of the new refrigerator and the cost of fixing the old one is $900 - 300 = 600$ dollars.

Now, let's start with choice (C) and guess that $x = 36$. Then the Martins will have saved $36(15) = 540$ dollars. This is a bit too small so we can eliminate choices (A), (B), and (C).

Let's try choice (D) next and guess that $x = 40$. Then the Martins will have saved $40(15) = 600$ dollars. This is correct so that the answer is choice (D).

For more information on this technique, see **Strategy 1** in ***"The 32 Most Effective SAT Math Strategies."***

* **Algebraic solution:** We solve the equation $15x = 900 - 300 = 600$. Divide each side of this equation by 15 to get $x = \frac{600}{15} = 40$, choice (D).

5. Geometry

* The perimeter of triangle ABC is $3(10) = 30$. Since triangle ABC is equilateral, the length of one side is $\frac{30}{3} = 10$, choice (B).

6. Number Theory

* The machine mints coins at the rate of 60(60)(10) = 36,000 coins per day. So to mint 360,000 coins it will take $\frac{360{,}000}{36{,}000}$ = 10 days, choice (A).

Note: There are 60 seconds in a minute and 60 minutes in an hour.

7. Statistics

* **Solution by converting averages to sums:** We change the average to a sum using the formula

Sum = Average · Number

The **Average** is given to be 12, and the **Number** is 2 (we are averaging 2 numbers). Therefore the **Sum** is $x + 3x = 2(12)$. So $4x = 24$, and therefore $x = \frac{24}{4} = 6$, choice (C).

For more information on this technique, see **Strategy 20** in ***"The 32 Most Effective SAT Math Strategies."***

Solution by starting with choice (C): Let's start with choice (C) and guess that $x = 6$. Then $3x = 3(6) = 18$, and the average of x and $3x$ is $\frac{6+18}{2} = 12$. This is correct. So the answer is choice (C).

For more information on this technique, see **Strategy 1** in ***"The 32 Most Effective SAT Math Strategies."***

8. Logic

* Let's draw a picture

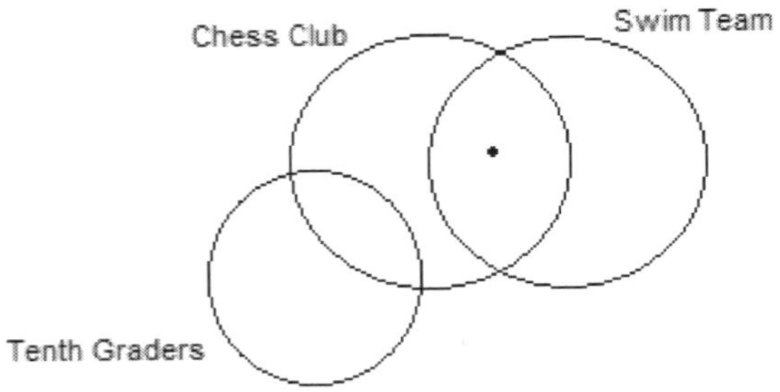

Note that saying that some members of the chess club are on the swim team is the same as saying that there is at least one member of the chess club that is on the swim team. This is indicated by the dot in the figure above.

Also note that the fact that no members of the swim team are tenth graders is indicated in the figure by making sure that the circles corresponding to the swim team and tenth graders do not intersect.

And finally note that we made the circles corresponding to the chess club and tenth graders intersect because we were not told that they do not. But there is no dot inside because we were also not told that they do intersect.

Finally note that the dot represents a member of the chess club that is on the swim team and is also not a tenth grader. So the answer is choice (C).

For more information on this technique, see **Strategy 9** in ***"The 32 Most Effective SAT Math Strategies."***

9. ALGEBRA

Solution by picking a number: Let's choose a value for x, say $x = 5$. The equation then becomes $3(5) + n = 5 + 1$, or equivalently $15 + n = 6$. It follows that $n = 6 - 15 = -9$. **Put a nice big, dark circle around -9 so that you can find it easily later.** Substituting $x = 5$ into each answer choice gives the following:

(A) 21
(B) 11
(C) -3
(D) -9
(E) -19

Since (A), (B), (C), and (E) each came out incorrect, the answer is (D).

Important note: (D) is **not** the correct answer simply because it is equal to -9. It is correct because all four of the other choices are **not** -9. **You absolutely must check all five choices!**

For more information on this technique, see **Strategy 4** in ***"The 32 Most Effective SAT Math Strategies."***

* **Algebraic solution:** We subtract $3x$ from each side of the given equation to get $n = -2x + 1 = 1 - 2x$, choice (D).

10. Number Theory

Solution by starting with choice (C): First note the following.

$\boxed{2} = \{2,4,6,8,...\}$ $\boxed{3} = \{3,6,9,12,...\}$ $\boxed{5} = \{5,10,15,20,...\}$

Now let's start with choice (C). We can eliminate choice (C) because 10 is not in $\boxed{3}$. We can eliminate choice (D) because 21 is not in $\boxed{2}$. We can eliminate choice (B) because 6 is not in $\boxed{5}$. We can eliminate choice (A) because 5 is not in $\boxed{2}$. So the answer must be choice (E).

For more information on this technique, see **Strategy 1** in ***"The 32 Most Effective SAT Math Strategies."***

* **Quick solution:** Since 2, 3, and 5 are prime, the multiples of 2, 3, and 5 are precisely the multiples of (2)(3)(5) = 30. Since every multiple of 60 is a multiple of 30, the answer is choice (E).

11. Geometry

* Since $\overline{CF}$ bisects angle *BOD*, angles *BOC* and *COD* have the same measure. Since $\overline{AD}$ is a straight line, angles *AOB*, *BOC* and *COD* have measures that add to 180 degrees. We are given that the measure of angle *AOB* is 80 degrees. So *BOC* and *COD* have measures that add to 180 – 80 = 100 degrees. Therefore they each have a measure of 50 degrees. Finally, angles *EOF* and *BOC* are vertical angles and therefore they have the same measure. So the measure of angle *EOF* is 50 degrees, choice (B).

12. Algebra

Solution by starting with choice (A): Let's start with choice (A) and guess that $k = 3$. Then $\sqrt{\frac{5k}{3}} = \sqrt{\frac{5(3)}{3}} = \sqrt{5}$. This is not an integer, so we can eliminate choice (A).

Let's try choice (B) next and guess that $k = 5$. Then $\sqrt{\frac{5k}{3}} = \sqrt{\frac{5(5)}{3}} = \sqrt{\frac{25}{3}}$. This is also not an integer, so we can eliminate choice (B)

Let's try choice (C) and guess that $k = 15$. Then $\sqrt{\frac{5k}{3}} = \sqrt{\frac{5(15)}{3}} = \sqrt{25} = 5$. This is an integer. So the answer is choice (C)

Remark: We started with choice (A) here because the word "least" is in the problem. Otherwise we would have started with choice (C).

For more information on this technique, see **Strategy 2** in ***"The 32 Most Effective SAT Math Strategies."***

* **Quick solution:** We are looking for the smallest positive integer that is divisible by both 3 and 5. This is (3)(5) = 15, choice (C).

Notes: (1) We need the integer to be divisible by 3 to cancel with the 3 in the denominator.

(2) We need the integer to be divisible by 5 to make the expression in the numerator a perfect square.

13. GEOMETRY

* It is easiest to try to place the middle figure first into each of the three choices.

In I, there is only one place where the middle figure will fit, and once it is placed, you can see there is nowhere to put the rightmost figure.

In II, there is again only one way to place the middle figure, and then the left- and rightmost figures fit nicely below and above the middle figure, respectively.

In III, the middle figure cannot be placed at all.

Therefore the answer is choice (C).

14. Number Theory

* 21 = (3)(7)
22 = (2)(11)
23 is prime
24 = (2)(12), but 12 is not prime
25 = (5)(5), but the two numbers are not different
26 = (2)(13)
27 = (3)(9), but 9 is not prime
28 = (2)(14), but 14 is not prime
29 is prime.

So the integers satisfying the given conditions are 21, 22, and 26. There are three of them, choice (D).

15. Geometry

Algebraic solution: By the Pythagorean Theorem,

$$10^2 = (7-x)^2 + (7+x)^2 = 49 - 14x + x^2 + 49 + 14x + x^2 = 2(49 + x^2)$$

So $100 = 2(49 + x^2)$, and therefore $49 + x^2 = \frac{100}{2} = 50$, choice (A).

Some details: $(7-x)^2 = (7-x)(7-x) = 49 - 7x - 7x + x^2 = 49 - 14x + x^2$ and $(7+x)^2 = (7+x)(7+x) = 49 + 7x + 7x + x^2 = 49 + 14x + x^2$.

* **Solution by guessing:** If we guess that $x = 1$, then $7 - x = 7 - 1 = 6$, and $7 + x = 7 + 1 = 8$. Since $6^2 + 8^2 = 36 + 64 = 100 = 10^2$, $x = 1$ is correct.

Finally, $49 + x^2 = 49 + 1^2 = 49 + 1 = 50$, choice (A).

For more information on this technique, see **Strategy 3** in ***"The 32 Most Effective SAT Math Strategies."***

16. Functions

* The figure does not say "figure not drawn to scale." Therefore we can assume it is. It looks like $h(-1) = 0$. So $a = -1$, choice (A).

For more information on this technique, see **Strategy 6** in ***"The 32 Most Effective SAT Math Strategies."***

A little more precision: If there are two x-intercepts on the graph of a quadratic function, then they are at the same distance from the x-coordinate of the vertex. The x-coordinate of the vertex is 2. From the given picture we see that the x-coordinate of one of the x-intercepts is less than 0. So it is more than 2 units away. It follows that the rightmost x-intercept is more than 2 units to the right of 2. So its x-coordinate is greater than $2 + 2 = 4$. This only leaves choice (A) for the answer.

17. ALGEBRA

* The second expression is 0 when $x = -1$ and $x = -h$. The constant term is the product of these roots, so $7 = (-1)(-h) = h$. The coefficient of x is the negative of the sum of these roots, so $k = h + 1 = 7 + 1 = 8$, choice (D).

Note: For the previous solution we used the following general theory:

Let $\boldsymbol{r}$ and $\boldsymbol{s}$ be the roots of the quadratic equation $\boldsymbol{x^2 + bx + c = 0}$. Then

$$\boldsymbol{b = -(r + s)} \quad \text{and} \quad \boldsymbol{c = rs}.$$

Solution by plugging in numbers: Let's plug in some simple values for x.

$x = 0$: The first expression gives us 7 and the second expression gives us h. Therefore $h = 7$.

$x = -1$: The first expression gives us $(-1)^2 - k + 7 = 1 - k + 7 = 8 - k$, and the second expression gives us 0. So $8 - k = 0$, or $k = 8$, choice (D).

Note: It turned out that $x = -1$ is all that was needed.

For more information on this technique, see **Strategy 4** in ***"The 32 Most Effective SAT Math Strategies."***

Algebraic solution: Multiply out the second expression (FOIL) to get

$$x^2 + hx + x + h = x^2 + kx + 7$$
$$x^2 + (h + 1)x + h = x^2 + kx + 7$$

Equating the constant terms on the left and right yields $h = 7$. Setting the coefficient of x on the left equal to the coefficient of x on the right yields $k = h + 1 = 7 + 1 = 8$, choice (D).

Remark: Since this is one of the last few questions in the section we can quasi-eliminate choice (E).

See **Strategy 10** in ***"The 32 Most Effective SAT Math Strategies"*** for more on Quasi-Elimination.

18. GEOMETRY

* The slope of the line is $m = \frac{10}{4} = \frac{5}{2}$. Since the hypotenuse of a right triangle is the largest side, the two smaller numbers must be in the ratio 5 to 2. This eliminates choice (C), (D), and (E).

The triangle is a right triangle. Therefore the sides of the triangle must satisfy the Pythagorean Theorem. $2^2 + 5^2 = 4 + 25 = 29$. So the hypotenuse of the triangle must have length $\sqrt{29}$. Therefore the answer is choice (A).

Remarks: (1) The Pythagorean Theorem is one of the formulas given at the beginning of each math section of the SAT.

(2) In the formula $c^2 = a^2 + b^2$ for the Pythagorean Theorem, c is the length of the hypotenuse of the right triangle. The hypotenuse is always the longest side.

(3) If the line j passes through the origin (the point (0, 0)) and the point (a, b) with $a \neq 0$, then the slope of line j is simply $\frac{b}{a}$.

(4) In general, the slope of a line is $m = \frac{rise}{run} = \frac{y_2 - y_1}{x_2 - x_1}$.

(5) We can also get the slope of $\overline{AB}$ by observing that to get from O to (4,10) we need to travel up 10, then right 4. So $m = \frac{rise}{run} = \frac{10}{4} = \frac{5}{2}$.

19. FUNCTIONS

* $f(\sqrt{t}) = 2\sqrt{t} - 1$. So we are given that $\frac{1}{2}(2\sqrt{t} - 1) = 4$. We multiply each side of this equation by 2 to get $2\sqrt{t} - 1 = 8$. Adding 1 to each side of this equation gives us $2\sqrt{t} = 9$. We now divide by 2 to get $\sqrt{t} = \frac{9}{2}$. Finally, we square each side of this equation to get $t = \frac{81}{4}$, choice (E).

Solution by picking numbers: Let's choose a value for k, say $k = 3$. We substitute 3 in for k into each answer choice.

(A) 6
(B) 9
(C) 10
(D) 13
(E) 14

We can eliminate choices (B) and (D) because they are not even (they are odd).

Now 6 = 2(3), so we cannot eliminate choice (A). Also, 10 = 2(5), so we cannot eliminate choice (C). Finally, 14 = 2(7), so we cannot eliminate choice (E).

Let's try an even integer next, say $k = 4$. We substitute 4 in for k into the remaining three answer choices.

(A) 8
(C) 12
(E) 18

All three of these integers are even.

Now 8 = 2(4) and 12 = 2(6). So we can eliminate choices (A) and (C). Therefore the answer is choice (E).

Remark: We should still check that choice (E) works. Indeed, 18 = 2(9). So 18 is twice the value of an odd integer.

For more information on this technique, see **Strategy 2** in ***"The 32 Most Effective SAT Math Strategies."***

*** Direct solution:** An odd integer has the form $2k + 1$ for some integer k. Thus, twice an odd integer has the form $2(2k + 1) = 4k + 2$, choice (E).

SECTION 8

1. COUNTING

* **Solution by listing:** Let's list 8 dinners and 3 desserts. We will use the numbers 1 through 8 to represent the dinners, and the letters A, B, and C to represent the desserts. Now let's list all dinner-dessert combinations.

1A	2A	3A	4A	5A	6A	7A	8A
1B	2B	3B	4B	5B	6B	7B	8B
1C	2C	3C	4C	5C	6C	7C	8C

We see that there are 24 dinner-dessert combinations, choice (A).

For more information on this technique, see **Strategy 21** in ***"The 32 Most Effective SAT Math Strategies."***

* **Solution using the counting principle:** (8)(3) = 24, choice (A).

Remark: The **counting principle** says that if one event is followed by a second independent event, the number of possibilities is multiplied. The 2 events here are "choosing a dinner," and "choosing a dessert."

2. ALGEBRA

* The sum of $3x$ and 5 can be written $3x + 5$. The product of x and $\frac{1}{3}$ can be written $(x)(\frac{1}{3}) = \frac{1}{3}x$. We are given that these two quantities are equal. So $3x + 5 = \frac{1}{3}x$, choice (E).

3. PROBABILITY

* The probability is $\frac{15}{90} = \frac{1}{6}$, choice (C).

Remarks: (1) Here we have used the **Simple Probability Principle** which says the following. To compute a simple probability where all outcomes are equally likely, divide the number of "successes" by the total number of outcomes.

(2) We can quickly reduce the fraction $\frac{15}{90}$ in our graphing calculator by typing 15 / 90 MATH ENTER ENTER.

4. Number Theory

Solution by picking numbers: Let's try to choose some values for *x* and *y* that satisfy the given equation.

Certainly $x = 1$, $y = 2$ works.

We can also double each of these numbers to get $x = 2$, $y = 4$. Note that $\frac{2}{4}$ can be reduced to $\frac{1}{2}$.

Similarly, we can triple 1 and 2 to get $x = 3$, $y = 6$. We can also multiply 1 and 2 by 4 to get $x = 4$, $y = 8$. And we can multiply by 5 to get $x = 5$, $y = 6$.

So the answer is "More than four," choice (E).

* **Quick solution:** Just note that if we multiply 1 and 2 by any number (as long as it is the same number), the resulting fraction will be equal to $\frac{1}{2}$. So the answer is choice (E).

Remark: If you are having trouble seeing this, try cross multiplying to get $y = 2x$. Now note that if we choose any value for *x*, then we can just let *y* be double that value. This leads to infinitely many pairs.

5. Data Analysis

* Let's just estimate the number of books sold for each two-month period.

(A) $7 + 40 = 47$
(B) $40 + 10 = 50$
(C) $10 + 33 = 43$
(D) $33 + 25 = 58$
(E) $25 + 30 = 55$

We are looking for the smallest number. So the answer is choice (C).

Remark: It is best to be safe here. Just do the five computations. It doesn't take that long.

6. Geometry

* Let's add the given information to the picture.

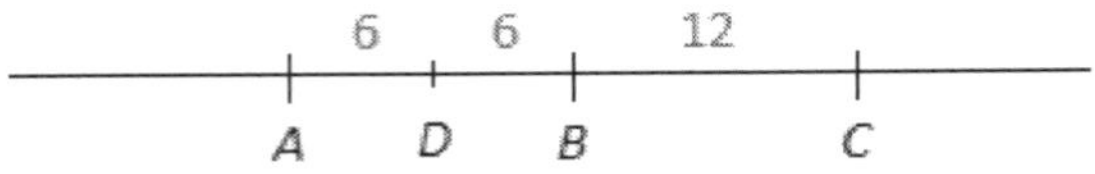

Note that $AB = BC = 12$, and so $AD = DB = 6$. So $DC = 6 + 12 = 18$, choice (D).

7. Algebra

Solution by picking a number: Let's choose a value for n, say $n = 3$. Then $(6 \times 10^{-n}) + (1 \times 10^{-n}) = (6 \times 10^{-3}) + (1 \times 10^{-3})$ = **.007**. **Put a nice big, dark circle around .007 so that you can find it easily later.** Substituting $n = 3$ into each answer choice gives the following:

(A) .7
(B) .007
(C) .000007
(D) .006
(E) .000006

Since (A), (C), (D), and (E) each came out incorrect, the answer is (B).

Important note: (B) is **not** the correct answer simply because it is equal to .007. It is correct because all four of the other choices are **not** .007. **You absolutely must check all five choices!**

For more information on this technique, see **Strategy 4** in ***"The 32 Most Effective SAT Math Strategies."***

* **Algebraic solution:** $(6 \times 10^{-n}) + (1 \times 10^{-n}) = (6 + 1) \times 10^{-n} = 7 \times 10^{-n} = \frac{7}{10^n}$, choice (B).

8. GEOMETRY

* A circle has a total of 360 degrees. Therefore $\frac{1}{4}$ of an arc of a circle has $\frac{1}{4}(360) = 90$ degrees, and $\frac{1}{5}$ of an arc of a circle has $\frac{1}{5}(360) = 72$ degrees. The difference is $90 - 72 = 18$ degrees, choice (B).

9. FUNCTIONS

* $f(x)$ is negative when its graph is below the x-axis. This happens when x is between 0 and 6. So $0 < x < 6$, choice (B).

10. GEOMETRY

* Note that we are computing the volume of the pedestal. We compute this by adding the volumes of each of the four layers, beginning at the top.

The top block has a volume of $(1)(1)(1) = 1$ cubic foot.

The second block down has a volume of $(2)(2)(1) = 4$ cubic feet.

The third block down has a volume of $(3)(3)(1) = 9$ cubic feet.

The bottom block has a volume of $(4)(4)(1) = 16$ cubic feet.

The total is $1 + 4 + 9 + 16 = 30$ cubic feet, choice (C).

11. ALGEBRA

Solution by picking a number: Let's choose a value for x, say $x = 3$. Then $4(2^x) = 4(2^3) = 4(8) = 32$. Since $4(2^x) = 2^y$, we have $2^y = 32$. So $y = 5$. Since we want x in terms of y, we should put a nice, big dark circle around **3**. We now substitute 5 in for y in each answer choice, and eliminate any choices that do not come out to 3.

(A) 3
(B) 4
(C) 5
(D) 6
(E) 7

Since (B), (C), (D), and (E) came out incorrect, we can eliminate them. The answer is therefore choice (A).

For more information on this technique, see **Strategy 4** in ***"The 32 Most Effective SAT Math Strategies."***

Remark: Normally we would choose a value for y here (since y appears in the answer choices), but the computations are a bit easier if we choose x instead.

* **Algebraic solution:** $4(2^x) = 2^2 2^x = 2^{2+x}$. So $2^{2+x} = 2^y$. Since the bases are now the same, so are the exponents. Therefore $2 + x = y$. We subtract 2 from each side of this equation to get $x = y - 2$, choice (A).

12. Geometry

* The angle measures can be represented by $2x$, $3x$, and $4x$. Since the angle measures in a triangle sum to 180 degrees, $2x + 3x + 4x = 180$, or equivalently, $9x = 180$. So $x = \frac{180}{9} = 20$.

The measure of the largest angle is $4x = 4(20) = 80$ degrees, and the measure of the smallest angle is $2(20) = 40$ degrees. The difference is then $80 - 40 = 40$ degrees, choice (C).

13. Algebra

Solution by picking a number: Let's choose a value for n, say $n = 3$. The cost of a phone call that lasts for 3 minutes is

$$50 + 30 + 30 = 110 \text{ cents} = \$\mathbf{1.10}.$$

Put a nice big, dark circle around 1.1 so that you can find it easily later. Substituting $n = 3$ into each answer choice gives the following:

(A) $f(3) = 2.4$
(B) $f(3) = 1.4$
(C) $f(3) = 1.7$
(D) $f(3) = 1.1$
(E) $f(3) = 2.1$

Since (A), (B), (C), and (E) each came out incorrect, the answer is (D).

Important note: (D) is **not** the correct answer simply because it is equal to 1.1. It is correct because all four of the other choices are **not** 1.1. **You absolutely must check all five choices!**

For more information on this technique, see **Strategy 4** in ***"The 32 Most Effective SAT Math Strategies."***

*** Algebraic solution:** If a call is made that lasts n minutes, then the first minute costs 0.50 dollars and the next $n - 1$ minutes cost $0.30(n - 1)$ dollars. So the total cost is $0.50 + 0.30(n - 1)$ dollars, choice (D).

14. GEOMETRY

Solution by picking numbers: Let's choose values for x and y, say $x = 100$ and $y = 40$. Now let's fill in some of the angles in the picture.

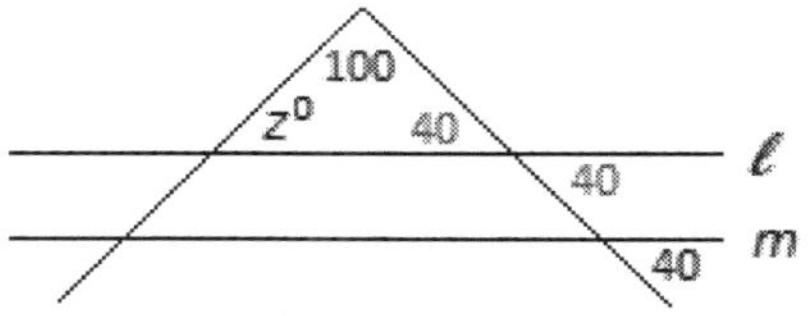

Note that when two parallel lines are cut by a **transversal**, each pair of **corresponding angles** formed has the same measure. The two rightmost angles are alternate interior angles and therefore they have equal measure.

Also, the two upper 40 degree angles are **vertical angles**. Vertical angles have equal measure.

Now note that since a triangle has angle measures that sum to 180 degrees, $z = 180 - 100 - 40 =$ **40**. **Put a nice big, dark circle around 40 so that you can find it easily later.** Substituting $x = 100$ and $y = 40$ into each answer choice gives the following:

(A) 140
(B) 60
(C) 80
(D) 120
(E) 40

Since (A), (B), (C), and (D) each came out incorrect, the answer is (E).

Important note: (E) is **not** the correct answer simply because it is equal to 40. It is correct because all four of the other choices are **not** 40. **You absolutely must check all five choices!**

For more information on this technique, see **Strategy 4** in ***"The 32 Most Effective SAT Math Strategies."***

* **Geometric solution:** The missing angle in the triangle measures y degrees. To see this note that

(1) When two parallel lines are cut by a **transversal**, each pair of **corresponding angles** formed has the same measure

(2) Vertical angles have equal measure.

Since a triangle has angle measures that sum to 180 degrees, we have that $x + y + z = 180$, or equivalently, $z = 180 - x - y$, choice (E).

15. NUMBER THEORY

* We can begin by canceling an n in the numerator with the n in the denominator.

$$\frac{\cancel{n}}{n-1} \cdot \frac{1}{\cancel{n}} \cdot \frac{n}{n+1} = \frac{5}{k}$$

$$\frac{1}{n-1} \cdot \frac{n}{n+1} = \frac{5}{k}$$

Now let's match up the numerators by letting $n = 5$. It follows that

$$k = (n-1)(n+1) = (5-1)(5+1) = (4)(6) = 24$$

This is choice (C).

16. ALGEBRA

Solution by picking numbers: Let's choose values for m, y, and p, say $m = 10$, $y = 20$, and $p = 6$. This means that originally 10 coworkers are contributing a total of 20 dollars. So each coworker is contributing 2 dollars. But if 6 of the coworkers fail to contribute, then the remaining 4 must pay 5 dollars each. So each coworker must contribute an extra **3** dollars. **Put a nice big, dark circle around 3 so that you can find it easily later.** Substituting $m = 10$, $y = 20$, and $p = 6$ into each answer choice gives the following:

(A) 2
(B) 5
(C) 30
(D) 8
(E) 3

Since (A), (B), (C), and (D) each came out incorrect, the answer is (E).

Important note: (E) is **not** the correct answer simply because it is equal to 3. It is correct because all four of the other choices are **not** 3. **You absolutely must check all five choices!**

For more information on this technique, see **Strategy 4** in ***"The 32 Most Effective SAT Math Strategies."***

*** Algebraic solution (not recommended):** Originally each coworker must contribute $\frac{y}{m}$ dollars. But after p fail to contribute, each of the remaining coworkers must contribute $\frac{y}{m-p}$ dollars. The difference is

$$\frac{y}{m-p}-\frac{y}{m}=\frac{ym}{m(m-p)}-\frac{y(m-p)}{m(m-p)}=\frac{ym-ym+yp}{m(m-p)}=\frac{py}{m(m-p)}.$$

This is choice (E).

Actions to Complete After You Have Read This Book

1. **Continue to practice SAT math problems for 10 to 20 minutes each day**

   Keep practicing problems of the appropriate levels until two days before the SAT. For additional practice use *28 SAT Math Lessons To Improve Your Score In One Month*.

2. **Use my Facebook page for additional help**

   If you feel you need extra help that you cannot get from this book, please feel free to post your questions on my Facebook wall at www.facebook.com/SATPrepGet800.

3. **Review this book**

   If this book helped you, please post your positive feedback on the site you purchased it from; e.g. Amazon, Barnes and Noble, etc.

4. **Visit my website www.SATPrepGet800.com**

   You will find free content here that is updated weekly to help with your SAT preparation.

5. **Follow me on twitter**

   www.twitter.com/SATPrepGet800

About the Author

Steve Warner, a New York native, earned his Ph.D. at Rutgers University in Pure Mathematics in May, 2001. While a graduate student, Dr. Warner won the TA Teaching Excellence Award.

After Rutgers, Dr. Warner joined the Penn State Mathematics Department as an Assistant Professor. In September, 2002, Dr. Warner returned to New York to accept an Assistant Professor position at Hofstra University. By September 2007, Dr. Warner had received tenure and was promoted to Associate Professor. He has taught undergraduate and graduate courses in Precalculus, Calculus, Linear Algebra, Differential Equations, Mathematical Logic, Set Theory and Abstract Algebra.

Over that time, Dr. Warner participated in a five year NSF grant, "The MSTP Project," to study and improve mathematics and science curriculum in poorly performing junior high schools. He also published several articles in scholarly journals, specifically on Mathematical Logic.

Dr. Warner has over 15 years of experience in general math tutoring and over 10 years of experience in SAT math tutoring. He has tutored students both individually and in group settings.

In February, 2010 Dr. Warner released his first SAT prep book "The 32 Most Effective SAT Math Strategies." The second edition of this book was released in January, 2011. In February, 2012 Dr. Warner released his second SAT prep book "320 SAT Math Problems arranged by Topic and Difficulty Level." Between September 2012 and January 2013 Dr. Warner released his three book series "28 SAT Math Lessons to Improve Your Score in One Month."

Currently Dr. Warner lives in Staten Island with his two cats, Achilles and Odin. Since the age of 4, Dr. Warner has enjoyed playing the piano—especially compositions of Chopin as well as writing his own music. He also maintains his physical fitness through weightlifting.

BOOKS BY DR. STEVE WARNER

17070102R00166

Made in the USA
Middletown, DE
04 January 2015